AF263609

Interaction

Fifty Years of Fred Sandback and Dia Art Foundation

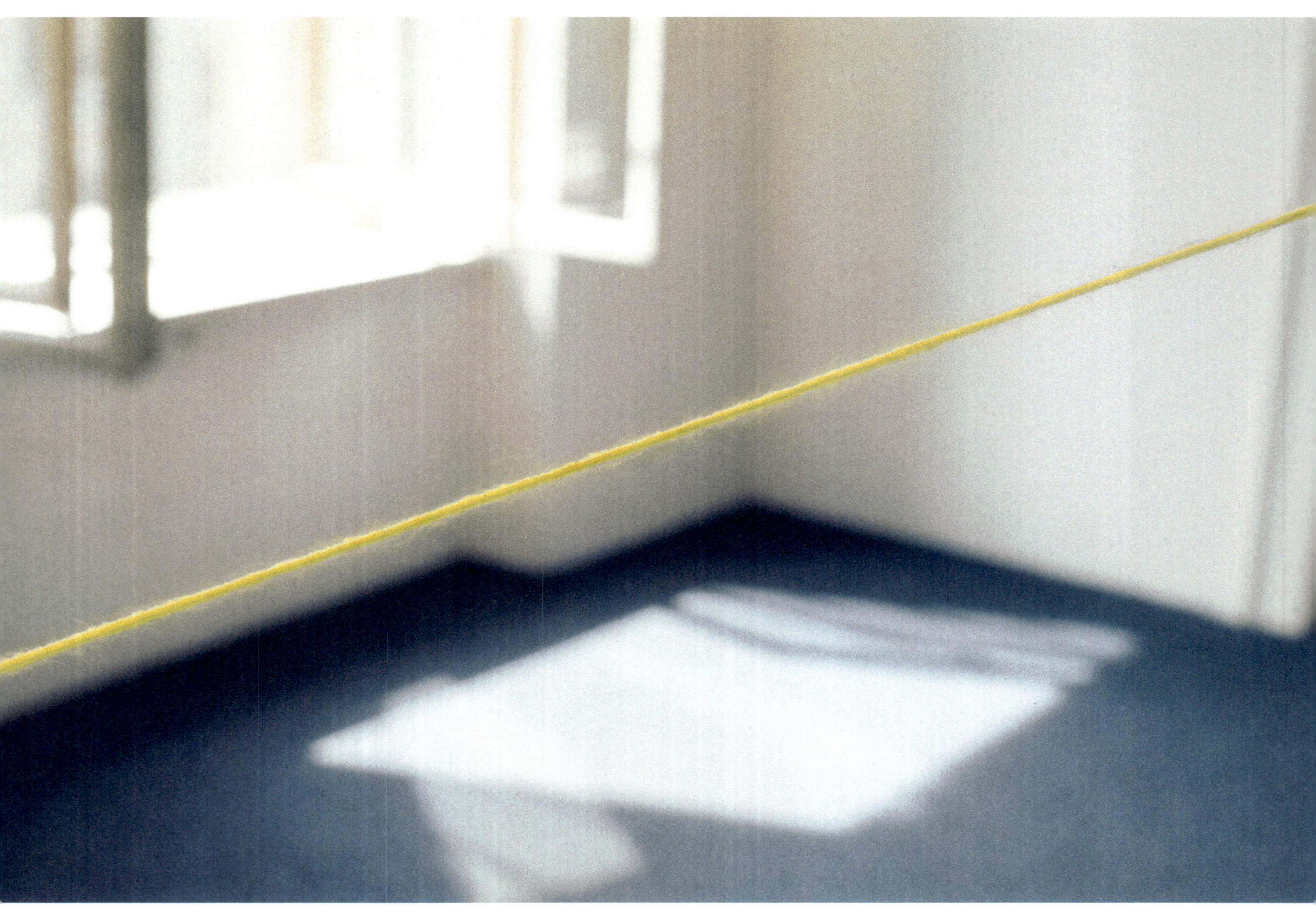

Interaction

Fifty Years of Fred Sandback and Dia Art Foundation

Fred Sandback Archive

Dancing Foxes Press, Brooklyn, New York

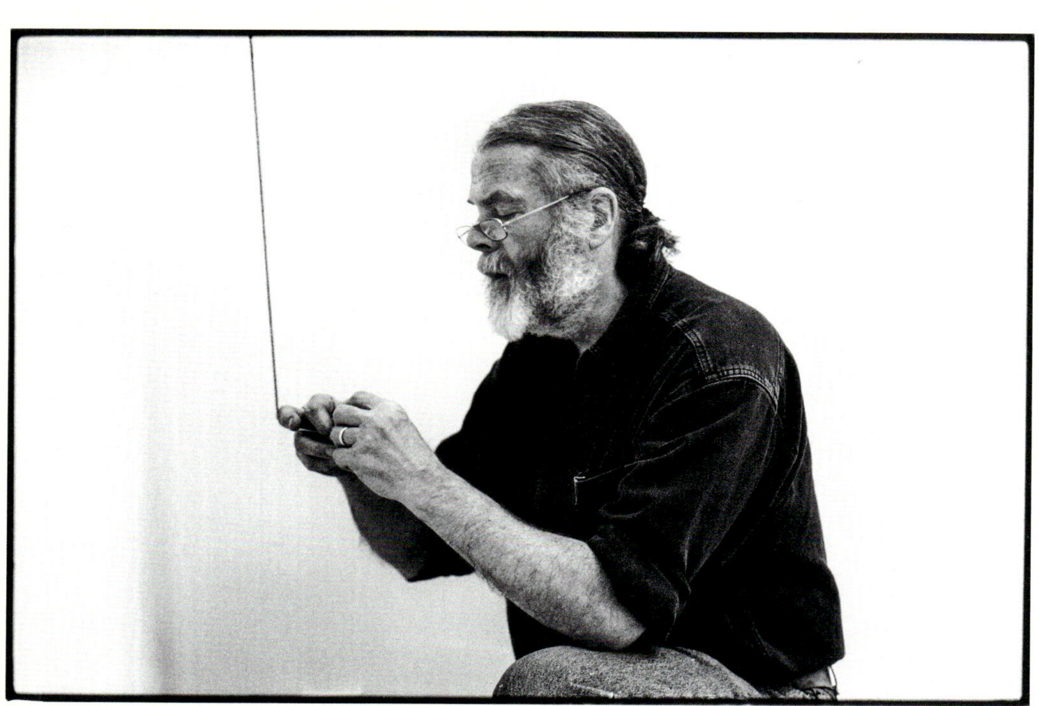

I did have a strong gut feeling from the beginning though, and that was wanting to be able to make sculpture that didn't have an inside. Otherwise, thinking about the nature of place, or a place— my being there with or in it—and the nature of the interaction between the two was interesting. And at that point the thinking was perhaps more interesting than the doing, though it's of course the latter that has sustained my interest.

—Fred Sandback, "Remarks on My Sculpture 1966–86," 1986

This book was published on the occasion of the fifty-year anniversary of Dia Art Foundation, New York, in 2024.

Edited by Karen Kelly and Barbara Schroeder
Editorial assistant: Noa Wesley
Copyediting: Sophie Taylor
Proofreading: James Camp
Design: Katy Homans

This book is typeset in Archer and Akzidenz-Grotesk and printed on Gardapat Kiara 150 gsm.

All artwork and text by Fred Sandback
© Fred Sandback Archive
All text © the authors

Text by Lynne Cooke is reprinted from *Dia:Beacon*, edited by Lynne Cooke and Michael Govan (New York: Dia Art Foundation, 2003). This slightly edited version is published with permission from Dia Art Foundation and the author.

Text by Corinna Thierolf was translated from the original German by Ishbel Flett.

Published in 2024 by the Fred Sandback Archive and Dancing Foxes Press, Brooklyn, New York

Cataloging-in-publication data is on file with the Library of Congress.
ISBN: 978-1-954947-12-2

Dancing Foxes Press
16 Lefferts Place
Brooklyn, NY 11238
dfpress.org

Distributed by
ARTBOOK | D.A.P.
artbook.com

Printed and bound in Italy by Trifolio, Verona, Italy

Photo and Collection Credits:

Every effort has been made to trace copyright holders for the use of copyrighted material. The publisher apologizes for any errors or omissions and would be grateful if notified of corrections that should be incorporated in future editions of this book.

Cover and p. 111: photo by Nic Tenwiggenhorn, courtesy Dia Art Foundation; pp. 2, 17, 20, 22 (top left and right), 23–24, 26, 27 (left), 28, 31 (left), 32–33, 36, 41 (top), 44, 47, 52–56, 59–60, 62, 64–65, 79, 93, 96, 98–99, 101–10, and 112: courtesy Fred Sandback Archive; p. 4: photo by Thomas Cugini, Zurich, courtesy Fred Sandback Archive; p. 8: photo by Susan Osberg; p. 12: collection and courtesy Annemarie Verna Galerie, Zurich; p. 14 (left): photo by Heide Stolz, © Estate of Walter De Maria; p. 14 (right): photo Galerie Heiner Friedrich, courtesy Thordis Moeller, Millerton, New York, © Estate of Walter De Maria; p. 15: Collection Museum MMK für Moderne Kunst, former collection of Karl Ströher, Darmstadt, courtesy Fred Sandback Archive; pp. 16 and 18–19: photo by Ron Amstutz, courtesy Fred Sandback Archive; p. 22 (bottom): courtesy Kunstparterre, Munich; p. 25: photo by Mary Bachman, courtesy Fred Sandback Archive; p. 27 (right): photo by John Berens, courtesy Ayn Foundation; p. 31 (right): Collection Staatliche Kunstsammlungen Dresden, courtesy Fred Sandback Archive; p. 37: Wikimedia Commons, https://w.wiki/_t2WH (accessed May 7, 2024); p. 38 (left): Collection Yale University Art Gallery; p. 38 (right): The Museum of Modern Art, New York; p. 39 (left): The Museum of Modern Art, New York, © 2024 Judd Foundation / Artists Rights Society (ARS), New York; p. 39 (right): © 2024 The Estate of Robert Morris / Artists Rights Society (ARS), New York; pp. 41 (bottom) and 43: courtesy David Zwirner; p. 42: © 2024 The LeWitt Estate / Artists Rights Society (ARS), New York; p. 45: © 2024 Anthony McCall; p. 48 (left): Wikimedia Commons, https://w.wiki/_t2W2 (accessed May 7, 2024); p. 48 (right): Licensed under CC0. Source: Science Museum GrouPage Set squares.1922-254/1Science Museum Group Collection Online, https://collection.science museumgrouPageorg.uk/objects/co428023/set -squares-squaring-drawing-instruments-set -squares (accessed May 7, 2024); p. 57: Mies van der Rohe Archive, gift of the architect, © 2024 Artists Rights Society (ARS), New York / VG Bild-Kunst, Bonn; pp. 70–77: photo by David Ludlow, courtesy Fred Sandback Archive; p. 78: photo by Moritz Bernoully, courtesy Proyectos Monclova, Mexico City; p. 81: courtesy Dia Art Foundation; pp. 82 and 85: photo by Cathy Carver, courtesy Dia Art Foundation; pp. 83, 84, and 86–87: Collection Dia Art Foundation, photo by Cathy Carver, courtesy Dia Art Foundation; p. 90: video by Sanden Wolff, © and courtesy Dia Art Foundation; pp. 114 and 117–32: photo by Bill Jacobson Studio, courtesy Fred Sandback Archive

Cover: Fred Sandback installing his work at Dia Beacon, Beacon, New York, 2003. Photo by Nic Tenwiggenhorn

Frontispiece: *16 Variations of 2 Diagonal Lines*, 1972. Acrylic yarn (yellow), situational dimensions, overall dimensions vary with each installation using spatial relationships established by the artist. Installation view, Galerie Heiner Friedrich, Munich, 1972

Page 4: Fred Sandback, Annemarie Verna Galerie, Zurich, 2000. Photo by Thomas Cugini, Zurich

Page 8: *Construction of Four Parallel Leaning Planes (from 133 Proposals for the Heiner Friedrich Gallery)*, 1969. Acrylic yarn (blue and green), situational dimensions, overall dimensions vary with each installation using spatial relationships established by the artist. Installation view, Dia Beacon, 2024

Contents

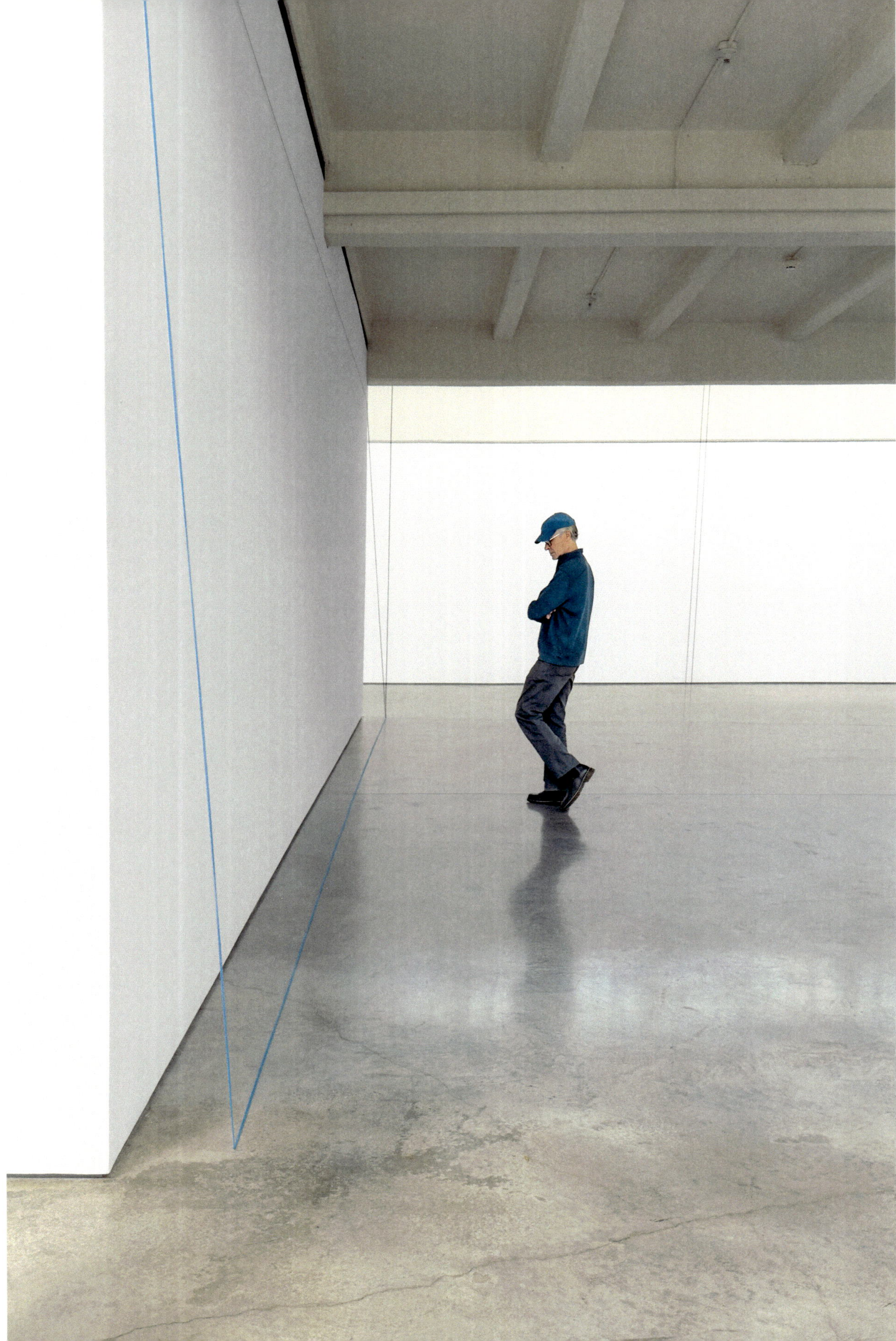

Foreword

If it all seems too bizarre to you, don't hesitate in throwing it all away in the wastepaper basket.

—Fred Sandback[1]

The profound and complex relationship between Fred Sandback and Dia Art Foundation dates back to the late 1960s, near the beginning of the artist's career. Even before he received his MFA from Yale School of Art and Architecture, the young artist connected with one of Dia's future founders, Heiner Friedrich.[2] Almost every year over the following decade, Sandback mounted solo exhibitions at Friedrich's galleries in Munich, Cologne, and New York City.

Sandback, who was not producing art that was "easily acquired or preserved … felt a great need for a sense of material continuity and permanence,"[3] and it was in his ongoing relationship with Dia Art Foundation that he found it. In 1981, Dia, together with the artist, inaugurated the Fred Sandback Museum in Winchendon, Massachusetts, which remained open for fifteen years. In time, Sandback would have solo exhibitions at Dia Art Foundation in SoHo; Dia Center for the Arts in New York City; and Dia Beacon, his last installation before his death in 2003. A posthumous exhibition of Sandback's prints took place at the Dan Flavin Art Institute in Bridgehampton in 2004. Sandback's work is on view at Dia Beacon today, just as he installed it back in 2003.

Like many artists striving to depart from centuries-old traditions of representational painting—particularly those in the then-recent movement of Abstract Expressionism—Sandback discovered the potency of variation within a confined universe of visual, material, and methodological parameters in sculptural and spatial realms. This rich diversity existed in the artwork and extended beyond it, engaging in a continuous dialogue with space—shaping and shaped by it, perceptible and comprehensible only through direct experience in the present moment. Numerous artists echoed this spatial and temporal awareness; Dan Flavin termed it *situational*, Robert Irwin *conditional*. Even in this book, *site aware* and *context dependent* variously describe this mode of artistic engagement. While these terms may not be interchangeable, they underscore the fundamental role of exteriority in Minimalist and Conceptual art practices and the viewer's role in completing the artistic equation. As Sandback

1. Fred Sandback, interview by *Sans Titre*, January 11, 1992, was first published in French in *Sans Titre, Bulletin d'Art Contemporain* (Lille, France), no. 16 (January–March 1992): 1–2. Available at https://www.fredsandbackarchive.org/publications.

2. Dia was founded in 1974 by Helen Winkler Fosdick, Heiner Friedrich, and Philippa de Menil (now Fariha al-Jerrahi).

3. Fred Sandback, "Remarks on My Sculpture 1966–86," in *Fred Sandback: Sculpture 1966–1986* (Mannheim, Germany: Kunsthalle Mannheim, 1986), 14.

aptly put it, "My marks are the gap between the spectator and the space that allow him to create his own conception of reality."[4]

This book celebrates Sandback and Dia's relationship—more than twenty years after the artist's installation opened to the public at Dia Beacon—as well as Dia's fiftieth anniversary. It also establishes a new iteration of the enduring relationship with many voices—both old friends and new—reflecting on its nuances.

In "The Work Is the Focus: On the Collaboration between Fred Sandback, Heiner Friedrich, and Dia Art Foundation," art historian and curator Corinna Thierolf highlights Sandback and Friedrich's shared objective of elevating the artist's work beyond commercial constraints and challenging conventional notions of sculpture. While she traces these relationships in time, Thierolf contextualizes Sandback and Friedrich, placing Dia Art Foundation in a wider framework.

Architectural designer and editor Julian Rose presents, in "Red Lines through the White Cube: Fred Sandback's Revisionary Architecture," a deep study of the spatial and architectural dimensions of Sandback's work and his "refusal of the binary structuring" that continues to inform contemporary artistic and institutional dynamics. Rose eloquently elucidates the axonometric specificities of Sandback's work, illuminating the artist's spatial concerns via isometric drawing and its relation-ship to the avant-garde; he concludes with an investigation of the white cube, post-studio practices, and the institutional spaces in today's global milieu.

In "Existing, Not Existing: Sculpture's Spaces in the Fred Sandback Museum," one of the most seasoned Sandback specialists, Edward A. Vazquez, author of *Aspects: Fred Sandback's Sculpture*, examines the importance of the Fred Sandback Museum, considering the genesis and life of this space while highlighting both the institutional complexities of the endeavor and the slippage between the public and private dimensions of the artist's practice.[5]

In August 2023, Matilde Guidelli-Guidi, Dia curator and department cohead, and director of exhibitions Curtis Harvey explored Dia's extensive support of artists and its establishment of single-artist museums during the 1970s, focusing, in particular, on the impactful relationship between the institution and Sandback. Their dialogue illuminates Sandback's unique approach to site-specificity and his skillful adaption of his sculptures to various architectural spaces. Emphasizing Sandback's conceptual understanding of space, they discuss his use of everyday materials like yarn and his rejection of traditional art-making notions to create encounters that transcend institutionalization and evoke a sense of tranquility for viewers sharing space with his sculptures.

4. Sandback, interview by *Sans Titre*.

5. Edward A. Vazquez, *Aspects: Fred Sandback's Sculpture* (Chicago: University of Chicago Press, 2017).

Much of the articulation of Minimalist and Conceptual art histories in and around Dia results from the rigorous and discerning work of Lynne Cooke, who was Dia's curator for almost two decades. In her essay "Fred Sandback at Dia Beacon," Cooke elucidates the interdependence between space and art and the particularities of Sandback's Dia Beacon installation. Cooke recognizes Sandback's departure from literal representation and pinpoints the interplay between vacancy and volume in his work as it relates to viewers in an affective phenomenological experience.

While installing his exhibition at Museo Tamayo in 2002, Sandback was "asked what he needed to understand the space, its architecture, and floorplan, and he responded with a smile, 'A chair, please.'"[6] Unlike many involved in this book and at Dia, I did not have the pleasure of meeting Fred Sandback. However, I have been exposed to his generosity, thoughtfulness, and deep sense of empathy through Amy Baker Sandback. It was in 2013, before my tenure at Dia, when I had the pleasure of spending time with Amy and Amavong Panya in Mexico City while we were installing *Un lugar en dos dimensiones: una selección de la colección Jumex + Fred Sandback* (*A Place in Two Dimensions: A Selection from the Jumex Collection + Fred Sandback*) at the Museo Jumex. I discovered then what I know now: the precision and care with which Amy has carried forward Fred's legacy. Dia is indebted to Amy, the Fred Sandback Archive, and David Gray for propelling and producing this publication and for years of wonderful allyship.

Dia is thankful to all contributors to this book and all who have been part of this story. The volume establishes another chapter in the multifaceted and long-standing relationship between Dia and Fred Sandback. *Interaction* is a new opportunity to revisit the richness of a lifelong partnership between the institution and the artist and to pay tribute to Sandback's uncompromising vision and creative fearlessness. Fred Sandback's art and life will continue to inspire and influence future generations.

Humberto Moro
Deputy Director of Program, Dia Art Foundation

6. Tobias Ostrander, *Fred Sandback*, ed. Friedemann Malsch and Christiane Meyer-Stoll (Berlin: Hatje Cantz, 2005), 186.

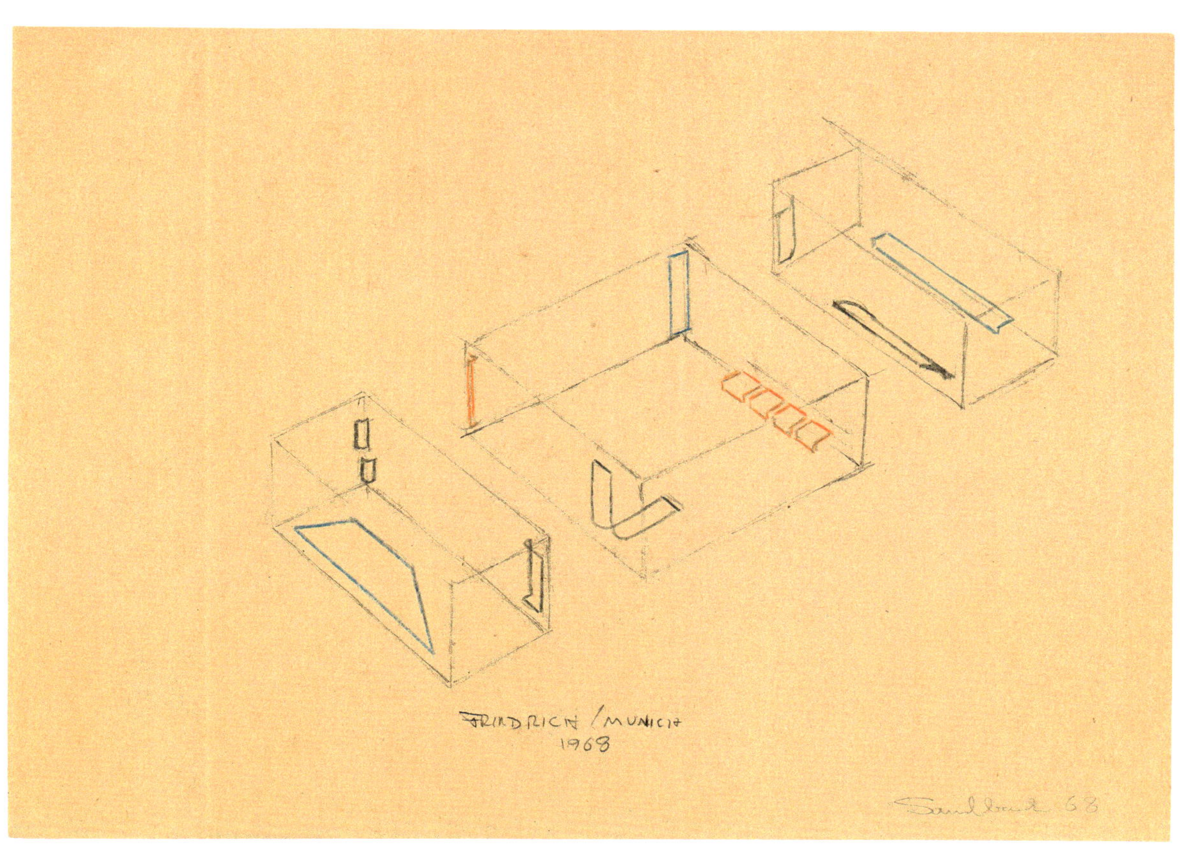

Untitled, 1968. Pencil and felt-tip pen on paper,
7¹¹⁄₁₆ × 10⅝ inches (19.5 × 27 cm). Sketch for
exhibition at Galerie Heiner Friedrich, Munich

The Work Is the Focus
On the Collaboration between Fred Sandback, Heiner Friedrich, and Dia Art Foundation

Corinna Thierolf

1. The archives I consulted did not hold documents that revealed the personal nature of Heiner Friedrich and Fred Sandback's relationship; instead, they evidenced the continuous nature of their exhibition planning. I especially rely here on the following sources: Stephan Urbaschek, *Dia Art Foundation: Institution und Sammlung, 1974–1985* (Marburg, Germany: Tectum Verlag, 2003); Lynne Cooke and Michael Govan, *Dia:Beacon* (New York: Dia Art Foundation, 2003); Günter Herzog, "Die Galerie Heiner Friedrich—München, Köln, New York, 1963–1980," in "Galerie Heiner Friedrich: München, Köln, New York, 1963–1980," ed. Heinz Holtmann, *Sediment: Mitteilungen zur Geschichte des Internationalen Kunsthandels ZADIK*, no. 21–22 (2013): 9–21; Corinna Thierolf, ed., *It Is the Art That Speaks: Heiner Friedrich in Conversation with Corinna Thierolf* (Munich: Schirmer/Mosel, 2018); and Kamilah N. Foreman, Matilde Guidelli-Guidi, and Sophia Larigakis, eds., *Dia: An Introduction to Dia's Locations and Sites* (New York: Dia Art Foundation, 2021); as well as materials from the Fred Sandback Archive, New York, which includes documents from Dia Art Foundation, New York; ZADIK | Central Archive for German and International Art Market Research | University of Cologne, Germany; and Thordis Moeller Archive, Millerton, New York. I wish to thank David Gray, Brigitte Jacobs van Renswou, Thordis Moeller, Nadine Oberste-Hetbleck, and Amy Sandback.

2. It has been rumored that Sandback and Friedrich met through Kasper König, but

The desire to bring focused awareness and extended visibility to Fred Sandback's oeuvre, which teeters on the brink of perception, lies at the heart of the fruitful long-term partnership between the artist and German gallerist Heiner Friedrich. Friedrich, who operated galleries in Munich, Cologne, and New York between 1963 and 1980, was a driving force behind the formation of Dia Art Foundation.[1]

The collaboration began in the late 1960s when the gallerist met Sandback on a visit to New York.[2] Subsequent visits expanded Friedrich's circle to include John Chamberlain, Walter De Maria, Andy Warhol, and La Monte Young, among others. This developing network, as Friedrich put it, "happened all at once in the mid-1960s. Our encounter with Dan Flavin came very early on. We met Donald Judd some time later and then of course we met Fred Sandback. Well let's say we had a lot to look forward to."[3]

In fact, unprecedented transatlantic dialogue between the United States and Europe marked the 1960s contemporary art world. In Germany, Friedrich, along with other notable gallerists such as Konrad Fischer, Rolf Ricke, and Rudolf Zwirner, spearheaded the exchanges. Like most of the artists they represented, these gallerists were in their thirties and had the intellectual curiosity and entrepreneurial drive to provide a forum for the art of their time. Inspired by innovative American gallerists, such as Richard Bellamy, Leo Castelli, Virginia Dwan, and Sidney Janis, their joint efforts defined and heightened the international visibility of postwar Western art and brought advanced art into museum collections at an early stage in their development. A comparison of their gallery programs shows that no individual figure can be credited with the lead role; rather, their collaboration, equally determined by mutual admiration and competition, fertilized the soil. From the 1960s onward, their alliance built a network that reached through much of Western Europe.[4]

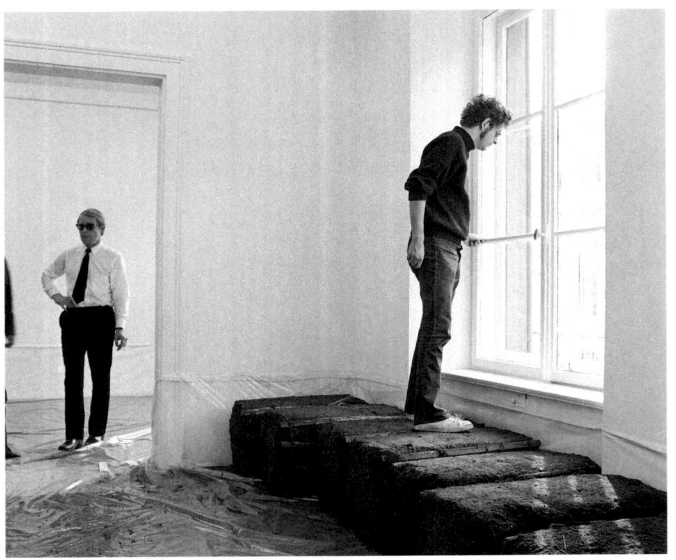 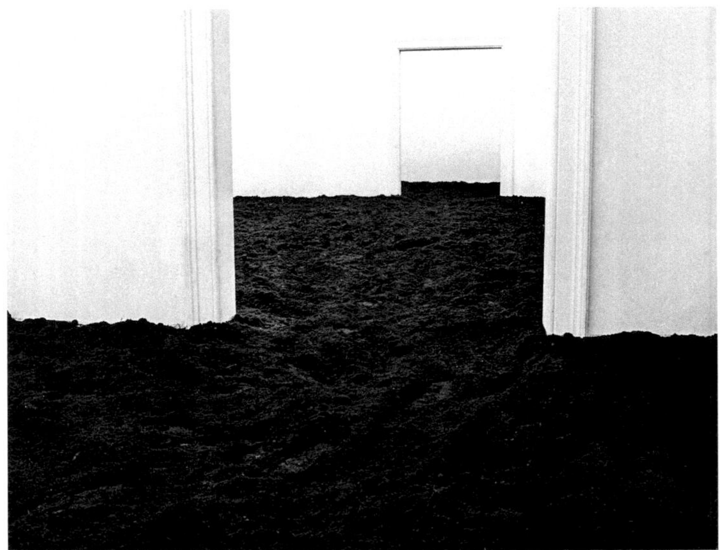

**Heiner Friedrich and Walter De Maria during
the installation of** *Munich Earth Room,* **1968**

Walter De Maria, *Munich Earth Room,* **1968**

this is unlikely: Konrad Fischer wrote to
König in May 1968, immediately after the
first exhibition of Sandback's sculpture at
his gallery, saying, "Our letter comes with
Fred Sandback to New York. His exhibition
is excellent. And he himself is a very nice
and intelligent person. Do get to know
him." Konrad Fischer, letter to Kasper
König, May 19, 1968, ZADIK (Zentralarchiv
des Internationalen Kunsthandels e.V.),
G20, IV, 2; see also "Kasper König: The
Formative Years," ed. Klaus Gerrit Friese,
*Sediment: Mitteilungen zur Geschichte des
Internationalen Kunsthandels ZADIK,* no.
23–24, (2014): 68.

3. Heiner Friedrich, in *It Is the Art That
Speaks,* 18.

4. The network also included Wide White
Space in Antwerp, Belgium; Enzo Sperone
in Turin, Italy; and Ileana Sonnabend in
Paris. It influenced art museums and
other public art institutions, particularly
in Aachen, Cologne, Darmstadt, Krefeld,
Leverkusen, and Mönchengladbach,
Germany; Amsterdam and Eindhoven,
the Netherlands; Bern, Switzerland; and
Stockholm, Sweden.

The artists Friedrich met found him to be not only an effective gallerist but
also a visionary partner who sought to overcome the commercial constraints of the
gallery scene.[5] Exhibitions in his Munich gallery were presented in such varied and
compelling succession that they enhanced and strengthened one another, creating
synergy between artists who made works of tremendous physical presence and others
whose art was nearly immaterial, artists who maintained stringent practices and artists
who worked with impassioned spontaneity. Indeed, this stimulating environment was
described as early as 1968 in a newspaper article about Sandback's first sculpture
exhibition in Munich, which came on the heels of De Maria's *Dirt Show/The Land
Show: Pure Dirt, Pure Earth, Pure Land.* For De Maria's exhibition, now known as *Munich
Earth Room,* the gallery's rooms had been filled knee-deep with earth: "Following the
forceful impact of the 'pure earth' covering the gallery floors . . . by American artist
De Maria, the gallery has now gone to the other extreme"—to the "pencil-thin" works
of Sandback.[6] Sandback himself described his work as "incorporat[ing] specific parts of
the environment, [while staying] coexistent with that environment, as opposed to
overwhelming or destroying that environment in favor of a different one."[7]

It was Friedrich's 1968 group exhibition *Drawings* that introduced Sandback
to a German audience and ushered in fifteen succeeding solo shows in Friedrich's
Munich, Cologne, and New York galleries.[8] The artist, at just twenty-four years old,
was the youngest in a show that also included a who's who of the cutting-edge art
scene in 1960s New York—Jo Baer, De Maria, Flavin, Eva Hesse, Judd, and Sol LeWitt,
known for their radical association with Conceptual art, Minimalism, and Process art.[9]

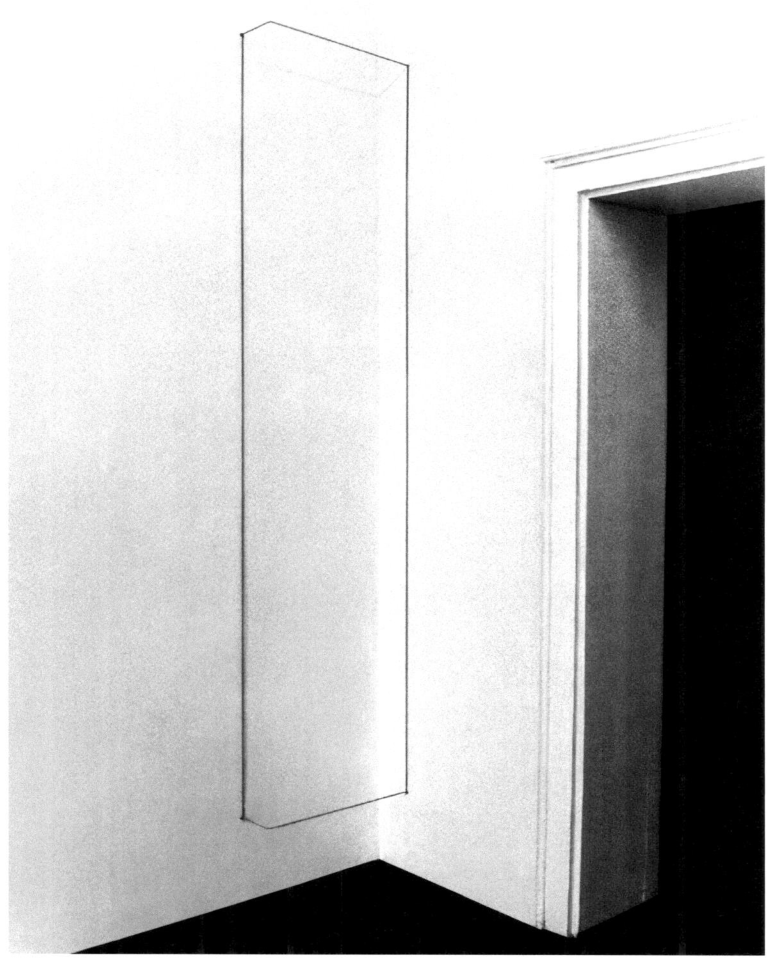

5. Friedrich's gallery represented many
artists who later were supported by Dia
Art Foundation, notably Americans John
Chamberlain, Walter De Maria, Dan
Flavin, Michael Heizer, Donald Judd, Fred
Sandback, Cy Twombly, Andy Warhol,
Robert Whitman, La Monte Young, and
Marian Zazeela, as well as German artists
including Joseph Beuys, Imi Knoebel,
Blinky Palermo, Gerhard Richter, and
Franz Erhard Walther.

Six months later, Friedrich's Munich gallery presented ten new Sandback works whose spatial reference points were concentrated on a corner, a wall, or the floor. Like traditional sculptures, these works could easily be moved from one room to another. By 1971, however, Sandback wished to devote a whole room to a single work; Friedrich readily accommodated the request and extended invitations to other artists in the gallery stable to do so as well.[10] Such solo presentations evolved into one-to-one relationships between artworks and the spaces they occupied; the concept of "one work, one room" would become the gallery's defining pursuit, one that would elevate artworks beyond mere marketable goods.

In order to carry this ambitious idea out, Friedrich invited the artists he worked with to make trips between Europe and the United States, which enabled them to make their art in situ, an unprecedented practice; the artists' role in the

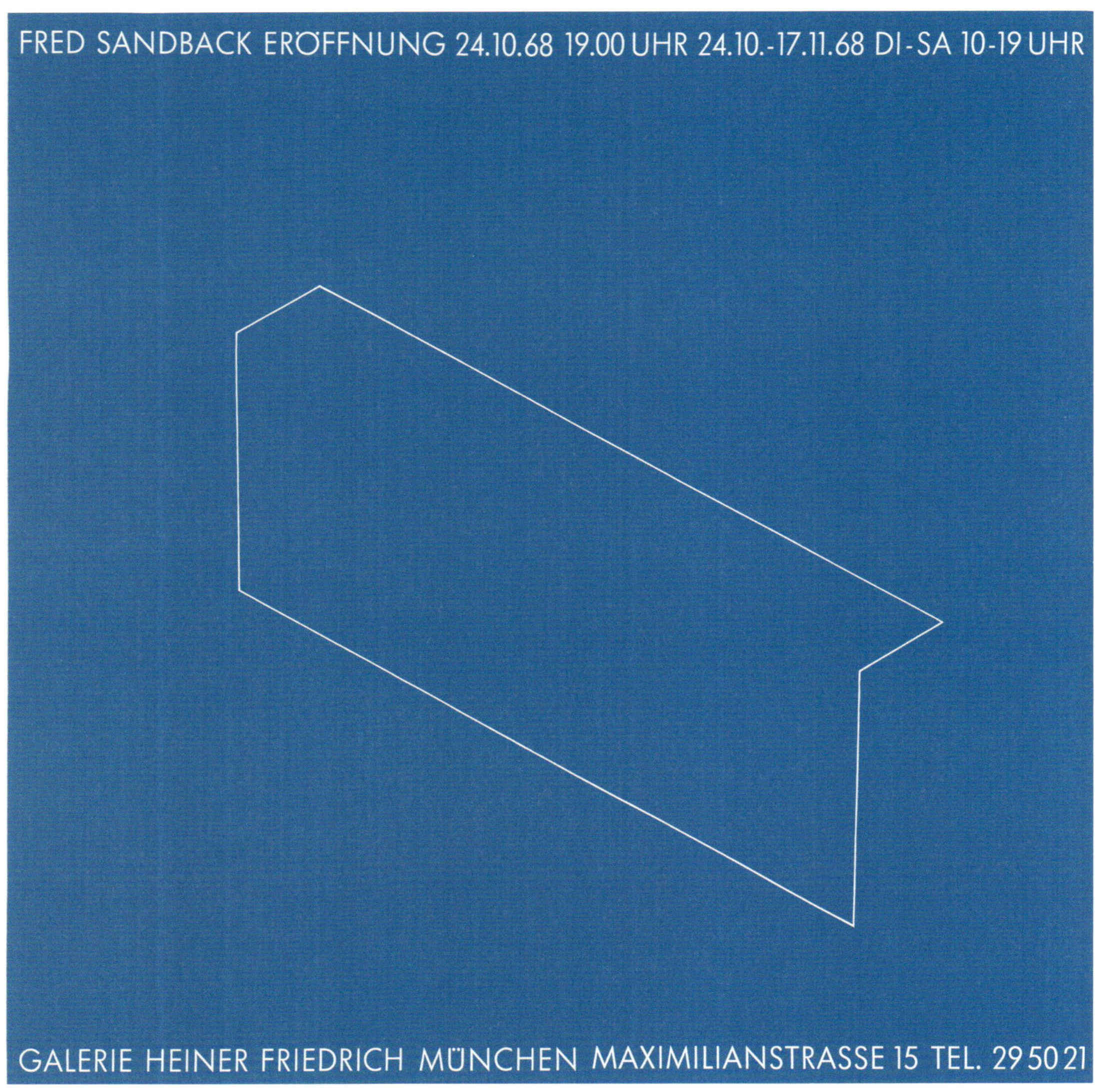

Poster for *Fred Sandback*, Galerie Heiner Friedrich, Munich, 1968

6. C. v. B, "Farbige Ströme quellen. Kurzberichte aus Münchner Galerien," *Abendzeitung München*, November 20, 1968.

7. Fred Sandback, "Notes," in *74 Front Street: The Fred Sandback Museum* (New York: Dia Art Foundation, 1982), 4. This text was first published in English and Italian in *Flash Art*, no. 40 (March–May 1973): 14; it is

installation of their work was not only innovative in the gallery world but also opened the gates separating artists from art lovers and collectors. Friedrich also provided the artists with substantial material support and fees for the creation of artworks, in addition to a percentage of sales income. He insisted that "the main connection with the artists was always the work of art."[11] Friedrich believed that artworks should be considered more than simple products—"Art is never a commodity; it was never a commodity and it will never be a commodity!"[12]—and asserted that the time span of an exhibition was too brief for a true experience of the works: "Every time an exhibition was installed: It was heaven! And when an exhibition came down: It was hell! . . . That created a lot of inner difficulties for me and led slowly to this notion of

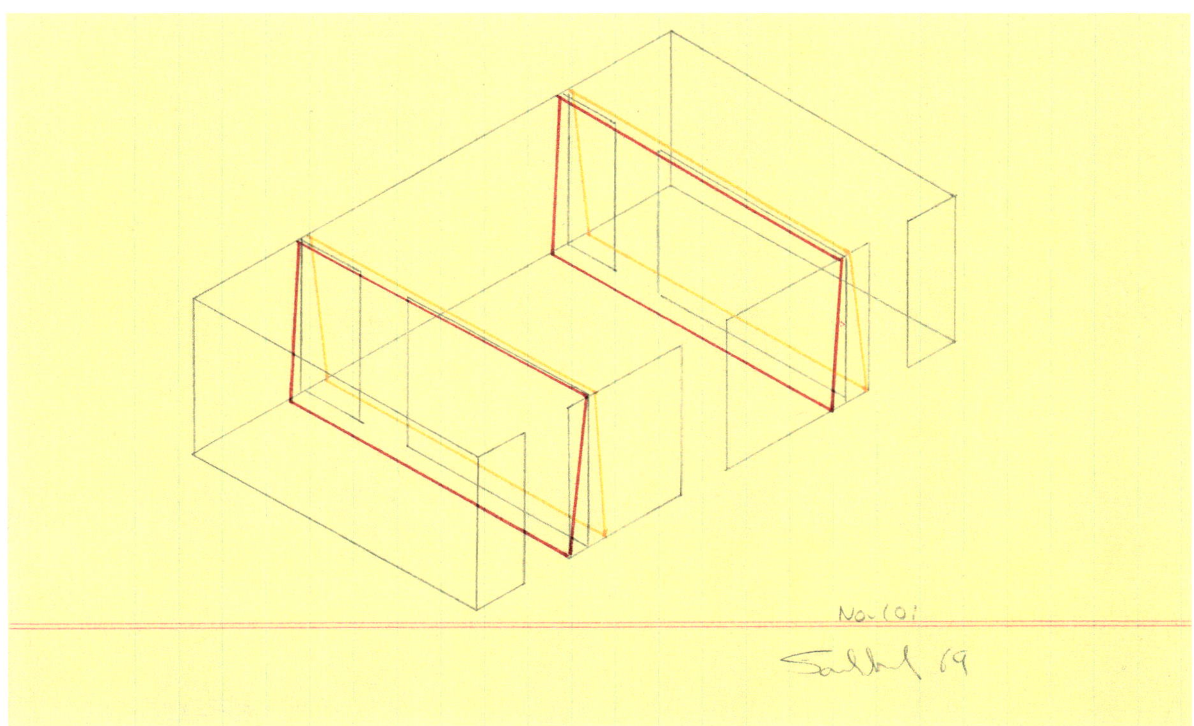

Untitled (no. 101, from 133 Proposals for the Heiner Friedrich Gallery), 1969. Ink and pencil on paper, 5 × 7⅞ inches (12.7 × 20 cm)

Untitled (One of Eight Situations for Heiner Friedrich), 1970. Acrylic yarn (black), situational dimensions, overall dimensions vary with each installation using spatial relationships established by the artist. Installation view, Galerie Heiner Friedrich, Munich, 1970

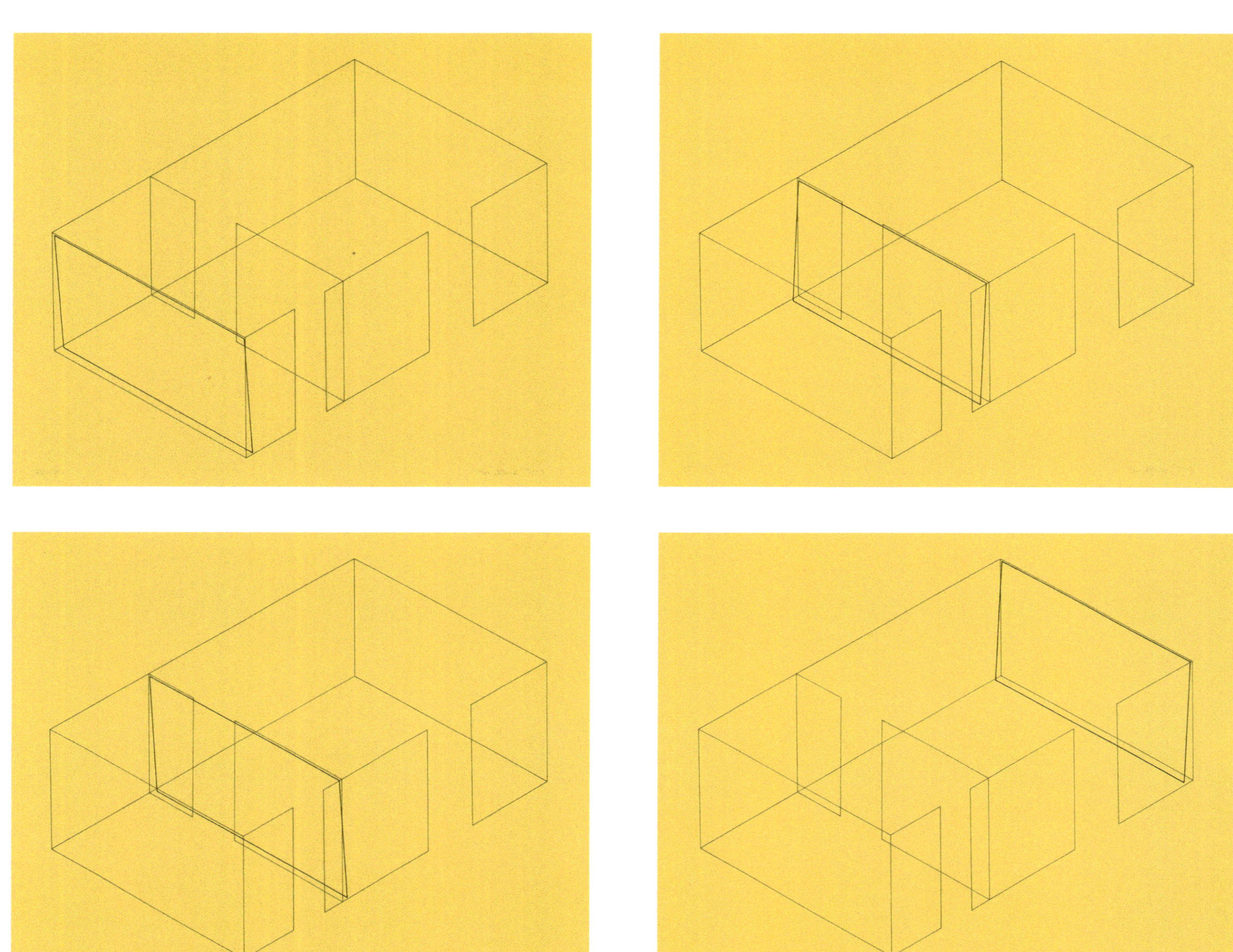

Eight Variations for Heiner Friedrich Gallery, 1971.
Screen prints on cardstock, 8 prints: 15 × 19¼ inches
(38.1 × 48.9 cm) each, edition of 50

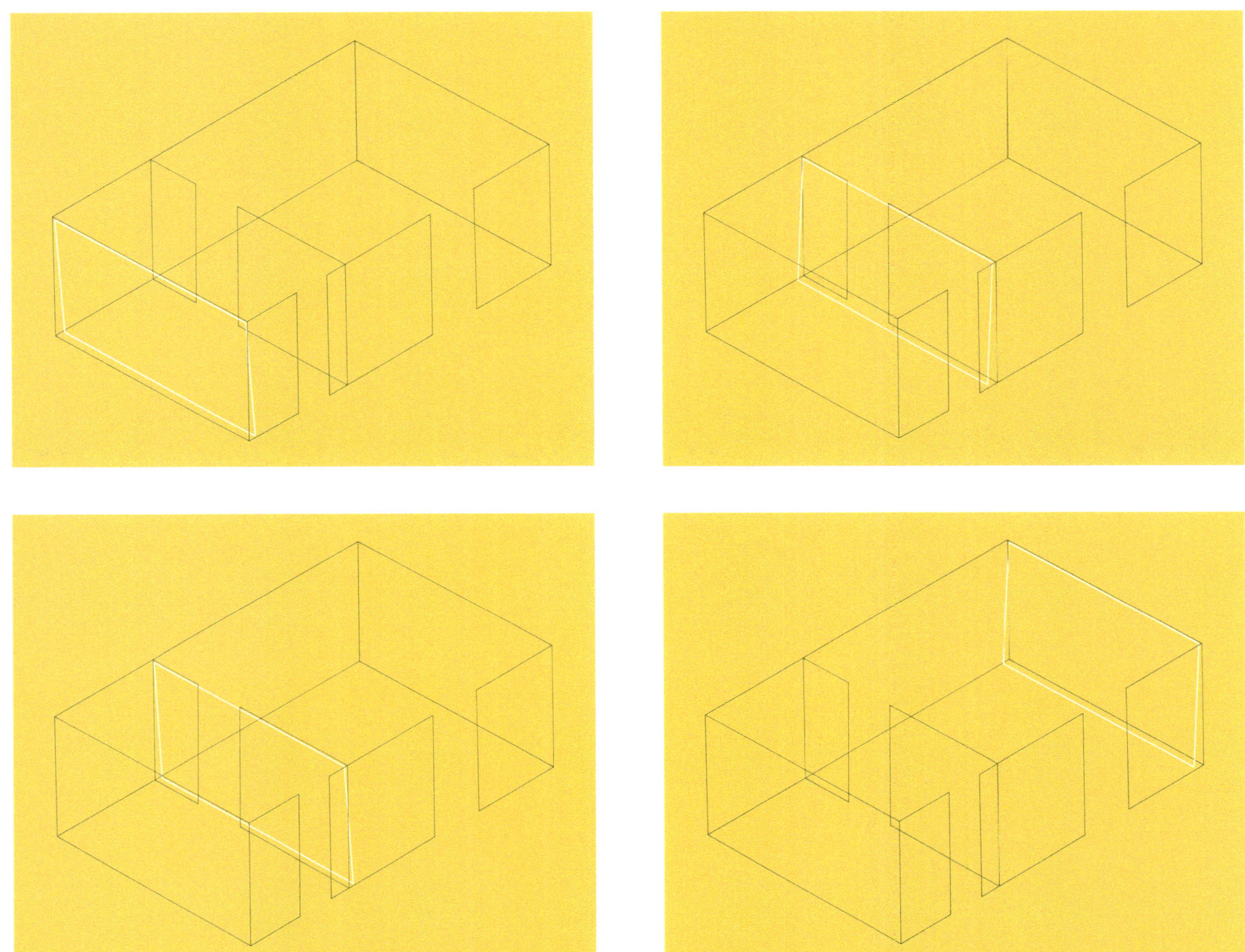

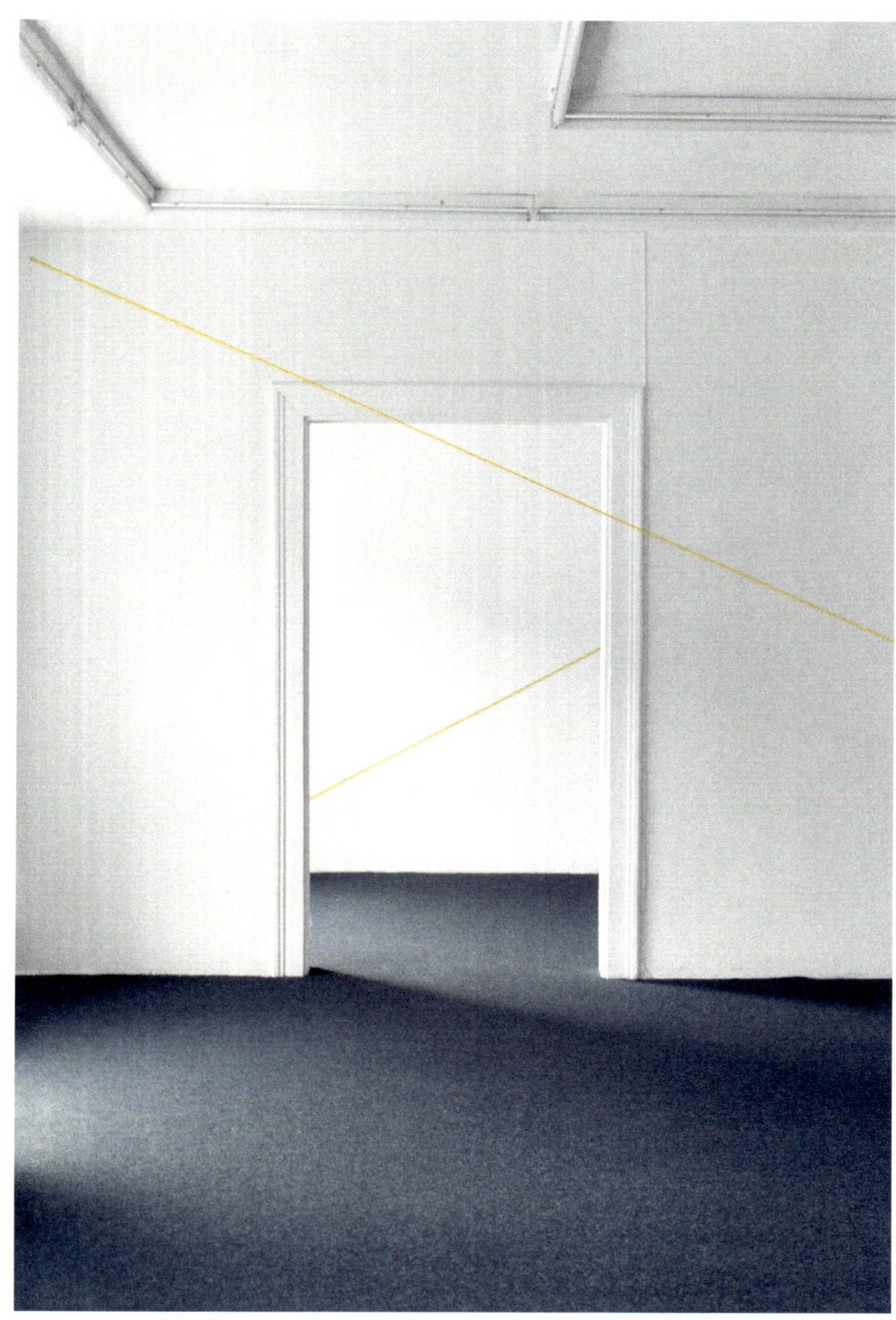

16 Variations of 2 Diagonal Lines, 1972. Acrylic yarn
(yellow), situational dimensions, overall dimensions
vary with each installation using spatial relationships
established by the artist. Installation view, Galerie
Heiner Friedrich, Munich, 1972

available online along with all other texts by Sandback at https://www.fredsandback archive.org/publications.

8. In a 2013 essay, Günter Herzog briefly mentioned this exhibition, bringing to light a forgotten fact that points to Sandback's first European recognition. Herzog, "Die Galerie Heiner Friedrich," 9–21. Herzog notes that "Darboven" and "Kiefer" also participated in the show. While Friedrich had worked with Hanne Darboven several times before, it would be the only known collaboration between Friedrich and Kiefer—if indeed it was Anselm Kiefer. Kiefer's archives contain no reference to the exhibition. (Waltraud Forelli, note to the author, Atelier Anselm Kiefer, July 26, 2023.)

9. This high-profile selection reflects Friedrich's rapid maturation in the contemporary-art field. Admitting his own inexperience at the time, he recently recalled, "It all happened at a time when I knew nothing about art. I knew classical antiquity and the Renaissance from my trips to Greece and Italy, but I was completely unprepared for the rest of it." Friedrich, in *It Is the Art That Speaks*, 18.

10. The idea seems to have gained traction when Walter De Maria installed *Munich Earth Room* in 1968. See his drawing proposals for the show in *Fred Sandback* (Ostfildern-Ruit, Germany: Hatje Cantz, 2005), 242. See also Dieter Schwarz, "Two Parts Fantasy and One Part Structure: Drawings of Fred Sandback," in *Fred Sandback: Drawings* (Düsseldorf, Germany: Richter Verlag, 2014), 15.

11. Friedrich, in *It Is the Art That Speaks*, 35.

12. Ibid., 31.

13. Ibid., 35.

14. Ibid., 52.

15. See Mark Godfrey, "Fred Sandback Drawings," in *Fred Sandback: Drawings*, ed. Dieter Schwarz (Düsseldorf, Germany: Richter Verlag, 2014), 134.

16. Those spaces have remained unchanged ever since: De Maria's *The New York Earth Room* (1977) at 141 Wooster Street

the 'manifestation of art in the long term.'"[13] Comparing the art of his time to that of Renaissance masters ("artists of the greatness of Michelangelo"), he claimed his mission to be "presenting art publicly and permanently."[14] The gallery's whole-hearted support for artists was unprecedented.

Sandback had first developed his own concept of room-filling sculpture in 1968 in preparatory drawings for his January 1969 exhibition at the Dwan Gallery in New York. A related group of drawings show that Sandback came up with a total of 133 variations on rectangles made from cord that would "lean" against the walls of Friedrich's Munich gallery, sculptures that would be realized over the course of the exhibition. As the gallery could show only one sculpture at a time, the absent variations were presented in the form of drawings, which provided something akin to a musical score and allowed visitors to conjure an imaginary world in which the full scope of the variations might play out.[15] In future exhibitions at Friedrich's galleries—in 1974 in Cologne and in 1978 in New York—Sandback again stretched the limits of an exhibition's space and time. In two exhibition sketches for Cologne, for example, six black and red lines intersecting over a floor plan represent notations for sculptures to be installed successively in the gallery over the course of six weeks.

Meanwhile, a corresponding desire to extend the duration of the shows in his galleries led Friedrich to envision "permanent" exhibitions. With this in mind, Friedrich closed his two New York galleries in 1977 and 1979 respectively, and almost immediately reopened them under the name Dia Art Foundation.[16] Dia, founded in 1974 by Friedrich, along with art historian Helen Winkler Fosdick and Friedrich's then wife, art patron Philippa de Menil (now Fariha al-Jerrahi), was rooted in an idealistic approach that enabled artists to make sited works of outstanding precision and scale, in addition to creating art for trade. This resulted in such publicly accessible works as Walter De Maria's *The Lightning Field* (1977) and Joseph Beuys's *7000 Eichen* (7000 Oaks, 1982), which set new paradigms for the art of the second half of the twentieth century. Dia's founders pursued a clear mission to closely collaborate with artists in placing their works on long-term view to the public. Funds were also allocated to build substantial collections of works by a select group of artists; fifty-nine sculptures, as well as many prints and a few drawings, by Sandback were eventually acquired. In addition, buildings and land were purchased to provide facilities where artists could develop projects to the highest standards without the constraints of administrative regulations. For Sandback, this resulted in the 1981 inauguration of the Fred Sandback Museum in Winchendon,

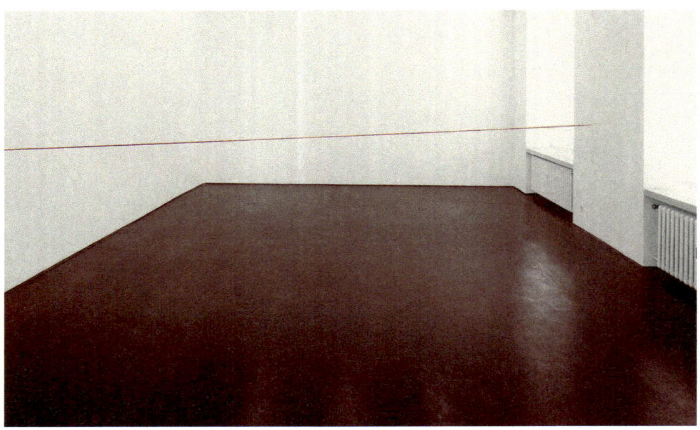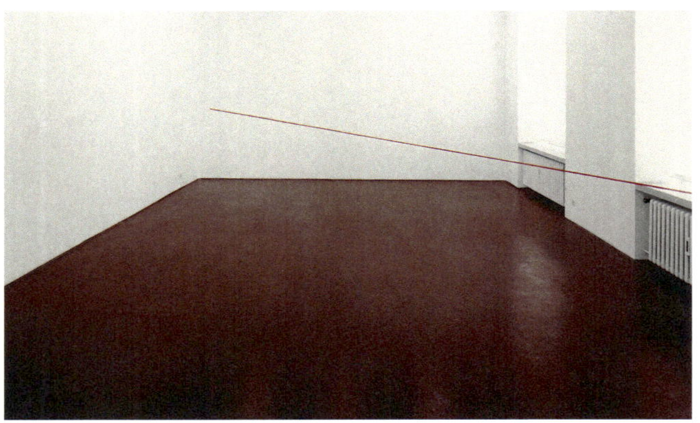

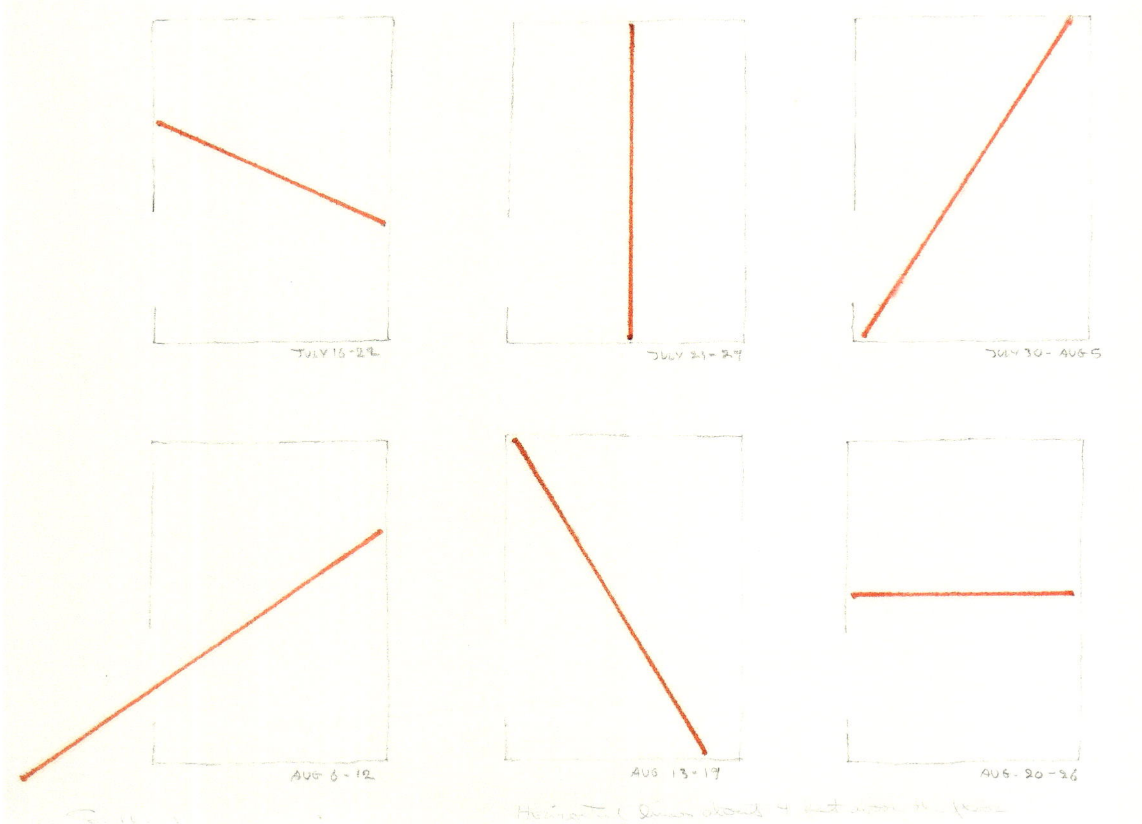

From *Untitled (Six Red Horizontal Lines)*, 1974.
Acrylic yarn (red), situational dimensions, overall
dimensions vary with each installation using spatial
relationships established by the artist. Installation
views, Galerie Heiner Friedrich, Cologne, 1974

*Untitled (Horizontal Lines about 4 Feet above the
Floor, Galerie Heiner Friedrich)*, 1974. Pencil and
felt-tip pen on paper, 8 × 10⅞ inches (20.3 × 27.5 cm)

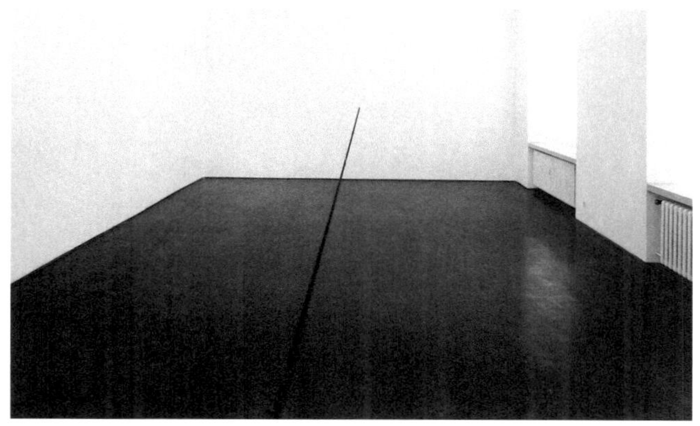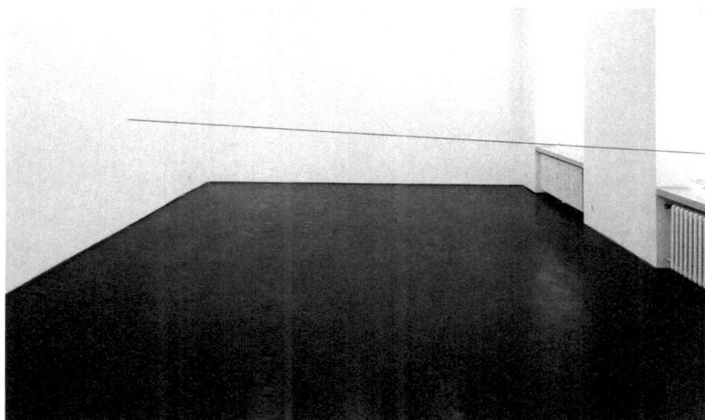

Massachusetts. Though open to the public, these spaces were not expected to bring a high volume of visitors so that those who came could truly *experience* them in full and without distraction.

Dia aimed for continuity. As the founders noted in their mission statement, which referred to chapels and sacred sites of the past, there is historically nothing new in the desire for permanence. Though they have continually been reinterpreted by staff and modified by changing cultural conditions, the institution's goals, as set forth in the early documents, endure for today's Dia Art Foundation.[17] Such steadfastness is rare in an era dominated by an art scene that is ever changing and moving ever faster. Today, long-term works commissioned during the early years of the institution, as well as recently acquired long-term projects—such as Nancy Holt's *Sun Tunnels* (1973–76) in the Great Basin Desert, Utah, and Cameron Rowland's *Depreciation* (2018) on Edisto Island, South Carolina—are maintained alongside Dia Beacon and Dia Chelsea, more traditional museum venues with works from the collection on view and temporary exhibitions. Viewers of Sandback's work at the foundation's upstate New York venue, Dia Beacon, a converted 1929 factory building, have a very different experience than those who visited Sandback's 1996–97 exhibition on the third floor of Dia Center for the Arts, a renovated warehouse in Manhattan dating from 1920, because each presentation precisely navigated distinct architectural environments. But the respite offered by Sandback's ultrafine and precise expressions in the sheltered nucleus of the Manhattan space, which starkly contrasted with the cacophany of the city street outside, is nevertheless analogous to that provided by Dia Beacon, with its expansive halls and Hudson Valley vistas. Holding fast to his belief in the value of extended engagement, Friedrich today operates the Ayn Foundation, an institution that is likewise devoted to long-term presentations, including an installation at Mana Contemporary in Jersey City, New Jersey, of fourteen Sandback works.

and *The Broken Kilometer* (1979) at 393 West Broadway.

17. Dia's founders remain on the board as emeritus trustees. See Rachel Churner, "The Present Has the Light: Heiner Friedrich in Conversation," May 6, 2019, https://www.manacontemporary.com/editorial/heiner-friedrich-in-conversation. For more information on Dia's exhibition making and core values, see Michael Govan, Marianne Stockebrand, and Gianfranco Verna, conversation with Fred Sandback, 26–32, and Michael Meredith, "Fred Sandback: Sculpture," 32–33, *Chinati Foundation Newsletter*, no. 7 (October 2002): 32.

DIA ART FOUNDATION

FOR IMMEDIATE RELEASE   FEBRUARY 22,1988

FRED SANDBACK: SCULPTURES
DIA ART FOUNDATION, 155 MERCER STREET

Four new sculptures by Fred Sandback will be exhibited at the Dia
Art Foundation, 155 Mercer Street, New York. The exhibition opens on Wednesday,
February 24, 1988, and will continue for this season through June 18, 1988.
Hours are Wednesday through Saturday, 12 noon to 6:00 p.m. Admission
is free.

The four new works exhibited here continue themes consolidated by Sandback
in two recent museum exhibitions in West Germany -- "Diagonal Constructions/
Broken Lines" at the Kestner-Gesellschaft in Hannover and "Vertical Constructions"
at the Westfalischer Kunstverein in Munster, both in 1987. The sculptures
are made from yarn, stretched taut, creating palpable spatial relationships
and subtle visual effects.

Sandback has written of his sculpture:

"The line is a means to mediate the quality or timbre of a situation,
and has a structure which is quick and abstract and more or less
thinkable, but it's the tonality or, if you want, wholeness of a
situation that is what I'm trying to get at. My intrusions are
usually modest, perhaps because it seems like it's that first moment
when things start to coalesce that is interesting.

"Most of my work is executed in and for a particular place. It's
always been conceived with at least a generalized sort of place
in mind, but these pieces are now bound to one site. This follows
from a desire to be working 'on location,' but also and more strongly
from my unwillingness to settle for the abstractness of more
generalized situations."

# # # # #

For further information, contact: Gary Garrels, Director of Programs
                                    Phone: 212-431-9232

Press release for *Fred Sandback: Sculptures,*
Dia Art Foundation, 1988

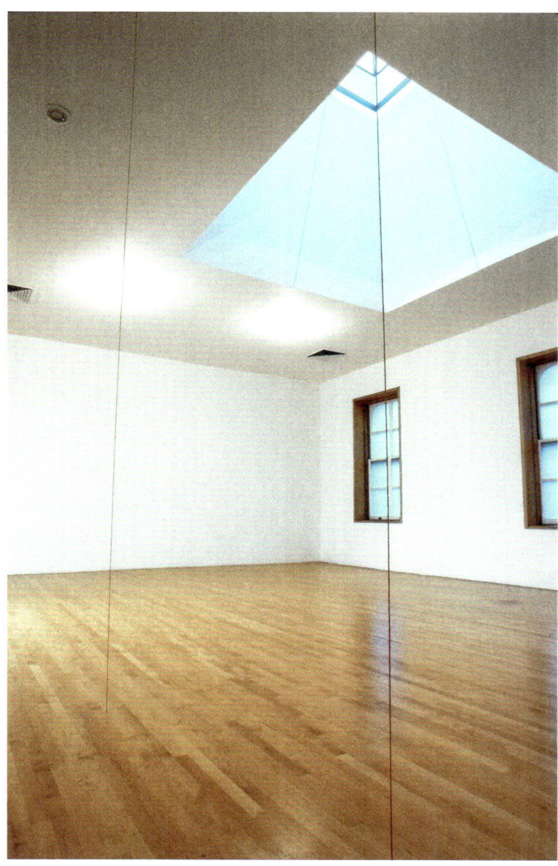

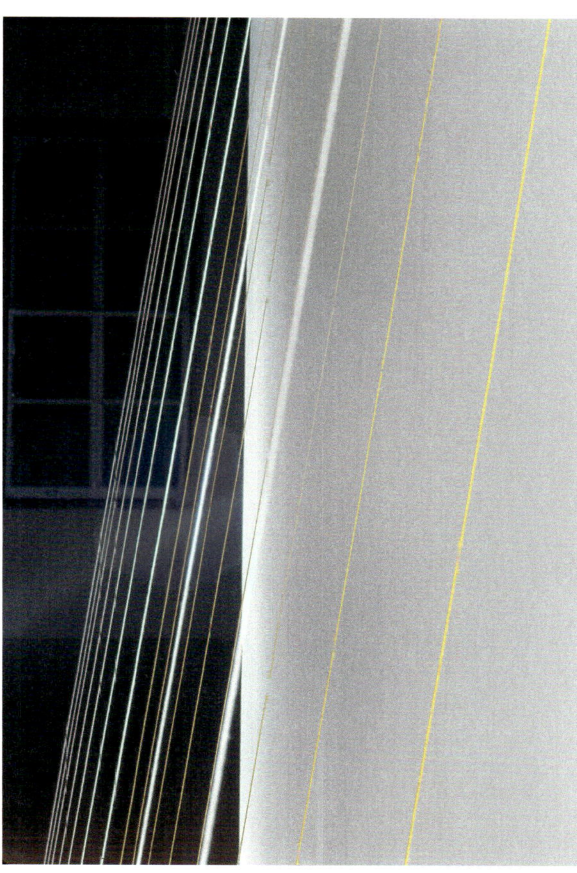

Installation views, *Fred Sandback:*
Sculptures, Dia Art Foundation, New York

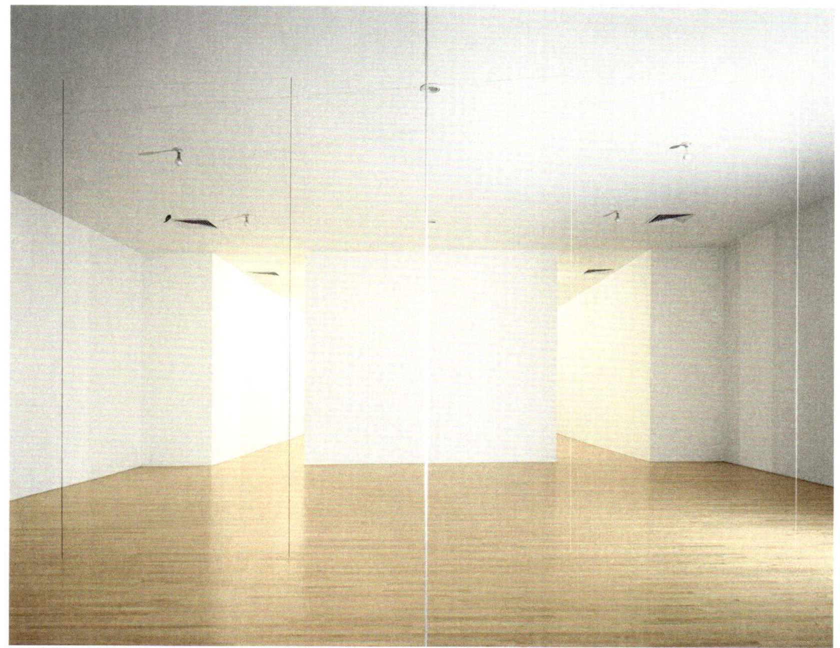

Chronology of
Fred Sandback's Collaborations with Heiner Friedrich

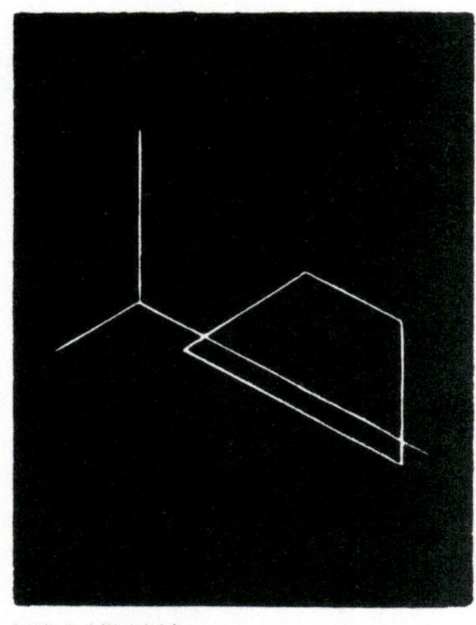

Invitation to *Fred Sandback: Frühe Skulpturen* and *Neue Grafik (Zeichnungen, Linolschnitte, Radierungen, Lithographien)*, Galerie Heiner Friedrich, Munich, 1975

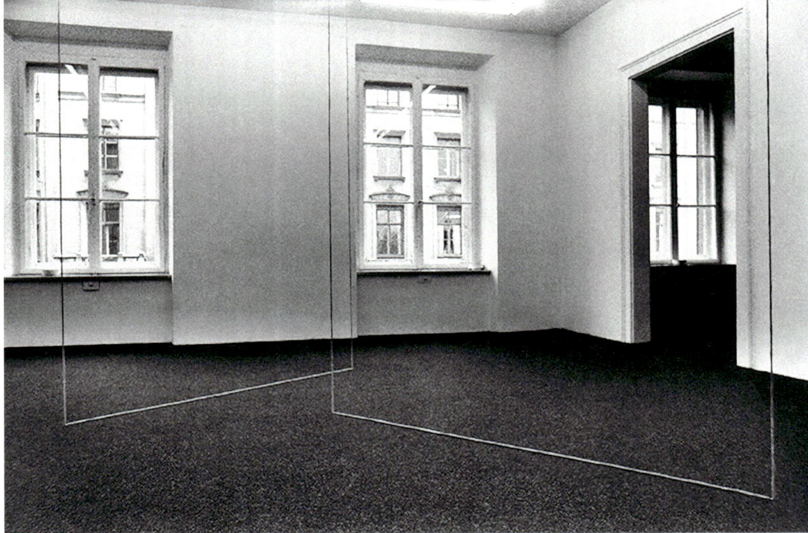

Installation view, *Fred Sandback: Neue Druckgraphik und Skulpturen, 1976 und 1977*, Galerie Heiner Friedrich, Munich, 1977

1968

Drawings: Andre, Baer, Bochner, Bollinger, Darboven, Flavin, Hesse, Judd, Kiefer, Kuehn, LeWitt, Mangold, De Maria, Morris, Moskowitz, Nauman, Novros, Ryman, Sandback, Smithson, Stella, Wells, Zox. Galerie Heiner Friedrich, Munich

Fred Sandback. Galerie Heiner Friedrich, Munich

1970

Fred Sandback. Galerie Heiner Friedrich, Munich

1971

Fred Sandback: Eight Variations for Heiner Friedrich Gallery. Galerie Heiner Friedrich, Munich

1972

Fred Sandback: 16 Variations of 2 Diagonal Lines. Galerie Heiner Friedrich, Munich

1973

Fred Sandback: 16 Variations of 2 Horizontal Lines. Galerie Heiner Friedrich, Munich

1974

Fred Sandback: Untitled (Six Horizontal Lines/Six Red Lines). Galerie Heiner Friedrich, Cologne

Fred Sandback: Zeichnungen. Galerie Heiner Friedrich, Munich

1975

Fred Sandback. Heiner Friedrich, Inc., New York

Fred Sandback: Frühe Skulpturen. Galerie Heiner Friedrich, Munich

Fred Sandback: Neue Grafik (Zeichnungen, Linolschnitt, Radierungen, Lithographien). Galerie Heiner Friedrich, Munich

1976

An Exhibition for the War Resisters League: Carl Andre, Larry Bell, John Chamberlain, Walter De Maria, Dan Flavin, Donald Judd, Sol LeWitt, David Rabinowitch, Fred Sandback, Richard Serra. Heiner Friedrich, Inc., New York

Fred Sandback. Heiner Friedrich, Inc., New York

Fred Sandback: Skulptur. Galerie Heiner Friedrich, Cologne

1977

Fred Sandback: Neue Druckgraphik und Skulpturen, 1976 und 1977. Galerie Heiner Friedrich, Munich

Handzeichnungen deutscher und amerikanischer Künstler: Baselitz, De Maria, Flavin, Judd, Knoebel, Palermo, Sandback, Turrell, Walther, Whitman. Galerie Heiner Friedrich, Cologne

1978

Fred Sandback: New Works. Heiner Friedrich, Inc., New York

Fred Sandback: Neue Arbeiten. Galerie Heiner Friedrich, Cologne

1981

Fred Sandback. Fred Sandback Museum, Winchendon, Massachusetts

1983

Fred Sandback: New Graphic Work and a Continuing Exhibition of Sculpture from 1967–1981. Fred Sandback Museum, Winchendon, Massachusetts

Fred Sandback: New Sculpture and a Continuing Exhibition of Prints and Drawings. Fred Sandback Museum, Winchendon, Massachusetts

1987

Fred Sandback: New Work and Work from 1967. Fred Sandback Museum, Winchendon, Massachusetts

1988

Fred Sandback: Sculptures. Dia Art Foundation, New York

1996–97

Fred Sandback: Sculpture. Dia Center for the Arts, New York

2003–19; reopened 2021

Dia Beacon, Beacon, New York

2004–5

Fred Sandback: Prints, 1971–79. Dia Art Foundation, Dan Flavin Art Institute, Bridgehampton, New York

2018–ongoing

Fred Sandback: Sculpture. Ayn Foundation at Mana Contemporary, Jersey City, New Jersey

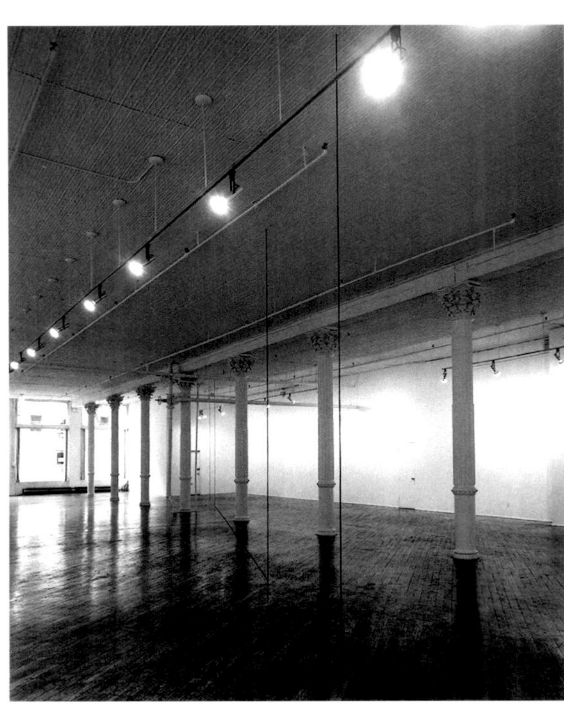

Installation view, *Fred Sandback: New Works*, Heiner Friedrich, Inc., New York, 1978

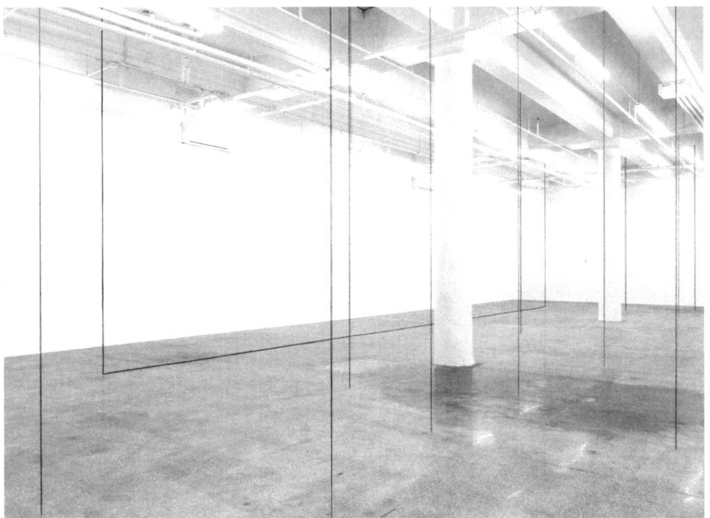

Installation view, *Fred Sandback: Sculpture*, Ayn Foundation at Mana Contemporary, Jersey City, New Jersey, 2018–ongoing

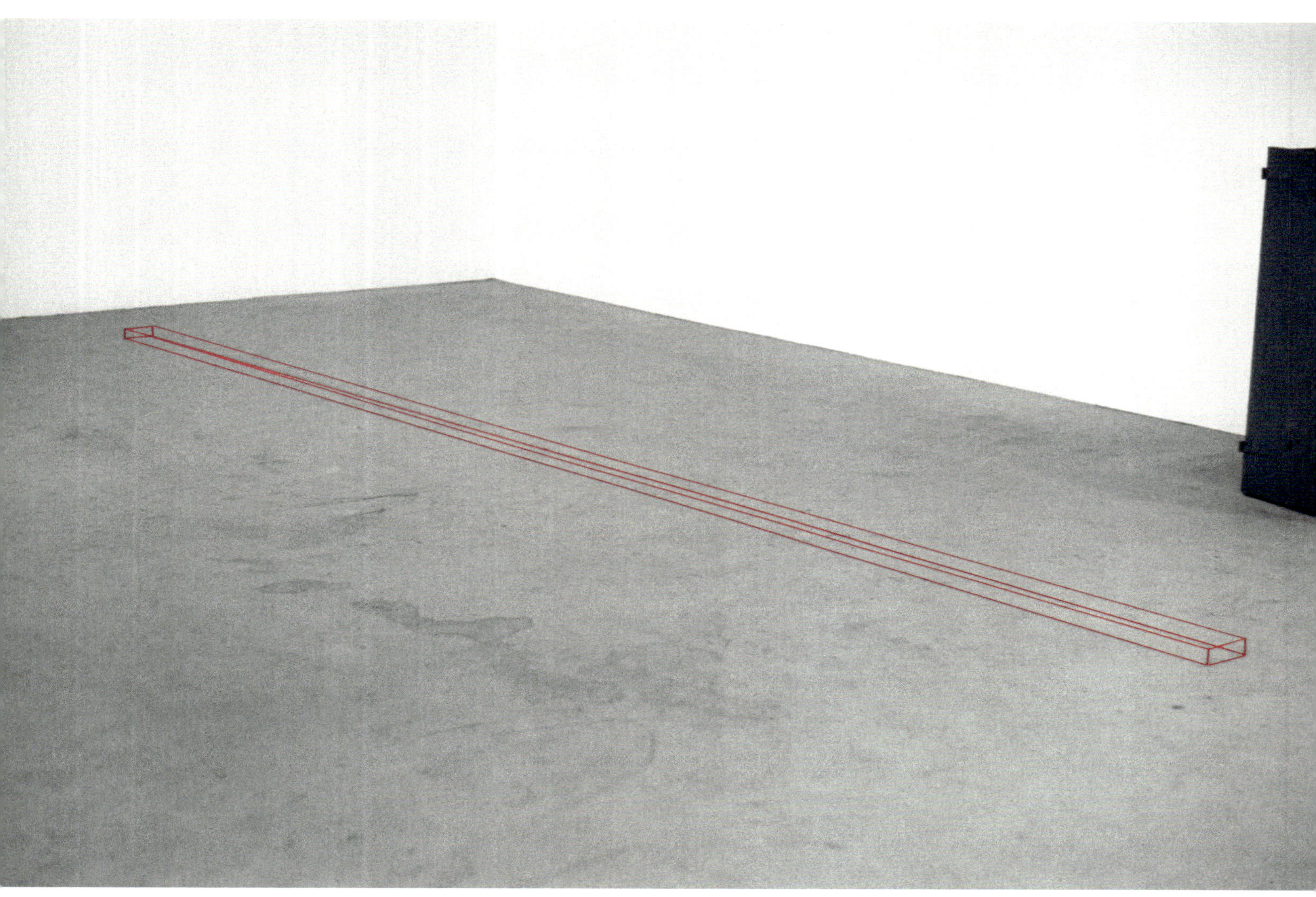

Untitled (Red Floor Piece), 1967. $\frac{1}{32}$-inch
elastic cord (red) and acrylic (red) on steel,
$1\frac{5}{8} \times 4\frac{1}{2} \times 264$ inches (4.1 × 11.4 × 670.6 cm).
Installation view in Sandback's studio,
Yale School of Art and Architecture, New
Haven, Connecticut

Red Lines through the White Cube

Fred Sandback's Revisionary Architecture

Julian Rose

Fred Sandback began his art practice with a conjuring act. In 1967, still an MFA student at the Yale School of Art and Architecture and dissatisfied with his initial experiments in sculpture, which he felt owed too much to conventions of modernist abstraction, Sandback had a breakthrough. As he described it some two decades later, "The first sculpture I made with a piece of string and a little wire, was the outline of a rectangular solid—a 2" × 4" lying on the floor."[1] In one sense, he was embarking on a path many cutting-edge American artists took in the 1960s. This was the decade of Minimalism, when artists reacted against the exuberant subjectivity that dominated Abstract Expressionism by reducing their work to raw materials and essential geometries. Among many examples, Carl Andre had been experimenting with placing sections of 12 × 12–inch timbers directly on the gallery floor since the early 1960s.[2] Surviving photographs show that Sandback stored spare materials on the floor of his studio at Yale; it is easy to imagine the young artist, fed up with his latest struggles carving or welding, looking down at a stack of lumber lying on the concrete and deciding to trace the outline of a single board in wire and string.

While this piece was grounded in Sandback's quotidian reality, his momentous decision to keep the work once removed from that reality—presenting only the ghostly silhouette of the board—set his practice apart from that of his contemporaries. The power of *Untitled (Red Floor Piece)* (1967) lies not in its shocking reduction of sculpture to brute material facticity but in the paradoxical way that it simultaneously evokes the board's presence and underscores its absence. In the artist's words, "It allowed me to play with something both existing and not existing at the same time. The thing itself—the 2" × 4" was just as material as it could be—a volume of air and light above the surface of the floor. Yet my forming of it, the shape and dimension of that figure, had an ambiguous and transient quality."[3] These two fundamental insights—first, that space itself can

1. Fred Sandback, "Remarks on My Sculpture 1966–86," in *Fred Sandback: Sculpture 1966–1986* (Mannheim, Germany: Kunsthalle Mannheim, 1986), 12. This text and all other published writings by Fred Sandback are online at https://www.fredsandbackarchive.org/publications.

2. In his *Elements* series, for example, begun in 1960, Andre used identical 36-inch sections of unfinished 12 × 12–inch lumber to create various geometric configurations.

3. Sandback, "Remarks on My Sculpture 1966–86," 12.

become a sculptural material, and second, that space can be shaped by merely tracing lines through it—propelled Sandback's work for the rest of his life.

Sandback was among many artists turning toward sculpture in the 1960s. If dramatic brushwork and painterly compositions were growing unpopular because they carried the aftertaste of an outmoded Abstract Expressionism, pictorial representation—the simulation of three-dimensional spaces and things on a two-dimensional canvas—was anathema, as it carried the full weight of the Western canon. As Donald Judd put it in his widely read and hugely influential article "Specific Objects," published in 1965, "Three dimensions are real space. That gets rid of the problem of illusionism . . . which is riddance of one of the salient and most objectionable relics of European art."[4] Two years later, Judd and Sandback developed a friendship while Judd was a visiting professor at Yale and Sandback his student. Perhaps under Judd's influence, Sandback would eventually abandon the evocation of an absent object manifest in *Untitled (Red Floor Piece)* to create more abstract geometries with lines woven through space.

Certainly, many commentators have read a lingering illusionism in this work. But only a few have noted something odd about the dimensions of *Untitled (Red Floor Piece)*: it is unusually long for a 2 × 4, 22 feet rather than the 8- or 10-foot lengths in which this lumber is typically sold, and slightly thinner than 2 and wider than 4 inches.[5] Can we say, then, that the artwork straightforwardly references an absent thing, presenting a three-dimensional picture of a real object? The bizarre fact is that the so-called 2 × 4 timbers ubiquitous in the American construction industry measure 1½ × 3½ inches. That half-inch gap is the difference between their nominal and actual dimensions, the implications of which are highly suggestive in relation to the work of Sandback, an artist deeply concerned with the nature of actuality itself.

In philosophy, the distinction between the nominal and the actual refers to the split between the realm of concepts and ideas—and the language used to represent and communicate them—and the concrete domain of physical reality, the material world as it exists independent of language and thought. In carpentry, the nominal dimensions refer to the size of the rough cut at the sawmill, when felled trees are cut green into 2 × 4–inch blanks. The wood is then dried, shrinking slightly from moisture loss, and finally planed on all four sides to create smooth surfaces, further reducing its dimensions.

Historically, the actual dimensions of a 2 × 4 were whatever resulted from this process, so 2 × 4s from different regions often varied in actual size. This worked fine when lumber was a locally produced resource and wood construction was largely

4. Donald Judd, "Specific Objects," *Arts Yearbook* 8 (1965): 78.

5. In a 2016 catalogue essay, Harry Cooper pointed out that such a section of wood would be "a very long two-by-four." See Harry Cooper, "Disillusion and Dissolution," in *Fred Sandback: Light, Space, Facts*, ed. Emily Wei Rales, Ali Nemerov, and Anne Reeve (Potomac, MD: Glenstone Foundation, 2016), 79. In his 2017 monograph, Edward A. Vazquez emphasized that the work's exact dimensions are 1⅝ × 4½ inches. See Edward A. Vazquez, *Aspects: Fred Sandback's Sculpture* (Chicago: University of Chicago Press, 2017), 22.

6. The best history of this evolution remains the report issued by the US Forest Products Laboratory in 1964: L. W. Smith and L. W. Wood, *History of Yard Lumber Size Standards* (Madison, WI: Forest Products Lab, 1964). Available online through the National Technical Reports Library: https://ntrl.ntis.gov/NTRL/dashboard/searchResults/titleDetail/PB2006102557.xhtml;jsessionid=85d9b84186b0633597fac72eb238.

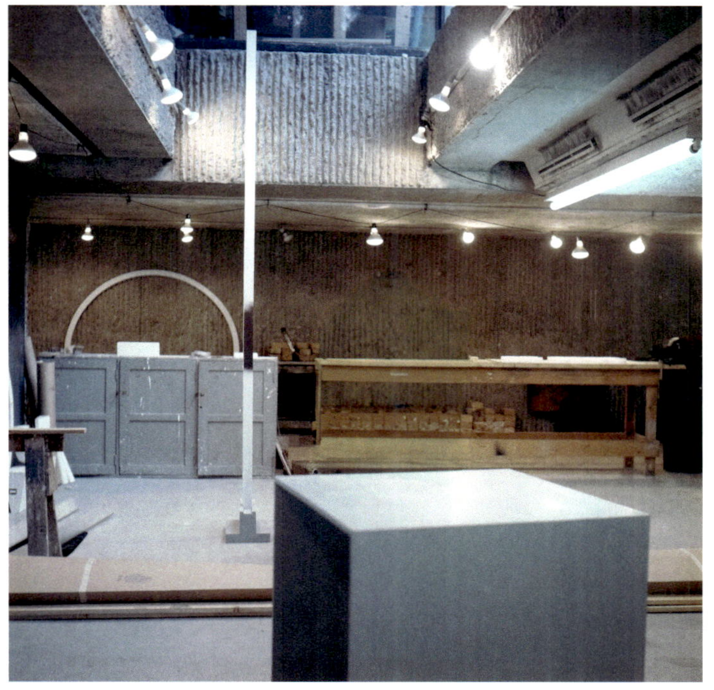 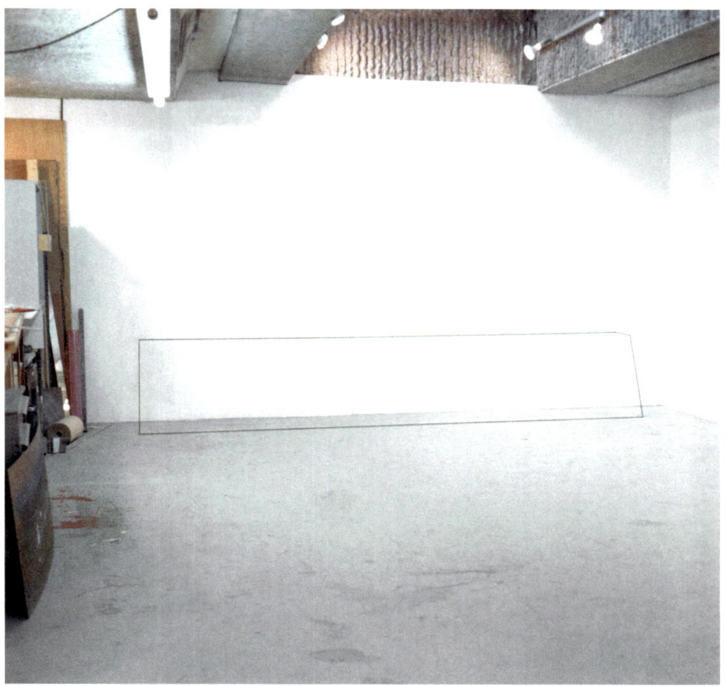

Given that *Untitled (Red Floor Piece)* measures precisely 1⅝ inches high—which is just within the industry-standard tolerance for the actual dimensions of a 2 × 4—it is entirely possible that Sandback based it on a piece of lumber in his studio or perhaps even used one as a jig to help him cut the thin steel rods to length. In any event, the piece's width of 4½ inches suggests that Sandback tweaked the final proportions of his sculpture until he felt they were suitable for its surrounding space. This contextual specificity came to define his work and echoes preindustrial construction methods.

artisanal—carpenters grew accustomed to the products of their local mill and often adjusted their size by hand on the job. By the late nineteenth century, the depletion of forests near urban centers meant that lumber was being shipped longer and longer distances, and it was important that all 2 × 4s be interchangeable, no matter where they were from. At the same time, the construction process itself industrialized, relying more on standardized components that could be assembled with less skilled labor; standardization was a crucial step in transforming lumber from a local craft material to a mass-produced commodity. Rule-of-thumb allowances for shrinkage and dressing suggested that no more than ⅛ inch would be lost from each side of a green 2 × 4 blank, so initial proposals were to standardize the size of these timbers at 1¾ × 3¾ inches. But the American lumber industry eventually realized that selling smaller timbers as "2 × 4s"—even if they were originally cut green to smaller dimensions, so were not even nominally 2 × 4 inches—would allow savings in both material and freight costs; thus, wood construction could remain competitive with new building materials, such as cement block. In 1964, the industry finally set the size of these boards at 1½ × 3½ inches, ignoring protests from retailers and customers that they were "selling air."[6]

A 2 × 4 is thus an object lesson in the reality of the built environment. Where architecture is concerned, there are no Platonic oppositions between the ideal and the real or between appearance and reality but rather an ever-shifting

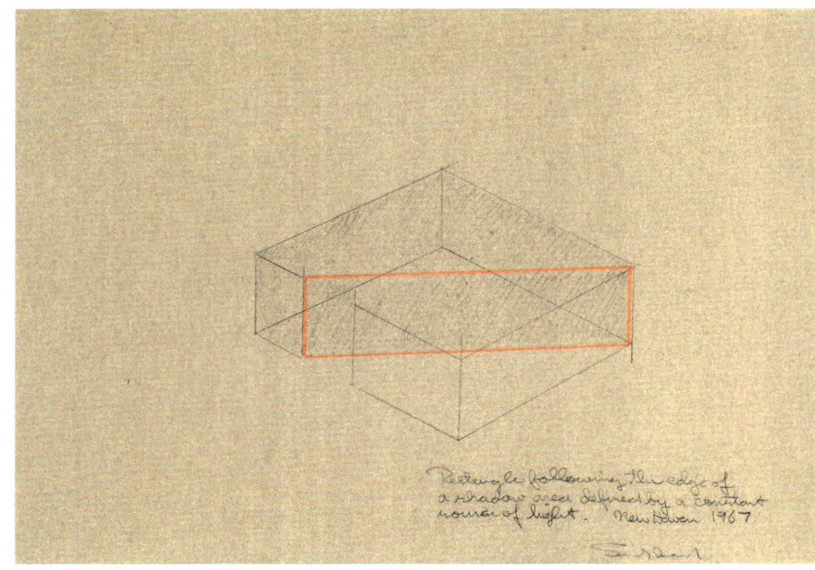

Rectangle Following the Edge of a Shadow Area Defined by a Constant Source of Light, New Haven, 1967. Pencil and felt-tip pen on paper, 7⅝ × 10½ inches (19.4 × 26.8 cm)

Untitled, 1969/1987. Pencil and pastel pencil on paper, 16¹⁵⁄₁₆ × 22 inches (43 × 56 cm)

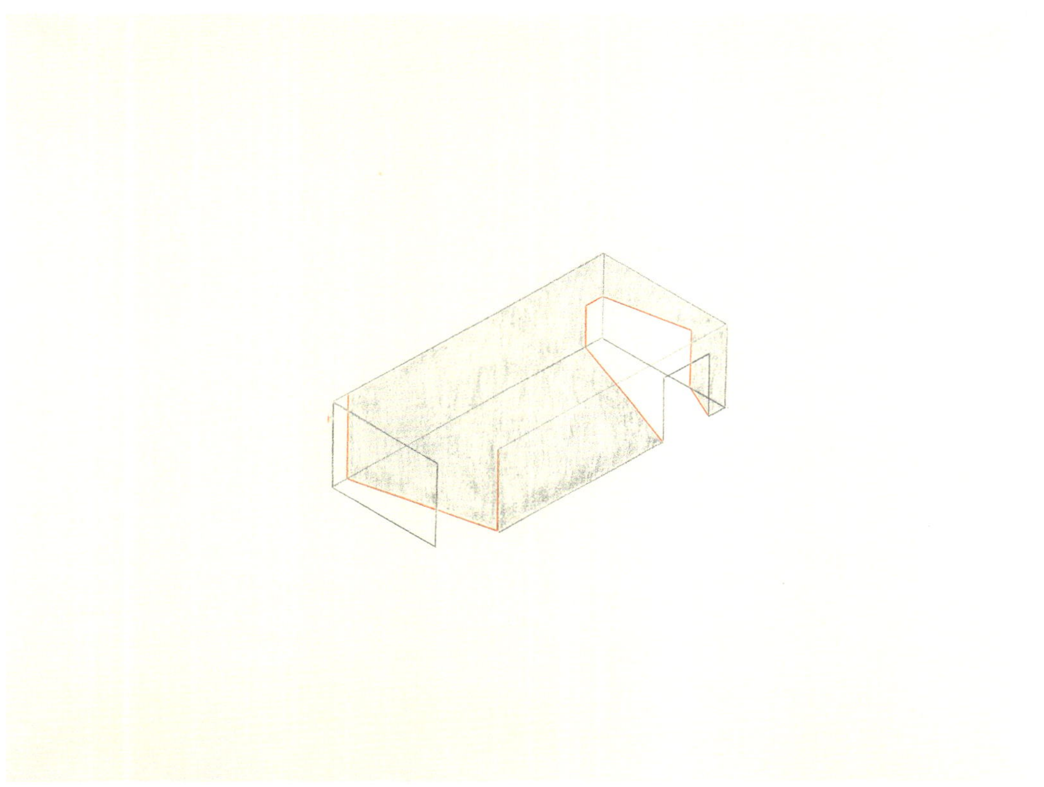

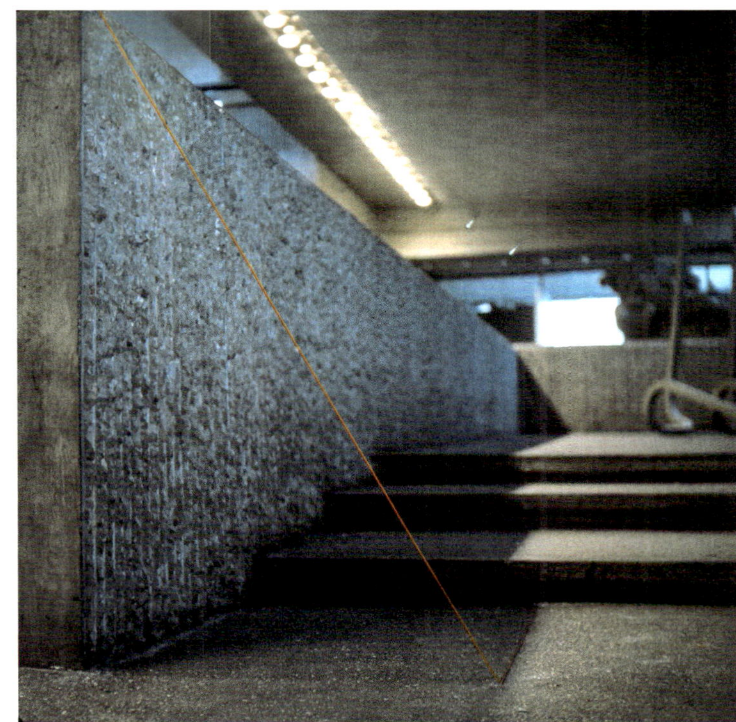

Untitled (Shadow Piece), 1967. Acrylic (orange) on elastic cord, situational dimensions, overall dimensions vary with each installation using spatial relationships established by the artist. Installation view, Yale School of Art and Architecture, New Haven, Connecticut

Shadow-Defining Piece on Stairs, 1967. Pencil and felt-tip pen on paper, 7⅝ × 10⅝ inches (19.4 × 27 cm)

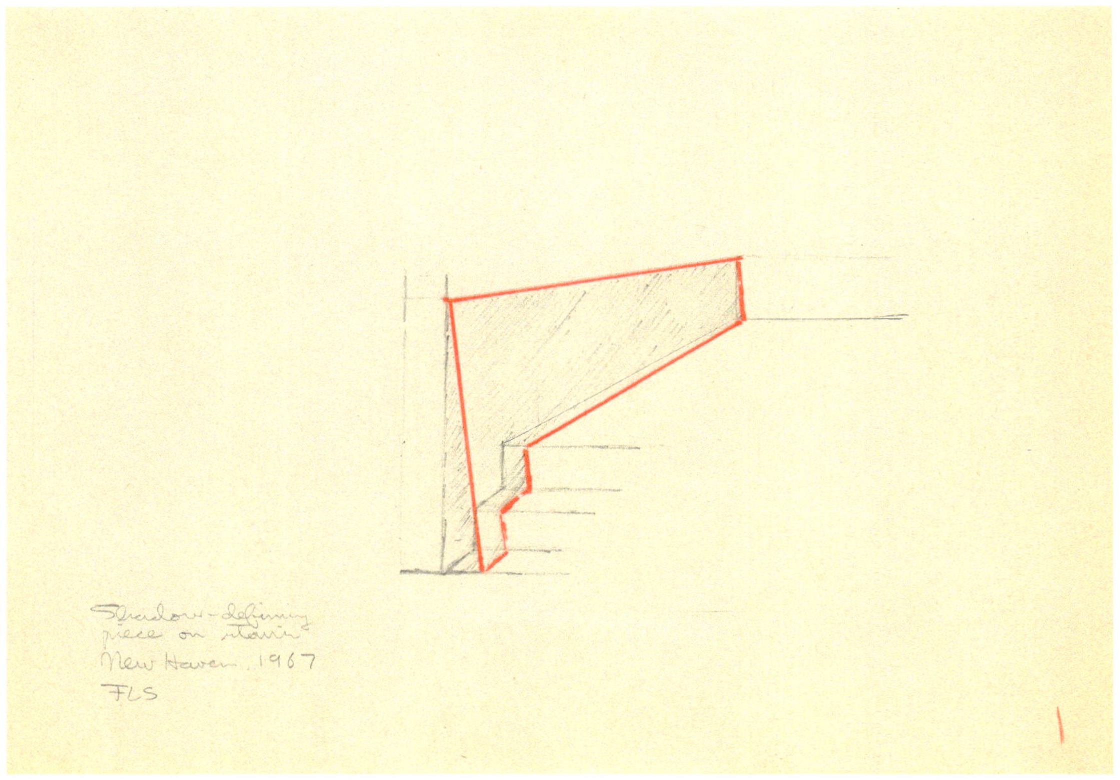

triangulation of design, representation, and construction; of the architect's idea, the drawing they make of it, and the builder's interpretation and material instantiation of that plan. Nor do these elements exist in a vacuum—their multivalent interactions unfold through a morass of invisible pressures and constraints created by cultural and economic forces.

Whether Sandback explicitly set out to explore all this in *Untitled (Red Floor Piece)*, there can be little doubt that this complex feedback loop would have appealed to him. And this inquiry into the 2 × 4's modes of existence adds dimension to Sandback's celebrated refusal of the binary structuring of so much art of his time: "Illusions are just as real as facts, and facts just as ephemeral as illusions."[7] More broadly, it suggests a new framework for thinking about his practice. Most commentators on Sandback's work note the artist's intimate connection to architecture—virtually inescapable given that the walls, floor, or ceiling of galleries literally provide the anchor points for his signature lines of yarn—but typically characterize architecture as a found condition to which the artist responds, a preexisting envelope for his sculpture. What if we instead consider architecture as a heuristic for Sandback's work, a theoretical ground as well as a material one?

Exploring how his practice partakes of architecture's complexities and depth—its protocols, intricacies, and processes—opens a host of new perspectives on his artwork. This approach is valuable, too, for situating the artist in relation to his contemporaries, given that he came of age in what Rosalind Krauss famously described as the "expanded field" of sculpture, when American artists involved architecture in their work in a multitude of ways. More specifically, it can help clarify the artist's relationship to Dia Art Foundation, whose ongoing support of his practice from its founding in 1974 decisively influenced his career. Dia is inextricably bound up with architecture in three ways: First, many of the foundation's flagship artists, notably Judd, Dan Flavin, Walter De Maria, and Sandback, directly engaged architecture in their work. Second, the foundation's commitment to permanent installations made it a collector not only of ambitious, large-scale artworks but of buildings to contain them. Third, over the years the signature look of Dia's spaces—that exceptionally crisp version of the white cube now known as the "Dia aesthetic"—has come to define the foundation's identity as much as the art exhibited within them.[8] This last point also throws Sandback's acute contemporary relevance into sharp relief: by directly engaging the physical and institutional conditions of his work's display, Sandback confronted head-on a series of problems that continue to structure the production, exhibition, and consumption of art in the present.

7. Fred Sandback, "Notes," in *Fred Sandback* (Munich: Kunstraum München, 1975), 11.

8. Rosalind Krauss, "Sculpture in the Expanded Field," *October* 8 (Spring 1979): 30–44. In a sense, Krauss's essay was an attempt to address in critical terms the same underlying cultural shifts that Dia sought to respond to in institutional terms.

9. Robin Evans, "Translations from
Drawing to Building," in *Translations from
Drawing to Building and Other Essays*
(Cambridge, MA: MIT Press, 1997), 165.

Counterintuitively, this architectural approach to Sandback's work means starting not with buildings but with drawings. In the discipline of architecture, drawings serve as the hinge between the conceptual and the actual, a duality also at the crux of Sandback's practice. Yet the artist's graphic catalogue is often considered either a distinct aspect of his oeuvre—with his drawings made, exhibited, studied, and collected as works of art in their own right—or a direct extension of his sculptures, themselves habitually described as "drawings in space."

The topic of representation remains a vexed one in Sandback's practice because of the rabidly anti-illusionistic rhetoric that dominated the art world during his formative years. This is where an architectural heuristic makes the first major contribution to our understanding of Sandback's work. In the art-world discourse of the sixties and seventies, representation was reflexively associated with the classical tradition of figurative painting and sculpture and with the evolution of linear perspective in Western art history. Architects, however, have developed their own nonperspectival visual language for depicting space, and their drawings, by and large, do not refer to people or things existing in the world but rather imagined buildings yet to be constructed. As the architectural historian Robin Evans explains, 'Drawing in architecture is not done after nature, but prior to construction; it is not so much produced by reflection on the reality outside the drawing, as productive of a reality that will end up outside the drawing. The logic of classical realism is stood on its head."[9]

Sandback's preference for one particular representational technique stands out: axonometric drawing. This system is known informally as parallel projection because although depth is depicted via diagonal lines, as in perspective, the lines remain parallel rather than converging toward a vanishing point. Sandback's earliest surviving graphic works are photostats of axonometric drawings of simple geometric shapes. Several are recognizable studies for sculptures he realized in steel rod, elastic cord, and acrylic yarn. The artist continued to use the technique for the next three and a half decades, producing hundreds of officially catalogued prints and drawings and countless informal sketches. Perhaps the clearest evidence of this preference is the fact that of the eighteen solo exhibitions Sandback had in the first five years of his career—that astonishingly high number itself a measure of his meteoric rise through the art world—nearly all had posters or invitations that depicted, in axonometric projection, one or several of the works to be exhibited within a wire-frame outline of the gallery space, turning this type of drawing into the artist's calling card.

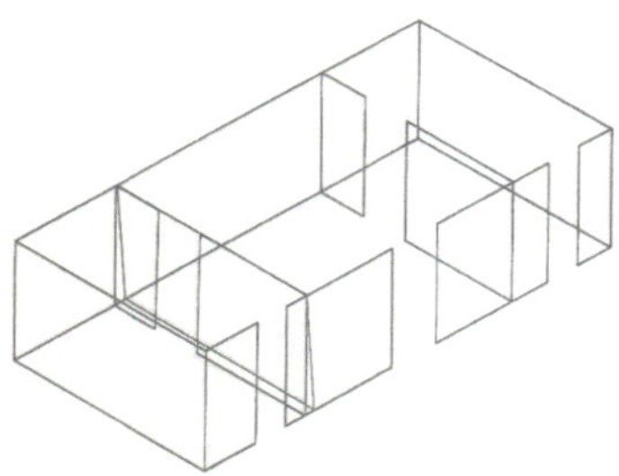

Invitation to *Fred Sandback*, Galerie Heiner Friedrich, Munich, 1971

Poster for *Fred Sandback: Five Situations; Eight Separate Pieces*, Dwan Gallery, New York, 1969

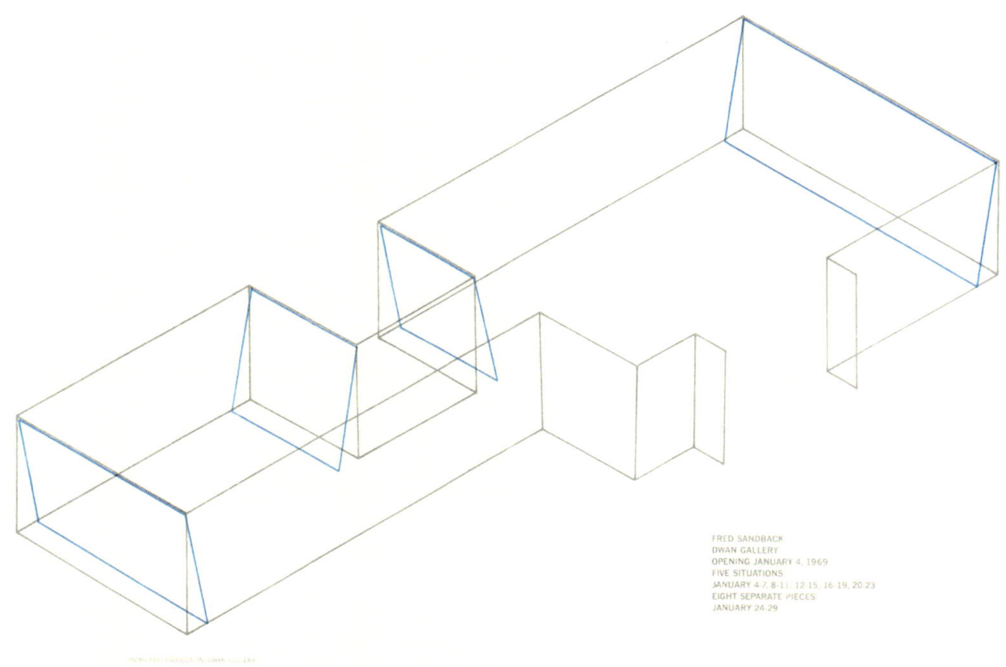

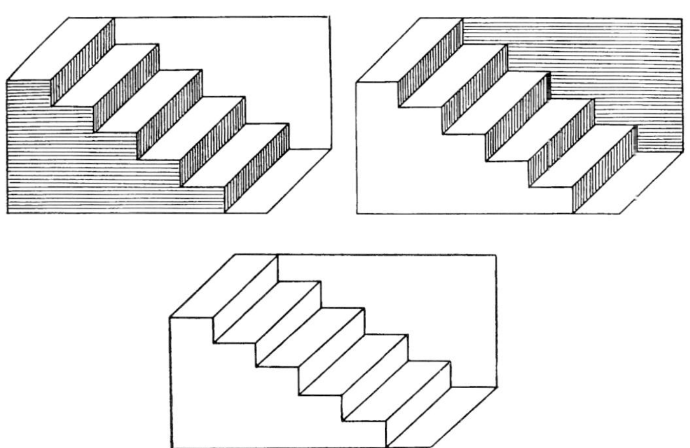

10. Yve-Alain Bois, "Metamorphosis of Axonometry," *Daidalos*, no. 1 (1981): 41–58. My own understanding of axonometric drawing is deeply indebted to this text, and I also benefitted enormously from participating in the seminar on the history of axonometry taught by Bois at Princeton University in the fall of 2019.

11. Erwin Panofsky, *Perspective as Symbolic Form*, trans. Christopher S. Wood (New York: Zone Books, 1991).

12. Yve-Alain Bois, "El Lissitzky: Radical Reversibility," *Art in America* 76, no. 4 (April 1988): 160–80.

13. El Lissitzky, "A. and Pangeometry," in *El Lissitzky: Life, Letters, Texts*, ed. Sophie Lissitzky-Küppers (London: Thames and Hudson, 1968), 348–53.

Artists and architects often used axonometric drawing in early twentieth-century European avant-garde movements, particularly De Stijl, Constructivism, and the Bauhaus. As Yve-Alain Bois argues in his definitive study of these deployments, axonometry functioned for the avant-garde as an antiperspective.[10] If linear perspective was a "symbolic form," as Erwin Panofsky famously posited, it largely symbolized the humanist ideology of the Renaissance from which it emerged.[11] It was a model of the world that literally centered—was, in fact, constructed around—the point of view of the viewing subject. An axonometric drawing is not constructed around a single viewpoint, and because its lines do not converge toward a single vanishing point, an axonometric drawing has a fundamental instability, a directional ambiguity; a shape drawn in axonometric projection can be perceived as either receding back into the page or popping up off it. The duality is analogous to that of the well-known duck-rabbit illusion; in fact several other optical illusions popular during the nineteenth century, such as the Schroeder stairs and the Necker cube, employ axonometric projection to produce similarly fluctuating readings. Constructivist architect and painter El Lissitzky, the most vocal opponent of perspective and advocate of axonometry during the early twentieth century, argued that such fluctuation fundamentally destabilizes the humanist subjectivity that linear perspective defines. In his analysis of Lissitzky, Bois indelibly elucidated this effect as "radical reversibility."[12]

While Lissitzky's antiperspective manifesto, "A. and Pangeometry" (1925), was neither easily accessible nor published in English until 1968, Sandback would likely have seen *Proun 99* (c. 1923–25), a painting by Lissitzky in the collection of the Yale University Art Gallery that prominently features an axonometric cube.[13] As an undergraduate in the spring of 1964, Sandback took a course with the eminent architectural historian Vincent Scully in which he likely would have been exposed to

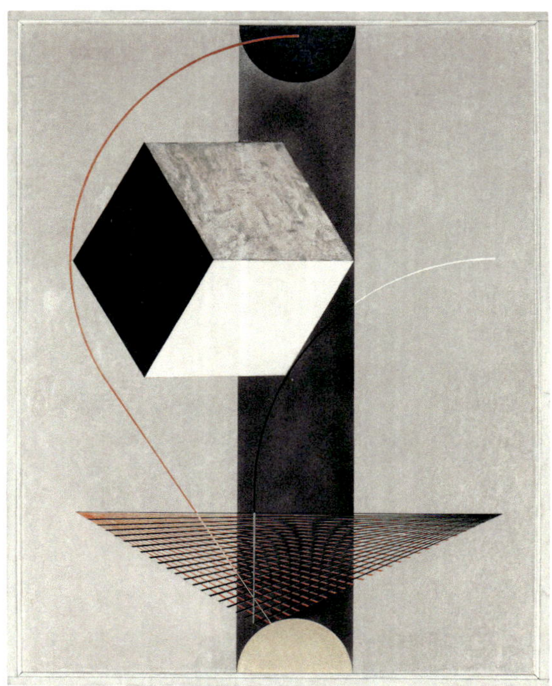

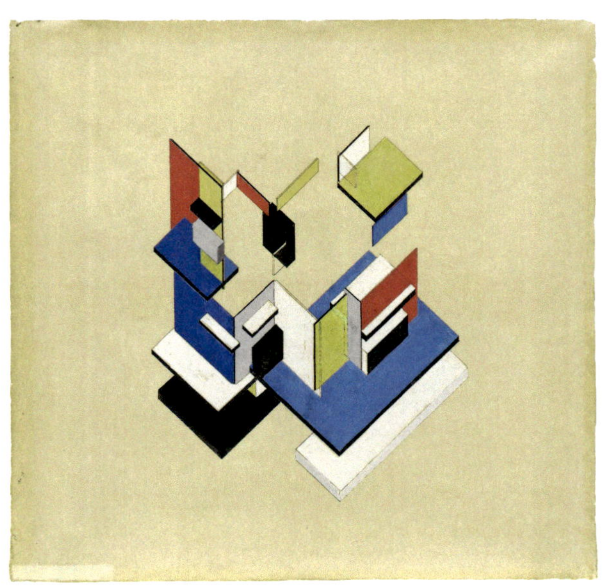

El Lissitzky, *Proun 99*, c. 1923–25. Water-soluble and metallic paint on wood, 50¹⁵⁄₁₆ × 39 inches (129 × 99.1 cm)

Theo van Doesburg, *Contra-Construction*, 1923. Gouache on lithograph, 22½ × 22½ inches (57.2 × 57.2 cm)

14. The course was "History of Art 53b: Modern Architecture." Although no syllabus or other materials from the course seem to have been preserved in Yale's archives, Scully published the first edition of his classic reference work *Modern Architecture* in 1961, and all the drawings mentioned here are reproduced in that volume.

15. Morris was at Yale the semester before Judd in spring 1967.

axonometric drawings by Le Corbusier, various Bauhaus architects, and key members of De Stijl, including the intricately interpenetrating colored planes of the famous series of drawings Theo Van Doesburg created in 1923, titled *Contra-Constructions*.[14] Sandback might even have gotten a dose of avant-garde axonometry straight from the source. Although the Bauhaus master Josef Albers retired from Yale in 1958, his influence there still loomed large over the following decade, and his fascination with the perceptual ambiguities of parallel projection—explored, for example, in his Multiplex and Interlinear series—is well known.

In the 1960s, there was also a marked resurgence in the use of axonometric drawing by many younger artists, including several of Sandback's teachers during his MFA years. When Judd was at Yale in the fall of 1967, he had been using parallel projection since he abandoned painting for sculpture in the early 1960s. Robert Morris, who also taught Sandback as a visiting professor, similarly made axonometric drawings, including for many sculptures that he would have industrially fabricated, such as the four steel boxes comprising *Untitled* (1967).[15] And by 1967, most of Judd's works were produced by others as well. Both artists typically used axonometric projection for fabrication drawings. Though adamantly anti-illusion and, more broadly, antirepresentation, they also eschewed craft and the romance of the artist's hand in favor of industrial manufacturing, creating a very architectural dilemma that pointed to a

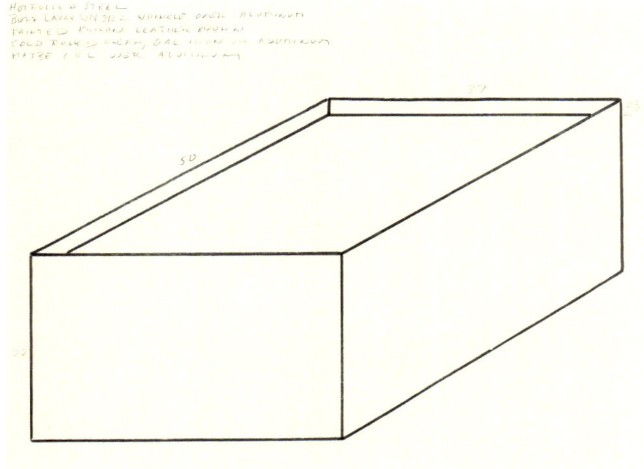

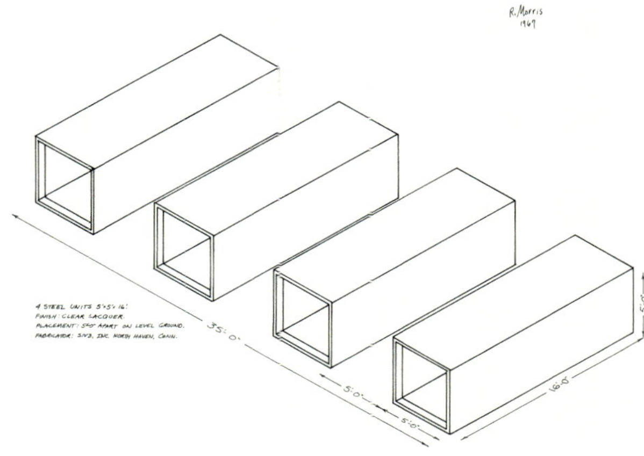

Donald Judd, Untitled, 1965. Felt-tip pen and pencil on paper, 10⅞ × 13½ inches (27.6 × 34.3 cm)

Robert Morris, *Untitled*, 1967. Ink on paper, 21¼ × 29¼ inches (54 × 74.3 cm)

paradox in their practices: both artists were deeply dependent on two-dimensional representations to communicate their ideas for three-dimensional artworks to the fabricators who would actually build them. Given his sharp attunement to the complex relationship between representation and reality, Sandback likely recognized this irony early—perhaps it even subtended his sly denial of the binary opposition between fact and illusion that structured the work of his professors and so many of his peers.

Sandback's method stands out from these precedents in crucial ways. He focused almost entirely on a specific subcategory of parallel projection: isometric drawing. In all types of axonometric drawing, parallel lines in actual space (say, two opposite edges of a cube) remain parallel on the page, rather than converging to produce the illusion of depth, as in linear perspective. To depict depth while keeping these lines parallel, at least one of the right angles that separate the three axes of Cartesian space (imagine one corner of a cube where three edges meet) must be distorted. This is the price of compressing three dimensions into two; if all three axes were separated by right angles, a cube would look flat on the page, lacking any depth—it would, in fact, appear square. In a trimetric drawing, the angles of all three axes are distinct; in a dimetric drawing, two are the same and one is different; and in an isometric drawing, all three are equal. Sandback also drew in other kinds of parallel projection and, occasionally, in perspective. (A drawing is a tool for realizing ideas, after all, not only an ideological statement, and even the violently antiperspective Lissitzky had occasional recourse to the technique.) The vast majority of Sandback's drawings, however, are not just axonometric but isometric.

In 1967, as Sandback was experimenting with isometrics at Yale, the prominent art critic Lucy Lippard published the article "Perverse Perspectives" in *Art International*. Noting the sudden proliferation of parallel projections in contemporary art, she suggested that this "tightly structured denial of pictorial logic" held a threefold appeal: it broke with the long tradition of linear perspective; its apparent rigor offered an antidote to the chaotic subjectivity of Abstract Expressionism; and, paradoxically, it nevertheless retained a high degree of perceptual complexity because of the inherently ambiguous directionality in its depiction of depth. In closing, Lippard argued that "the isometric projection of volumes" was one of artists' "most effective tools": "Though the actual measurements of a three-dimensional figure are presented rather than the traditional distortions of focal perspective, and the drawn result is thus closer to 'reality,' it is less familiar and therefore more exotic."[16]

Although her analysis of the broad trend is incisive, Lippard misunderstood the specific qualities of isometrics, exemplifying the persistent confusion in geometry and terminology that has plagued—and in many ways hindered—the interpretation of these drawings. Because the Cartesian axes in an isometric drawing are always separated by 120 degrees, all three axes appear equally foreshortened on the flat plane of the sheet of paper; because of this foreshortening, an object shown in isometric projection is depicted at approximately 80 percent of its actual size. When Lippard writes about "actual measurements," she describes something closer to plan oblique drawing, another common form of parallel projection.[17] Here, the drawing starts with a ground plan of an object, true to scale, lying flat on the paper as if seen from above but typically rotated so that lines depicting the object's height can be projected upward without occluding one another. Architects have long favored the plan oblique drawing because it prioritizes the ground plan of a building, shown without distortion. It is sometimes known informally as "military perspective" because military architects and engineers often took advantage of its expediency in planning fortifications.

And plan oblique projections certainly do appear exotic, as Lippard said. The combination of looking straight down onto the plan *and* back into receding depth simultaneously produces a vertiginous feeling and grotesque proportional distortions. Sol LeWitt, another American artist with a close connection to architecture, used plan oblique projection in the drawings for one of his most famous works, *Incomplete Open Cubes,* exhibited at John Weber Gallery in New York in

16. Lucy Lippard, "Perverse Perspectives," *Art International* 11, no. 3 (March 1967): 28.

17. In another example of this widespread confusion, the cover image of Sol LeWitt's book *Isometric Drawings* shows a cube in parallel projection, but it is not an isometric. It is, in fact, an elevation oblique, which is similar to a plan oblique, except that the elevation of the depicted object, rather than the plan, is shown true to scale and then the depth, rather than the height, is aggressively distorted. See Sol LeWitt, *Isometric Drawings* (New York: Paula Cooper Gallery and John Weber Gallery, 1982).

It should be noted here that while both isometrics and plan or elevation obliques are forms of parallel projection, obliques are not, technically speaking, axonometrics. Axonometric projection is a type of orthographic projection, which means that in all forms of axonometric (trimetric, dimetric, and isometric) the depicted object is visualized as rotated in relation to the plane of projection and then the projection lines linking the object to the plane are orthogonal to that plane. Plan and elevation oblique are forms of oblique projection, where the depicted object is visualized as parallel to the plane of projection and the projection lines themselves are oblique to that plane. (The parallel relationship between the plane of projection and one of the object's faces, for example its plan or elevation, is what allows that plane to be presented free of distortion.) In practice, however, the term *axonometric* is often used as a general description for all forms of parallel projection.

18. The show consisted of three forms of representation displayed together: the same series of 122 cubic frames was shown as physical models, photographs,

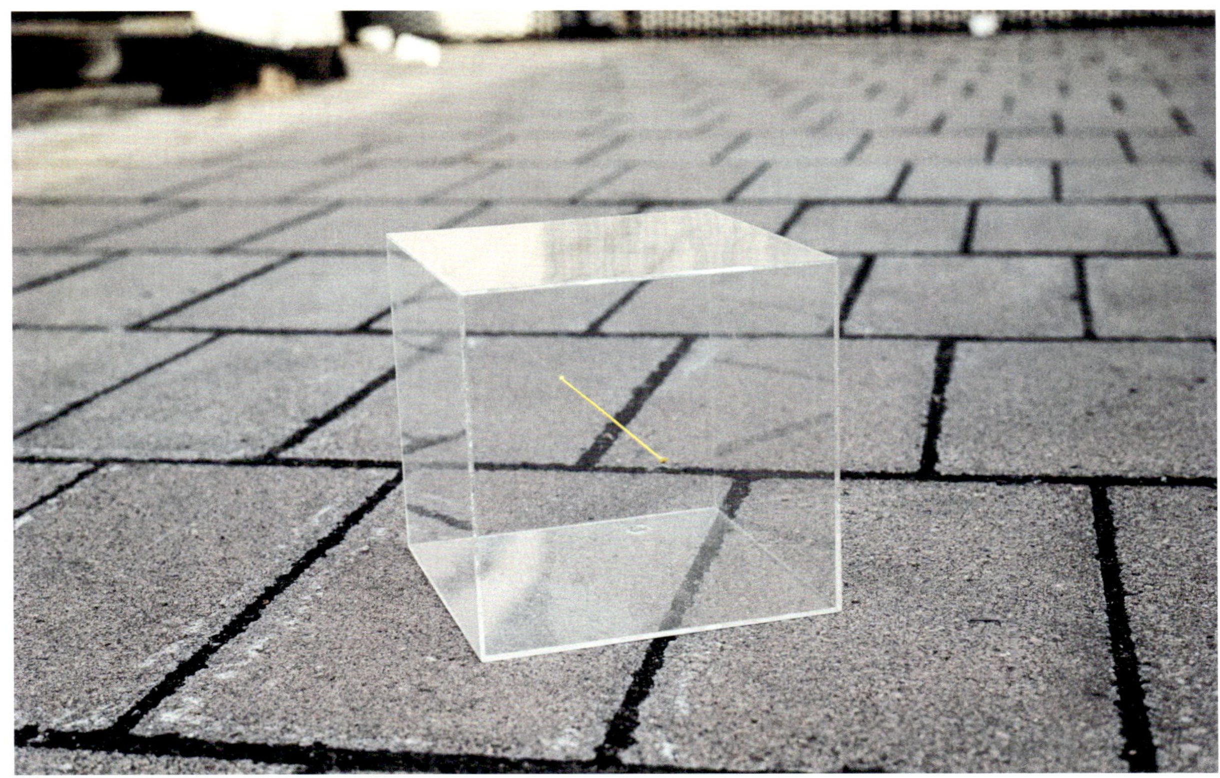

Untitled, c. 1966.
Plexiglass and rayon cord
(yellow), 8 × 8 × 8 inches
(20.3 × 20.3 × 20.3 cm)

Untitled, c. 1970s. Ink and
silver ink on isometric
paper, 8½ × 11 inches
(21.6 × 27.9 cm)

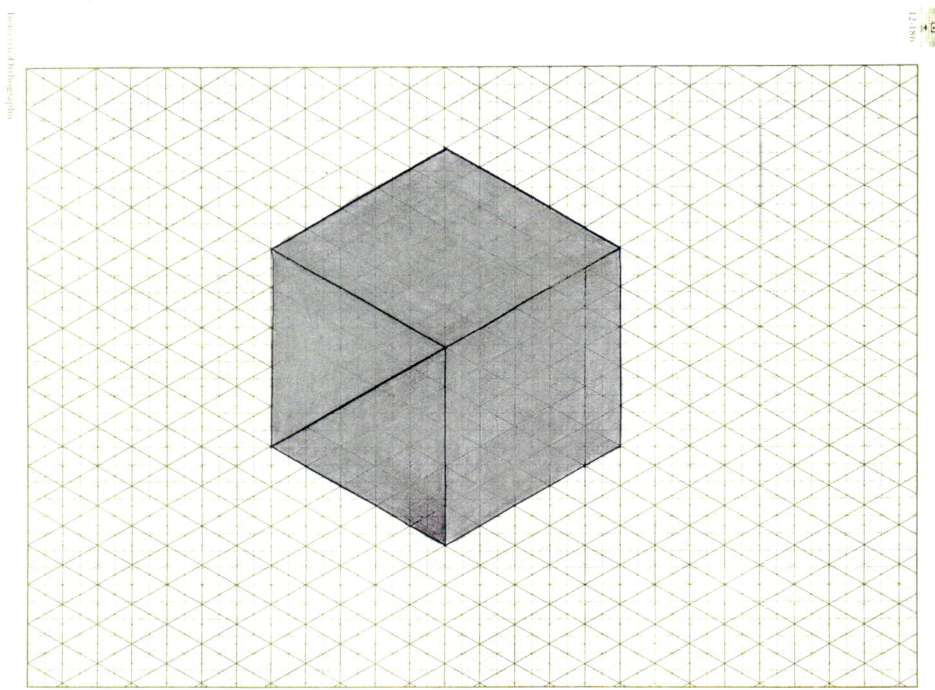

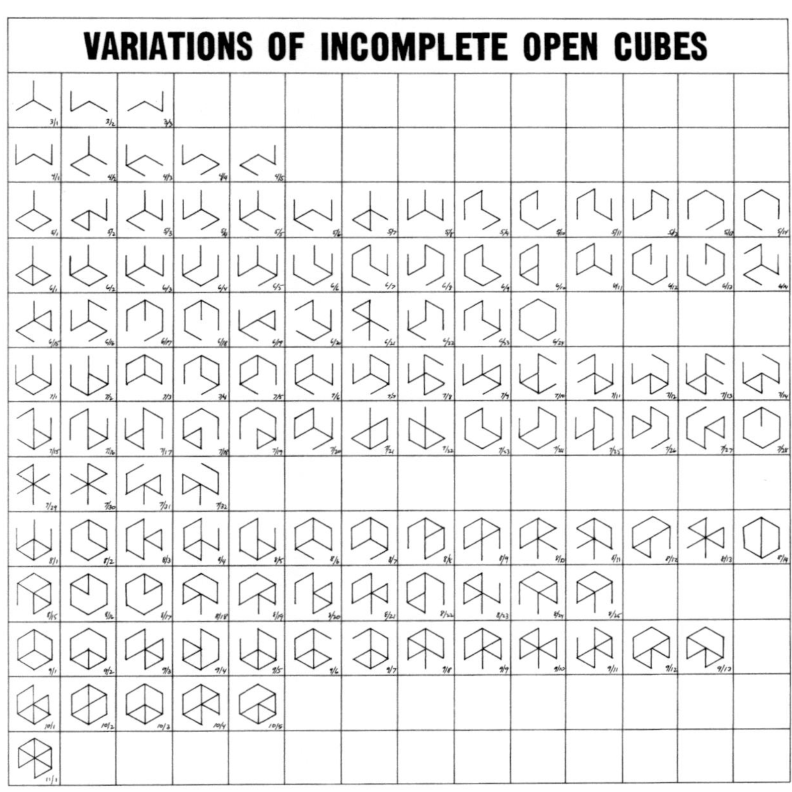

Sol LeWitt, poster for *Variations of Incomplete Open Cubes* (detail), John Weber Gallery, New York, 1974

and drawings. Perhaps because the drawings hung next to the photographs, LeWitt chose not to use isometric projection. Depending on the lens's focal length, the object's size, and its distance from the camera, a photograph looking down at an object from an oblique angle can appear quite similar to an isometric projection. In LeWitt's photographs, the lower corner of the cubes forms an angle that is very close to 120 degrees, although the angle of the top corner noticeably differs because of the distortion caused by the monocular perspective of the camera. Isometric drawings might have looked too similar to these photographs, in other words, so presumably LeWitt chose plan obliques as his preferred type of parallel projection at least in part for their alien appearance. It is also worth

1974. The resulting bizarre geometric distortions perfectly exemplify the strategy of obsessively following rational rules until they produce irrational results that drove so much of LeWitt's practice.[18]

Artists like LeWitt, Judd, Morris, and Andre (the last also an early adopter of parallel projection, particularly for studies of his wood sculptures) were all, to varying degrees, interested in the work of the early twentieth-century European avant-garde, and the resurgence of axonometric drawing among artists in the 1960s and 1970s can be understood as part of the broader reengagement with the legacy of early twentieth-century modernism sometimes characterized as the emergence of a "neo-avant-garde." The same is true among architects. Among many others, the "New York Five"—Peter Eisenman, Michael Graves, Charles Gwathmey, John Hejduk, and Richard Meier—were fascinated with parallel projection in no small part because of its association with some of the most radical figures of the early twentieth century. (Meier, in particular, was an acolyte of Le Corbusier, who had produced axonometrics of several of his most famous houses in the 1920s and 1930s.) Like LeWitt, these architects were especially drawn to plan oblique: their influential book *Five Architects* from

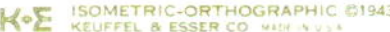

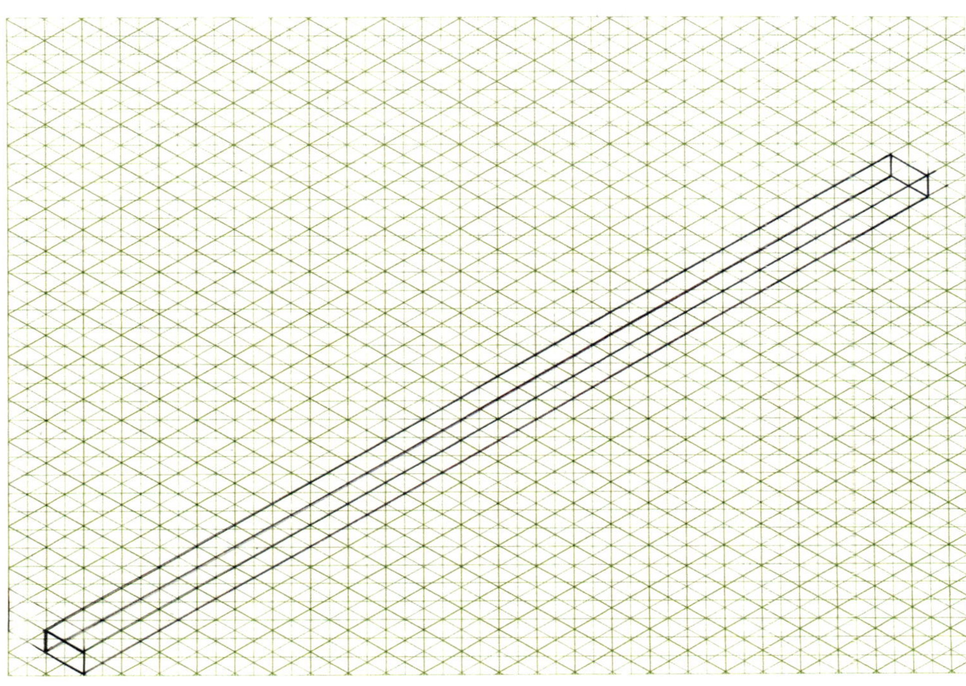

Untitled, c. 1970–74. Pencil on isometric
paper, 8½ × 11 inches (21.6 × 27.9 cm)

noting that he used isometrics in the thumb-
nail drawings for the poster that shows all
variations together on a single sheet, probably because of the comparatively greater
legibility of isometric projection.

19. *Five Architects: Eisenman, Graves,
Gwathmey, Hejduk, Meier* (New York: Oxford
University Press, 1975). In addition to these
nonisometric parallel projections, the book
also contains many traditional orthographic
drawings: plans, sections, and elevations.

20. Reyner Banham, "Iso! Axo! (All Fall
Down?)," in "Great Models: Digressions
on the Architectural Model," ed. Suzanne
Buttolph, *The Student Publication of the
School of Design* (North Carolina State
College), no. 27 (1978): 20.

21. Ibid., 19.

1975 contains exclusively this type of parallel projection, without a single isometric.[19]
In a sense, these drawings allowed architects to have their cake and eat it too—a building's plan was undistorted, requiring no translation from two to three dimensions. At
the same time, the aggressive distortion of the projected depth gave the drawings a
striking spatiality.

Not everyone approved. In 1978, a little more than a decade after Lippard's
article on perverse perspective, the influential architecture critic Reyner Banham
published a scathing assessment of what he described as the "axonometric revival"
in his field. At their best, Banham argued, architectural drawings "stand at the exact
point where the process of intellectual creation transforms into a process of physical
creation."[20] But the drawings by architects like the New York Five lost touch with
the material realities of building and became paper architecture, mere fantasy and
decoration—what he memorably termed a kind of architectural "masturbation."[21] A
show of architectural drawings at Leo Castelli Gallery in November 1977 that heavily
featured both axonometric and isometric projection particularly incensed Banham:
"The *reason* why such drawings get loose from the studio and turn up in Leo Castelli's

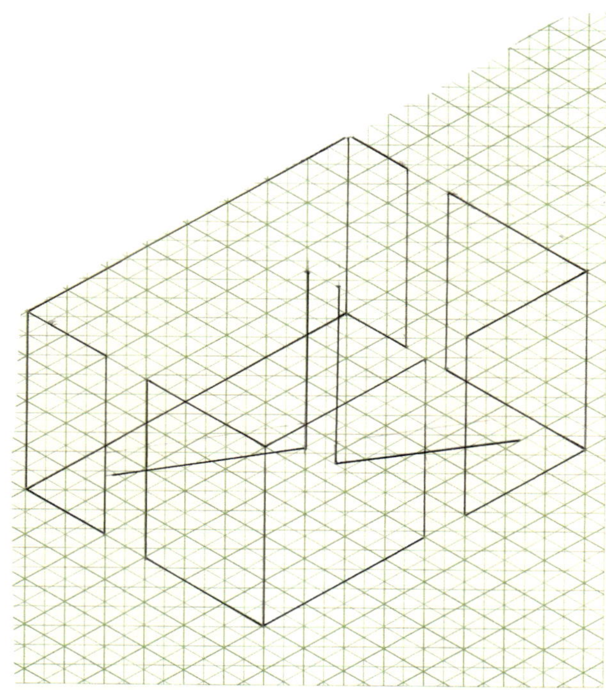

Untitled (Study for P.S. 1), c. 1977. Felt-tip pen and pencil on isometric paper. 7½ × 6¼ inches (19 × 15.9 cm)

Untitled (Partial Installation Drawing for the Exhibition at Magasin 3, Stockholm Konsthal), 1991 (detail). Pastel pencil and pencil on tracing paper with masking tape, 11¼ × 15 inches (28.5 × 38 cm)

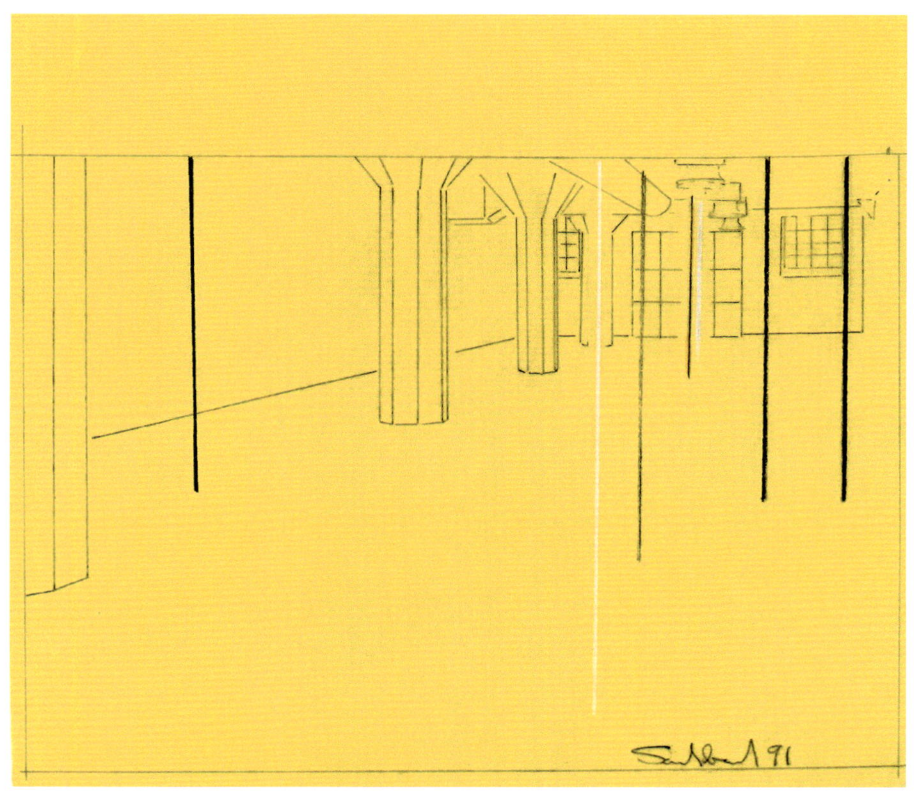

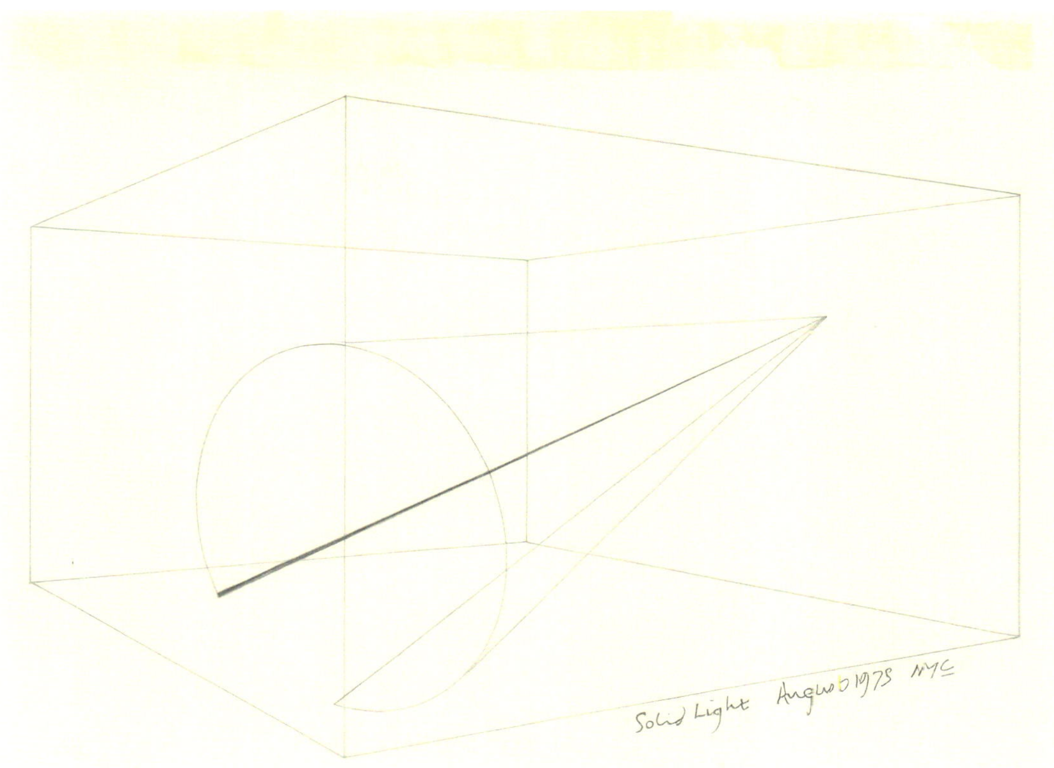

Anthony McCall, *Solid Light,* 1973. Ink on paper, 9¼ × 12 inches (23.5 × 30 cm). Installation drawing for *Line Describing a Cone,* 1973

gallery is that axo's and iso's make such entrancingly ambiguous patterns on the paper surface."[22]

In other words, one architect's radical reversibility is another's tacky Op art—depending on your perspective. Yet Sandback's drawings distinctly show that his concerns were spatial and material rather than merely visual, anchoring his isometrics precisely at Banham's transformative point between intellectual and physical creation. Unlike his peers, Sandback consistently drew not only his work but the entire volume of the gallery space surrounding it. Other artists who commonly used isometric and other forms of axonometric projection—including Judd, Morris, Andre, and LeWitt— typically drew artworks in isolation, at most hinting at a work's placement in space by adding a corner in the background. While artists associated with Land art, notably Alice Aycock, used isometric projection to show the structures they envisioned, these were, in essence, isolated objects in the landscape without an architectural context. Interestingly, artists who worked with light and projection—such as Dan Flavin, Anthony McCall, and James Turrell—often drew their work in situ but primarily used linear perspective, since they were especially concerned with how their atmospheric interventions created an immersive experience within the gallery space.

22. Ibid., 18.

45

Sandback's preference for isometric drawing and his consistent depiction of the entire gallery space suggest that his work had a radically nonhierarchical relationship to architecture. Isometrics, after all, are not only about ambiguity; they are also about interconnection and equivalence. Fundamentally, these drawings portray lines stretching in all directions as equal, with the same level of foreshortening and the same distortion of angles—hence the prefix *iso-*. Unlike plan obliques, isometrics do not prioritize the ground plan as the underlying source of compositional logic, as "true" proportions and dimensions in one axis are not preserved at the expense of additional distortion in others. There is no origin in an isometric drawing, no foundational geometry that must be drawn first. Sandback sometimes sketched over plans of exhibition spaces while conceptualizing new works, but it is impossible to draw an isometric directly over a ground plan because the isometric view changes the rectangle of a room into a parallelogram with two 120- and two 60-degree angles. To produce drawings such as his iconic poster for his first Dwan Gallery exhibition in 1969, Sandback translated both his work and the surrounding architecture into the emphatically equal medium of isometric space.

Sandback's drawings suggest the pragmatism and accessibility of isometric rendering, too—deeper implications already illuminated by the British mathematician and chemist William Farish, who was the first to codify this system of representation in the early nineteenth century. As a professor of machine design, Farish was preoccupied with the problem of representing intricately interconnected three-dimensional objects in two-dimensional drawings, which was extremely difficult in traditional approaches. Linear perspective might accurately illustrate how a given machine would look in a factory space, but it inevitably distorted and foreshortened its parts; orthographic projection, the traditional combination of ground plans, elevations, and cross sections used by architects to represent buildings, preserved the accurate dimensions of a machine's parts but presented them only as a series of two-dimensional slices, making it ineffective for illustrating complex three-dimensional connections.[23]

Farish proposed that it would be "much easier and simpler" to illustrate machines using a novel kind of parallel perspective in which the three Cartesian axes are separated by equal angles of 120 degrees and consequently lines extending in all directions are equally foreshortened.[24] "Even in the hands of a person who is but little acquainted with the art of drawing," he wrote, isometric projection would produce far more useful renderings than any other technique because the equal foreshortening ensured that accurate scale measurements could be made from anything depicted

23. In Farish's words: "Such a method . . . would be liable to great objections. It would be unintelligible to an inexperienced eye; and even to an artist, it shews but very imperfectly *that which is most essential, the connection of the different parts of the engine with one another*." William Farish, "On Isometrical Perspective," in *Transactions of the Cambridge Philosophical Society*, vol. 1 (Cambridge, UK: University Press, 1819), 2. Emphasis mine.

24. Ibid., 3.

TEN ISOMETRIC DRAWINGS
FOR
TEN VERTICAL CONSTRUCTIONS

FRED SANDBACK   1977

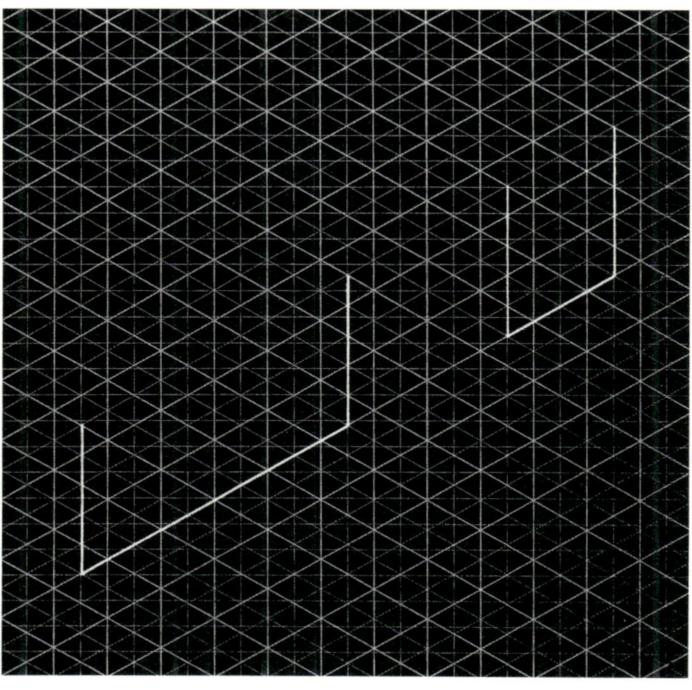

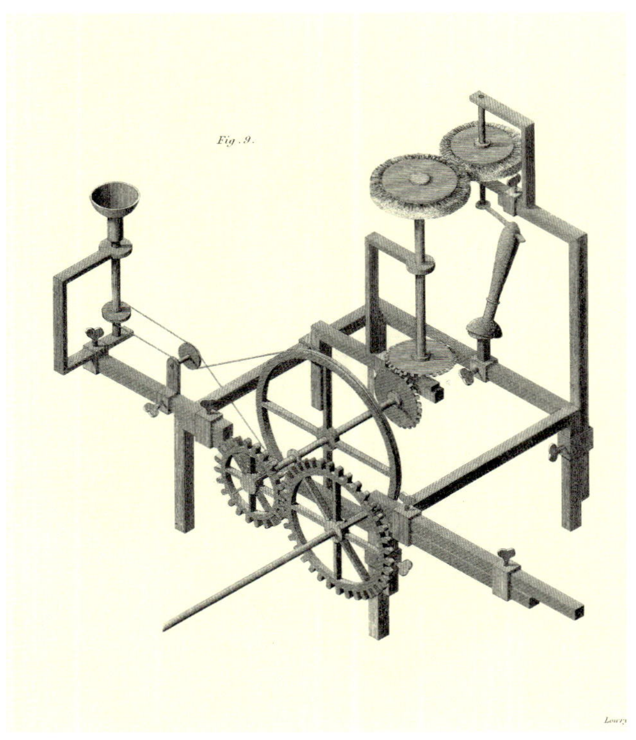

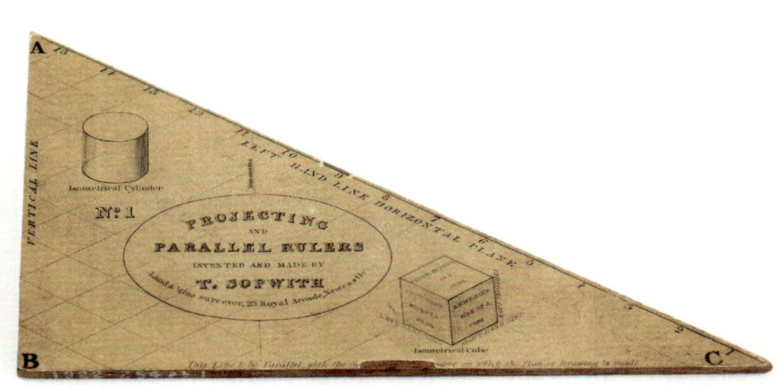

William Farish, isometric rendering of optical-grinding machine, 1822

One of three set squares for use in isometric projection, paper on wood, invented and manufactured by Thomas Sopwith, c. 1838

25. Ibid., 18.

26. "Isometric Drawing Paper," *Power* 34, no. 21 (November 21, 1911): 798. Discussing the same innovation, the trade magazine *American Carpenter and Builder* put it even more succinctly: "With this paper, isometric drawing is easy." "Isometric Drawing Paper," *American Carpenter and Builder* 12, no. 3 (December 1911): 82. A popular manual on isometric drawing published around the same time—its prolix subtitle an excursus on the utility of this technique—included an entire chapter on the use of this paper: "The Use of Isometric Paper," in Frank Richards and Fred H. Colvin, *Practical Perspective: A Treatise Showing Just How to Make All Kinds of Mechanical Drawings in the Only Practical Perspective*

in the drawing, no matter its angle or position.[25] The only problem was actually making the drawings; the typical drafting setup of the time was a T square combined with a rectangular drawing board, which could produce only 90-degree angles with ease. The widespread use of the 30-60-90 triangle, which could be combined with the T square to expediently produce the diagonals of an isometric, eventually solved the problem. Unsurprisingly, a 30-60-90 triangle and a T square hang on the wall in photos of Sandback's downtown studio at 561 Broadway.

Yet there is an even easier way to make these drawings: isometric graph paper, which was introduced at the turn of the twentieth century, when the explosive growth of industrialization in America required a widespread increase in the production of technical drawings. As one engineering publication put it in 1911, paper ruled with isometric lines made "any knowledge of isometric projection . . . unnecessary, as its isometric ruling makes it easy to complete such a drawing without arduous study or calculation."[26]

Sandback began regularly using isometric graph paper almost as soon as he started producing isometric drawings. His medium of choice was orthographic-isometric paper, usually the version manufactured by the Keuffel and Esser Company, a major producer of drafting supplies and surveying and engineering equipment for

(Isometric). Makes Everything Plain so that Any Mechanic Can Understand a Sketch or Drawing in this Way. Saves Time in the Drawing Room and Mistakes in the Shops. Contains Practical Examples of Various Classes of Work (New York: Norman W. Henley, 1908), 29–56.

27. The company was granted a copyright for the "K & E Isometric Drawing Kit—a Short Cut to Pictorial Drafting." See Library of Congress Copyright Office, *Catalogue of Copyright Entries, Part 4: Works of Art; Reproductions of a Work of Art; Drawings or Plastic Works of a Scientific or Technical Character; Photographs; Prints and Pictorial Illustrations, Including Prints and Labels Used for Articles of Merchandise* (Washington, DC: US Government Printing Office, 1943), 247. Along with this graph paper, an astonishing variety of drawing aids and manuals proliferated during the surge in industrial production caused by World War II. With so many working-age men serving on active duty, there were fewer skilled draftsmen to produce traditional engineering drawings and fewer skilled machinists and fabricators to interpret them.

Tools like isometric graph paper made producing these drawings far more accessible and their interpretation more intuitive, and their spread continued in the boom years after the war. Keuffel and Esser offered an incisive summary of this situation in the introduction to the isometric drawing equipment section of their first postwar catalogue, worth quoting in full: "Pictorial forms of drawing [i.e., non-perspectival three-dimensional projections such as axonometrics] are being used increasingly in industry. They aid workers to a quicker understanding of dimensions, construction details and assembly relationships. Of all forms of production drawing, the Isometric Method is the most practical, because an isometric drawing, besides presenting the object as it looks, is much easier to make than a perspective drawing. Furthermore, all measurements in the three major axes are true to scale in an isometric drawing and identical with those of the corresponding orthographic

much of the twentieth century. This isometric paper innovatively featured *both* an isometric, hexagonal grid and an orthographic, square grid, making it practical for any kind of drawing. Keuffel and Esser introduced their product in 1943 as part of an "isometric drawing kit" that also included a set of scales, protractors, and templates geared toward helping inexperienced draftsmen and fabricators cope with the wartime production boom.[27] By the time Sandback adopted it, the paper was ubiquitous, not only in fabrication shops and architecture and engineering offices but in artists' studios, although most of Sandback's contemporaries seem to have ignored its isometric potential and used it as standard gridded graph paper or simply sketched over it as if it were a blank sheet. Several of Andre's drawings on the paper survive; Lawrence Weiner used it, including for some of his Structure Poems; Robert Barry executed preparatory sketches for indoor and outdoor performances and installations on it; and Mel Bochner deployed it for studies of his sculptures and paintings. In fact, when Milton Glaser designed the poster for the now-legendary exhibition *Working Drawings and Other Visible Things on Paper Not Necessarily Meant to Be Viewed as Art,* organized by Bochner at the School of Visual Arts in 1966, he prominently featured a top-down view of a three-ring binder drawn on orthographic-isometric paper.[28]

Sandback's consistent use of the paper for its designated purpose ties him to a long, largely unknown history of isometric drawing. Just as linear perspective is inextricably bound up with the Western canon, art and architectural historians have so strongly associated isometrics and other forms of parallel projection with avant-garde practice—both their "emergence" in the 1920s and their "rediscovery" by the 1960s and 1970s neo-avant-garde—that more than two centuries of isometric drawing for more humble purposes remains obscured. Farish did not discuss visual complexity or perceptual ambiguity; he presented isometric drawing as easier to make and read than other forms of representation. Isometric paper was not introduced for its rich perceptual effects; it allowed inexperienced and unskilled draftsmen to quickly produce crucial working drawings for all kinds of engineering and industrial fabrication. Even today, while artists or architects might occasionally deploy isometric drawing as a coy historical reference, it remains a quotidian practice in many trades; many states include it in their licensing exams for master plumbers, who routinely deal with networks of complex three-dimensional connections. To isometrics' radical reversibility, then, we must add a proletarian pragmatism.[29]

drawing. The K&E Isometric Drawing Instruments listed on this and the two following pages have been specially designed to speed up and simplify the making of isometric production drawings." See *K&E Catalog: Drafting and Reproduction Equipment and Materials, Slide Rules*, forty-first edition, part one (Hoboken, NJ: Keuffer & Esser, 1949), 134.

28. This drawing was also Glaser's contribution to the show; he presumably chose the binder as his subject because the exhibition itself consisted of photocopied sheets collected in three-ring binders, with the binders placed on pedestals in the gallery. For other examples of this trend of using isometric paper for nonisometric drawing, see: https://www.tate.org.uk/art/artworks/andre-drawing-for-the-perfect-painting-t02136; https://www.nga.gov/collection/art-object-page.77627.html; and https://www.moma.org/collection/works/109516. This is not to say that other artists never used the paper for isometric drawing, only that they did not do so consistently. Two exceptions to this general tendency, both worth mentioning because the works depicted are often discussed in relation to Sandback, are the isometric drawing Andre made to propose his firebrick sculpture *Lever* for the Jewish Museum's famous 1966 show *Primary Structures* (the drawing was not exhibited but is reproduced in the exhibition catalogue) and the isometric drawing Bochner made proposing a masking-tape-and-felt-tip-pen "number line" piece for his 1971 exhibition at the Museum of Modern Art, New York. See, respectively, "Carl Andre," in *Primary Structures: Younger American and British Sculptors* (New York: Jewish Museum, 1966), n.p.; and https://www.moma.org/collection/works/35863.

29. While these two qualities might seem incompatible, even contradictory, both are inherent in the technique, and it is worth emphasizing that the individual executing the drawing has a great degree of control over which quality is emphasized in a given isometric. Through choices about

Sandback's drawings partake of both qualities of isometrics; they not only reveal his sculptures' relationships to the surrounding architecture with rigorous precision but also hint at their experiential complexity, clarifying and complicating his work at the same time. The artist seemed to relish both the technique's avant-garde associations and its potential to demystify his art by rendering it diagrammatically legible. Above all, isometric drawing made it easy for Sandback to play with architectural space. He welcomed simplicity and whimsy: in his short text "A Children's Guide to Seeing," he describes his work as "a somewhat distant cousin" to string games, like cat's cradle, that are found in cultures worldwide, concluding, "We all need a place for play."[30]

Where did Sandback choose to play? Photographs of his MFA studio show *Untitled (Red Floor Piece)* resting on a gray concrete floor, two white walls converging in the background. This generic space could be any of the white-cube galleries in which Sandback would exhibit over the next three and a half decades. But that artwork measured only 1⅝ inches tall, allowing the artist to crop the photograph frame tightly near the floor. Images of other works taken in this same studio, particularly the vertical pieces, reveal the craggy surface of bush-hammered concrete above the white drywall, which appears to extend some 8 feet up from the floor: this was not a generic context after all. It was, rather, one of the most famous—indeed infamous—buildings constructed in America in the 1960s: Paul Rudolph's Art and Architecture Building for Yale. And surely the years Sandback spent working and learning in this structure influenced his thinking about architecture as much as the people he encountered there, whether Scully, Morris, or Judd.

Rudolph's building, dedicated early in Sandback's sophomore year, was one of the first examples of Brutalist architecture constructed in the United States, and it landed squarely in the middle of hotly contested debates over the legacy of modern architecture. A "late" style, Brutalism complicates and extends the modernist architecture that emerged in the early twentieth century, tending toward more expressive materiality and more Baroque geometries. In the 1960s, some embraced this evolution. Ada Louise Huxtable, the longtime architecture critic for the *New York Times*, called the Yale building "a spectacular tour de force."[31] Others viewed it as an indefensible departure from modernism's roots. Writing in *Architectural Forum*, the architectural historian Sibyl Moholy-Nagy (widow of the Bauhaus artist and teacher László) argued that the building showed that architects like Rudolph "have left the safe anchorage of functionality, technology, and anonymous teamwork to start the long voyage home to architecture as an art."[32] A line can be traced from the first stirrings of architecture-as-art identified by Moholy-Nagy in ambitious 1960s architecture to the highly sculptural and expressive buildings that would become increasingly popular for art museums in the following decades, epitomized by the "Bilbao effect" famously attributed to Frank Gehry's design for the Guggenheim Museum, which opened in that city in 1997. As this trend continued, artists began complaining that their works were being upstaged by the buildings they were being exhibited in, and many responded with their own ever larger and more spectacular installations, locking art and architecture into a kind of arms race.

Sandback seems to have learned a more practical lesson from his early exposure to architecture-as-art. Rather than confronting architecture, he could tune it out. As his MFA studio shows, some drywall and a little white paint were enough to turn even the most expressive and aggressive architecture into the spatial equivalent of a blank canvas. For Sandback, then, the white cube was a kind of architectural Trojan horse, a way of ensuring that his work found favorable conditions wherever it was shown. Conceptually, the white cube is reflexively associated with modernism, partly because it has long been established as the preferred context for exhibiting modern art. Yet, in historical terms, the white cube is fundamentally postmodern; it emerged from the struggles of art and architecture to adapt to the aftermath of modernity. This is underscored by the history of Dia Art Foundation, which decisively normalized the idea of converting formerly industrial spaces into galleries, first in New York City and then around the world, offering an essential early paradigm for the role of culture in the postindustrial city.

Perhaps because of its interlayered associations with modernism, raw industrial spaces, and iconic Minimalist practices like those supported by Dia, the white cube is also commonly assumed to exemplify clarity and transparency, to embody total architectural neutrality. Dia, however, utilized the white cube to mask, obfuscate, or suppress the particulars of a place. Richard Gluckman, Dia's primary architect for more than twenty years, recalls that his first Dia-related project, in 1977, was not, in fact, to turn an old downtown factory into a chic new gallery space—although he would do that many times in the following decades. It was, instead, to convert the Gilded Age townhouse owned by two of Dia's founders, Heiner Friedrich and Philippa de Menil (now Fariha al-Jerrahi), to resemble a white-cube gallery by stripping out its ornate detailing before installing the work of several Dia artists.[33]

In 1978, in keeping with the foundation's ambition to create permanent museums dedicated to the work of single artists, Dia partnered with Sandback to buy

shading and line weight, using (or not using) dashed lines to represent "hidden" lines, including or omitting scale figures, and many other details, it is possible to either emphasize or minimize directional ambiguity by clarifying or obfuscating which surfaces or elements in a drawing lie in front of or behind the others. In other words, both Farish and Lissitzky were correct in their claims about isometric projection; each simply highlighted a different dimension of the technique.

30. Fred Sandback, *A Children's Guide to Seeing* (Houston: Contemporary Arts Museum, 1989), n.p. It is relevant here that isometric projection has proved enduringly popular in computer and video-game graphics.

31. Ada Louise Huxtable, "Winner at Yale: The New Art and Architecture Building Lives Up to Great Expectations," *New York Times*, November 10, 1963.

32. Sibyl Moholy-Nagy, "Yale's School of Art and Architecture: The Measure, A Critical Appraisal of the Building and Its Place in Contemporary Architecture," *Architectural Forum* 120, no. 2 (February 1964): 77.

33. Richard Gluckman, interview by Julian Rose, in Julian Rose, *Building Culture: Sixteen Architects on How Museums Are Shaping the Future of Art, Architecture, and Public Space* (New York: Princeton Architectural Press, 2024), 132–38.

ALSO LIST OF MY SCHEDULE
FOR PLACE AND MY USES

H. WANTS MORE DETAILED
COMPREHENSIVE EXPENSE SHEET
(MORE SHOULDNT BE ASKED
FOR LATER, SO IT SHOULD
BE COMPLETE AND
OVERESTIMATED)

74 FRONT STREET   WINCHENDON, MASS.

General function:

I think that the space would be best used as outlined in my
previous sketches:

The main area of the first floor (46'x46'x12') should be left
open as one space to house a series of large pieces on a rotating
long term basis.

The second large area on the main level (46'x32'x10') will have
two walls constructed to include and conceal the pillars. It
would be best used for the display of drawings and graphics,
though it could be used for constructions once the cellar area
was fully prepared for drawings and graphics.

The second floor(46'x46'x10') would function best broken up into
five separate spaces for sculpture.

The cellar will eventually serve well, as noted, for graphics and
drawings (maybe 3000+ sq. ft. are eventually usable)

The two irregular spaces on the main floor (about 500 sq. ft. each)
seem best suited to office space, administrative functions, storage
of constructions and graphics, etc.

---

74 FRONT STREET - PROPOSED RENOVATIONS:

Heating System:
Remove radiators from main areas in first and second floors.
The two side rooms and rear room, first floor, will be heated,
as will the basement front section. These sections will be
primarily used for drawings and graphics. Main floor rear
could also be used for sculpture.

Plumbing system:
Remove plumbing fixtures except for toilet and sink in main
floor left office and toilet in cellar.

Structural: /Cosmetic:

Unboard and reglaze five windows, second floor.

Partition second floor into four rooms, 1/2" sheetrock -
    2"x6" studs 24" o.c.
                                (2nd fl)
Remove wainscoting from peripheral walls and sheetrock them.
                        (covering windows side walls rear)
Remove wainscoting 1st floor main and rear sections - sheetrock.

First fl. rear - ceiling remove acoustical tile(?) replace or
    cover with ½" sheetrock

Frame out and sheetrock first floor front area street side wall
up to 9 ft. level - from there to ceiling with translucent plexi-
glas. Exterior of upper area to be redone with translucent plex
or with similar glass, whichever cheaper.

First floor main area - remove plywood floor section - replace
with hard maple flooring to match - approx. 400 fkxxqx sq. ft.

Exterior - scrape and paint window frames and cornice, paint
lower lever facade and provide cosmetic covering for cinder
block section.

Cellar: main section, build indicated partitions, sand and
polyurethane floor.

Sand and polyurethane all floors, 1st & 2nd floors

Heating Alternative: replace existing radiators in two main
areas with low finned-pipe types

Patch plaster in side rooms, main floor, remove partition in
left room, strip floors.

Spray paint all walls and ceilings throughout white.

Proposal to Dia Art Foundation outlining plans for the Fred Sandback Museum, Winchendon, Massachusetts

a building in Winchendon, Massachusetts, and transform it into the Fred Sandback Museum. Constructed in 1867, the building was originally a three-story Victorian bank. To prepare it for the exhibition of Sandback's work, extensive renovation of the space took place over two years, with most of the design and construction carried out by the artist himself. "I planned all of the restructuring of the building, and, as you can imagine, executed a lot of it, too," Sandback wrote in 1981.[34] Photographs of the work in progress show a completely gutted interior, with Sandback framing out 2 × 4 stud walls to shape and subdivide the space into his preferred proportions. Given his lively sense of humor, he perhaps sensed a faint irony here: his mature work had begun with a meditation on a 2 × 4, and now the 2 × 4 was his primary tool for shaping his own personal museum.

When Dia bought the former bank in Winchendon, Sandback also sought the foundation's support to build a new studio in the nearby town of Rindge, New Hampshire. He conceptualized the studio as an extension of the museum, suggesting it be open to the public. The studio building would also allow the artist to think about

34. Fred Sandback, letter to Amy Baker (now Amy Baker Sandback), September 12, 1981. Winchendon folder, Fred Sandback Archive, New York.

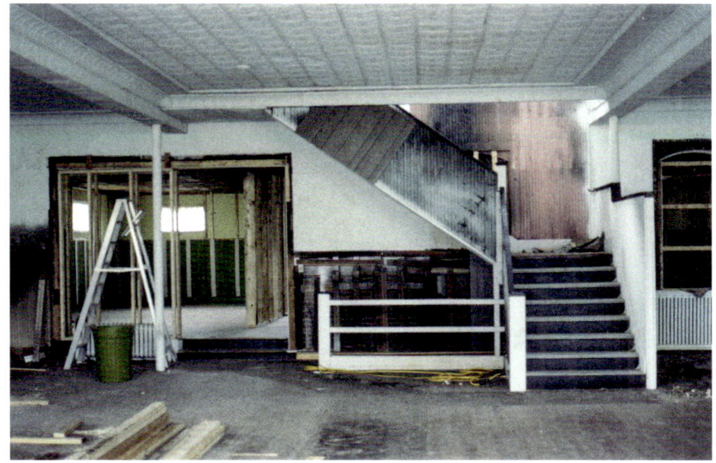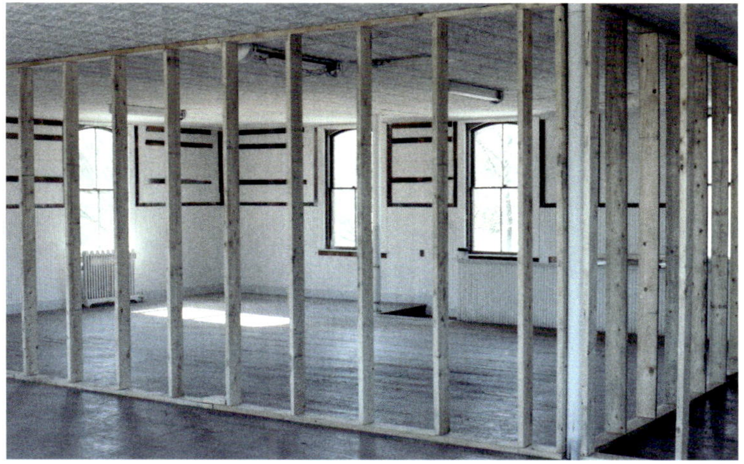

The Fred Sandback Museum in Winchendon, Massachusetts, under construction, c. 1979–80

35. Fred Sandback, letter to the Lone Star Foundation, sister organization to Dia Art Foundation, June 8, 1979. Fred Sandback Archive, New York.

his work in relation to new, ground-up construction, an opportunity not afforded by the renovation of the bank. As he explained in a letter written in the summer of 1979, he had decided to design and build the new studio "because of an increasing interest on my part in the architectural context in which my work may be experienced."[35] It was a fascinating proposition. An artist whose work was ubiquitously described as responsive to existing spaces—who had, at most, occasionally masked the more distinctive qualities of the architecture he encountered—would have the opportunity to imagine an entirely new space, conceived as the ideal place in which to make and show his work. What form would this new building take?

The studio no longer exists, but a small collection of surviving photographs gives the answer: it was a pristine white cube. Indeed, many of the studio images are almost indistinguishable from contemporaneous photos of the museum's interior in Winchendon, with polished wood floors and spotless white walls. Further, while the first floor of the bank building had distinctive tin ceilings that Sandback kept, simply painting them white, he appears to have installed a new plasterboard ceiling on the museum's second floor at almost the exact height of the ceiling in his studio. And this was no neutral architecture. Producing a white cube in this context was an impressive feat—the studio sits, after all, on a rugged, isolated plot of land in rural New Hampshire. The artist's drawings of the building show that the site's incline compelled Sandback to raise the studio off the ground on concrete piers to create a level floor. Harsh winters demanded a sloped roof to shed snow; Sandback's sketches show his experiments with various roof profiles, always built around the rectangular cross section of the interior. There was little connection between the interior space of the building and its exterior envelope, in other words, because both the climate and

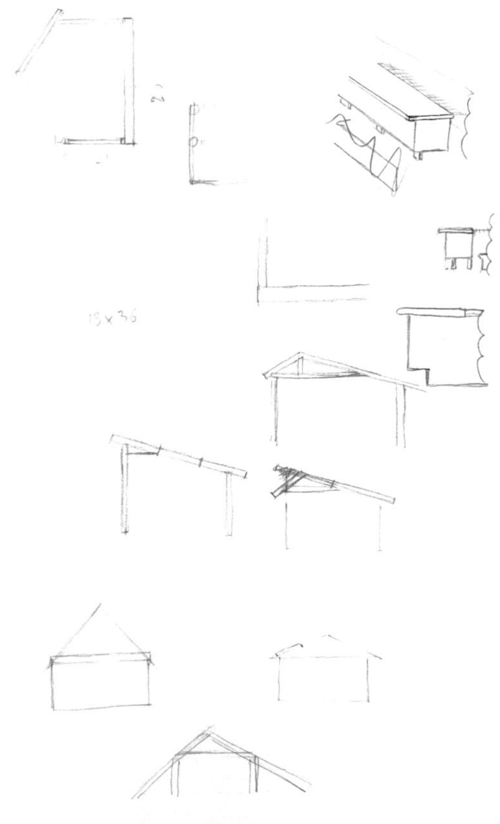

Sketches for roof profile of Rindge studio, c. 1979

36. These details are drawn from my conversation with the artist's son Peter Sandback on October 4, 2023. I am grateful to him for sharing his memories of the studio, invaluably supplementing surviving drawings and photographs.

the topography were hostile to a cubic structure. Sandback initially proposed that the building have no windows, only a skylight, to complete the isolation of the interior, but he abandoned this idea because of its high cost, ultimately installing a door with glass panels in addition to four large windows, two each on adjacent walls. (Limiting the windows to these two walls left him with one entirely white-walled corner to photograph works in.) He also included a drafting table and a flat file for drawing storage, separated from the rectangular volume of the main studio in a small alcove by the primary entrance.[36]

Why did Sandback settle on this design of all possible options? Tellingly, the artist conceived an untitled sculpture for the studio in 1982: an equilateral triangle in red yarn positioned in one corner of the rectangular room. He had experimented with similar triangular corner pieces as early as 1969, when he installed an 8-foot equilateral triangle of gray elastic cord in his Yale studio. But this red triangle was larger, scaled precisely to the studio's architecture so that its apex coincided with an upper corner of the room. Sandback also positioned the line defining the base of the triangle flush with

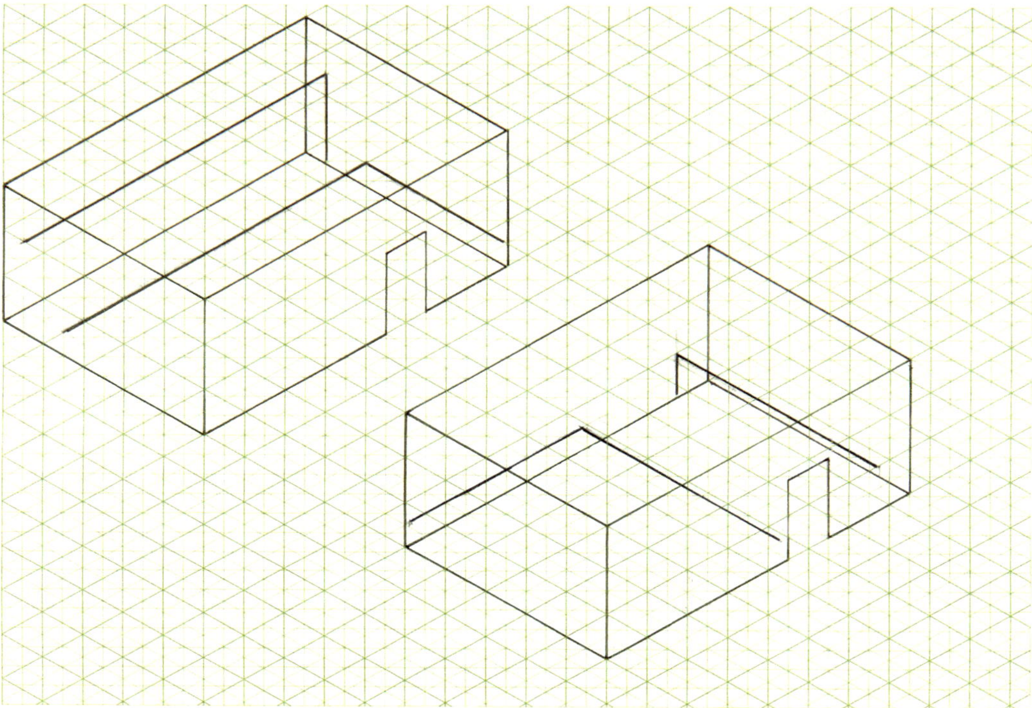

Untitled (Rindge Studio), c. 1981. Ink on isometric paper, 8½ × 11 inches (21.6 × 27.9 cm)

37. In six of these, the triangle appears
extremely distorted because the angle of
the isometric projection renders one of
its equal sides far longer than the other
two. But in two of the views, the triangle
appears—almost magically—completely
undistorted, a true equilateral, as it would
be if the shape were traced directly on
the floor and then shown in a floor plan
of the space. This is because Sandback
has positioned the work precisely within
the rectangular prism of the studio's
volume so that when the whole ensemble
is drawn in isometric projection, looking
toward the corner in which the piece is
installed (from either above or below), the
triangular plane defined by the piece is
exactly parallel to the sheet of paper on
which the isometric is drawn.

the studio floor. He produced an additional suite of drawings for this piece, unique in his oeuvre. On each of two long horizontal sheets of paper, he drew four views of the red triangle side by side: the eight drawings show the piece from eight different isometric views, as if looking down at the work from each of the four upper corners of the rectangular studio space, as well as looking up from the four lower corners.[37]

Isometric drawing is frequently described as lacking a point of view. It is true that an isometric view is not constructed from a fixed point in space, unlike a perspectival illusion, which always has both a vanishing point and a viewpoint. But, as Sandback's drawings of this piece remind us, isometrics do have a clear axis of view, which orients the spectating body in relation to the depicted object. And when the celebrated isometric "reversal" takes place, this orientation shifts: it is not only that one corner of a rectilinear volume pops forward or back, the space suddenly advancing rather than receding or vice versa, but also that the viewer is essentially looking in the opposite direction from the opposite side, having circled around the object and dropped precipitously (or risen vertiginously) through space.

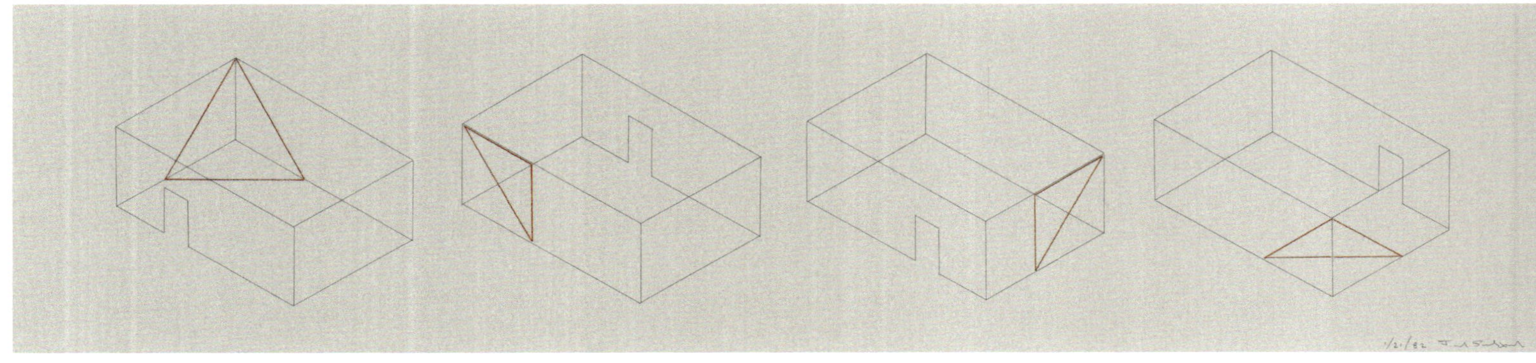

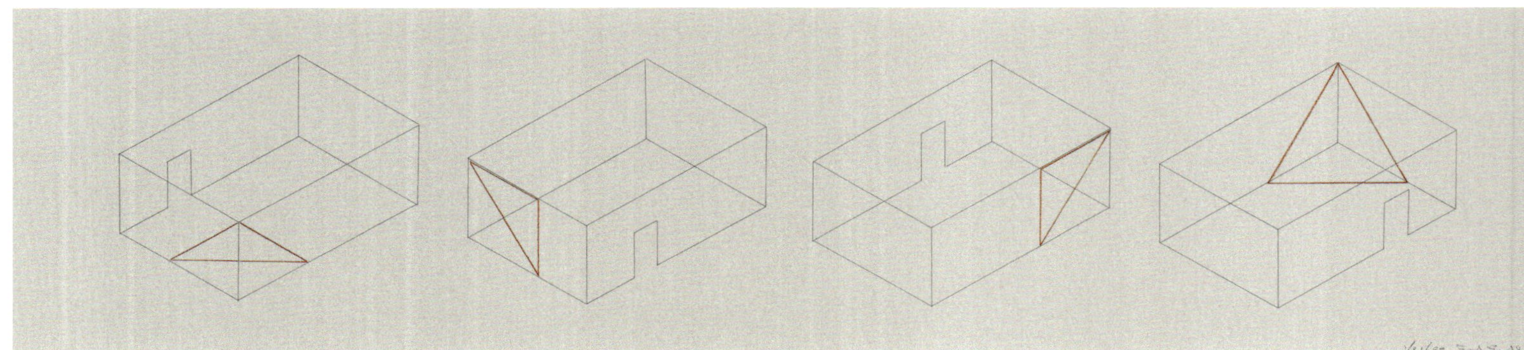

Untitled (Eight Constructions, Rindge Studio), 1982. Pencil and colored pencil on gray paper, two parts: 6 × 25½ inches (15.24 × 64.8 cm) each

38. The full passage reads: "Ses toiles, on le sait, étaient faites pour être accrochées dans n'importe quel sens, ce qui déjà implique un renoncement à la verticalité du tableau et du spectateur, gouvernés tous deux par la loi de la gravitation universelle." Yve-Alain Bois, "Exposition: esthétique de la distraction, espace de démonstration," *Cahiers du musée national d'art moderne*, no. 29 (Fall 1989): 76. Translation by the author.

39. Maria Gough, "Architecture as Such," in *Malevich*, ed. Achim Borchardt-Hume (London: Tate Publishing, 2014), 161.

Looking at Sandback's eight drawings, in other words, may be likened to flying through and around the white cube of his studio space. This levitational effect of isometrics also fascinated the avant-garde practitioners who used the technique in the early twentieth century. Bois reminds us that Lissitzky designed his canvases to hang in any direction on the wall, "which already implied a renunciation of the verticality of the painting and the viewer, both governed by the law of universal gravitation."[38] Malevich's preferred term for the fantastical constructions he drew in parallel projection was "Aerovisual Architecture," evincing what the scholar of Constructivism Maria Gough evocatively describes as "a futurist hunger for the phenomenological experience of flight."[39] But part of the poignancy of these experiments is that they stopped in two dimensions; translating their findings into three-dimensional space remained only a dream.

The modernist pioneer who came the closest to realizing this kind of weightless effect in actual space was probably Mies van der Rohe. This is ironic, in a sense, because he almost entirely eschewed parallel projection, preferring the architect's traditional triad of orthographic projections (plan, section, and elevation) in combination with linear perspective. However, his drawing nonetheless reveals an extraordinary conceptual kinship with Sandback. As Evans points out in his analysis of Mies's

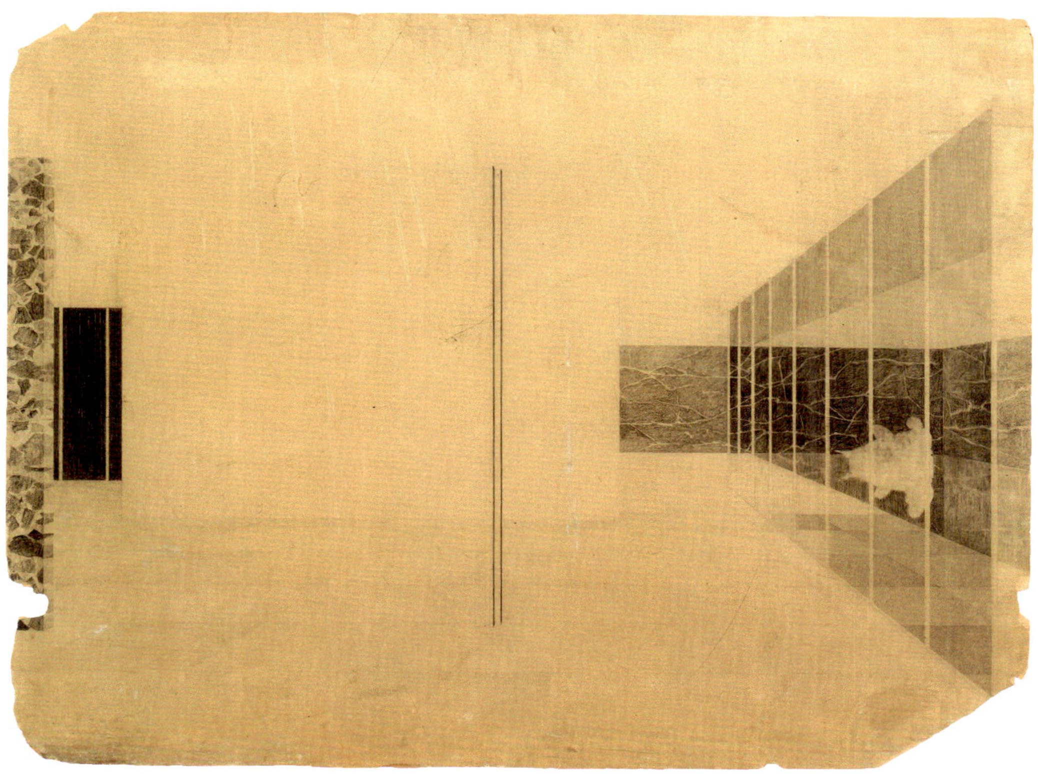

Mies van der Rohe, *German Pavilion, International Exposition, Barcelona, Spain (Interior perspective)*, c. 1928–29. Graphite on illustration board, 39 × 51¼ inches (99.1 × 130.2 cm)

iconic rendering of the interior of the 1929 Barcelona Pavilion, "In the foreground of the perspective, two vertical lines that indicate a column are drawn so close together that they look more like a stretched cord than a compressed column—wherein lies a clue."[40] The clue reveals a tectonic paradox: Mies's buildings "do not rise against the pull of gravity; gravity does not enter into it. They make you believe, against reason, that they do not partake of that most pervasive and relentless of all natural forces." It might be tempting to characterize this ethereal effect as purely visual, a kind of dematerialization, but Evans emphasizes that wherever gravity is implicated, there will inevitably be an intense corporeal impact. And so Mies offers not the illusion of a floating structure, which would indeed be a mere optical effect, but rather a destabilization of the body's relationship to the inexorable vertical axis of gravitational pull, resulting in "a gentle, dreamy disorientation in the observer."[41]

A similar effect will be familiar to anyone who has shared a room with one of Sandback's works. His ability to echo the weightlessness of isometric drawings in real space—to free the viewer from gravity, even for a moment—is one of his core achievements. To sustain this weightless effect, even his realized sculptures must remain slightly divorced from physical reality; hence the artist's eventual preference

40. Robin Evans, "Mies van der Rohe's Paradoxical Symmetries," in *Translations from Drawing to Building and Other Essays*, 241.

41. Ibid., 246.

42. Fred Sandback, conversation with Michael Govan, Marianne Stockebrand, and Gianfranco Verna, October 6, 2001, Chinati Foundation, Marfa, Texas, on the occasion of the opening of *Fred Sandback: Sculpture*, in *Chinati Foundation Newsletter*, no. 7 (October 2002): 26.

43. These essays were reprinted and expanded as Brian O'Doherty, *Inside the White Cube: The Ideology of the Gallery Space* (Berkeley, CA: University of California Press, 1999).

for acrylic yarn over the elastic cord he used in his earliest works. ("The problem with the elastic cord is that it always wants to sag, and this doesn't," he told an interviewer.[42]) Gravity is his work's enemy—which is why it is jarring to experience a work of Sandback's that has been bumped by a careless viewer and hangs slightly slack. This aligns with Sandback's preference—even in his studio—for the laboratory-like conditions of the white cube; a degree of abstraction, a distance from material things, sustains the productive illusions of his work.

Sandback's reliance on the framework of the white cube entails a certain modesty, too, which, in its own way, also defines his work. Many of Sandback's peers devoted endless energy to rebellion against the white cube, whether by physically attacking its white walls, rejecting its impermanence with doctrines of site-specificity, or fleeing from it entirely into the field of Land art. When critic Brian O'Doherty published "Inside the White Cube," his influential series of *Artforum* articles in 1976, he was hailed as a spokesman for a generation of artists that vehemently rejected the white cube as the default exhibition space.[43] While today O'Doherty is remembered primarily for exposing the white cube as anything but neutral and therefore justifying artistic assaults on its hidden ideologies, his actual message was much more pessimistic. The white cube is not just ideological, he argued, but inevitable, a fundamental part of the system through which art is produced and consumed. A half century later, most of the critiques launched by Sandback's contemporaries have been easily assimilated, tamed, and ushered back into the white-cube gallery or museum—or, worse, the white cubicle of the art-fair booth, that procrustean bed through which any cultural practice must pass to be viable as contemporary art today.

Dia embodied, in part, a shift in exhibition design—its galleries looking like (and eventually occupying) the same downtown lofts in which artists lived and worked. In retrospect, Sandback's choice of the white cube as his studio space reminds us that Dia was also, in many ways, the beginning both of what would come to be called "poststudio" practice and of architecture as institutional brand building, eventually normalizing a generic context crucial to the functioning of the global art world. It is the white cube, after all, that allows so many of the same artists and even the same institutions to move seamlessly among financial and cultural capitals, from New York to Paris to Abu Dhabi to Hong Kong. Sandback realized that truly site-specific sculpture was not viable in this brave new world, but he had the foresight to make his work context dependent, activating the white cube as a space of genuine play and experimentation, transforming it into something sublime.

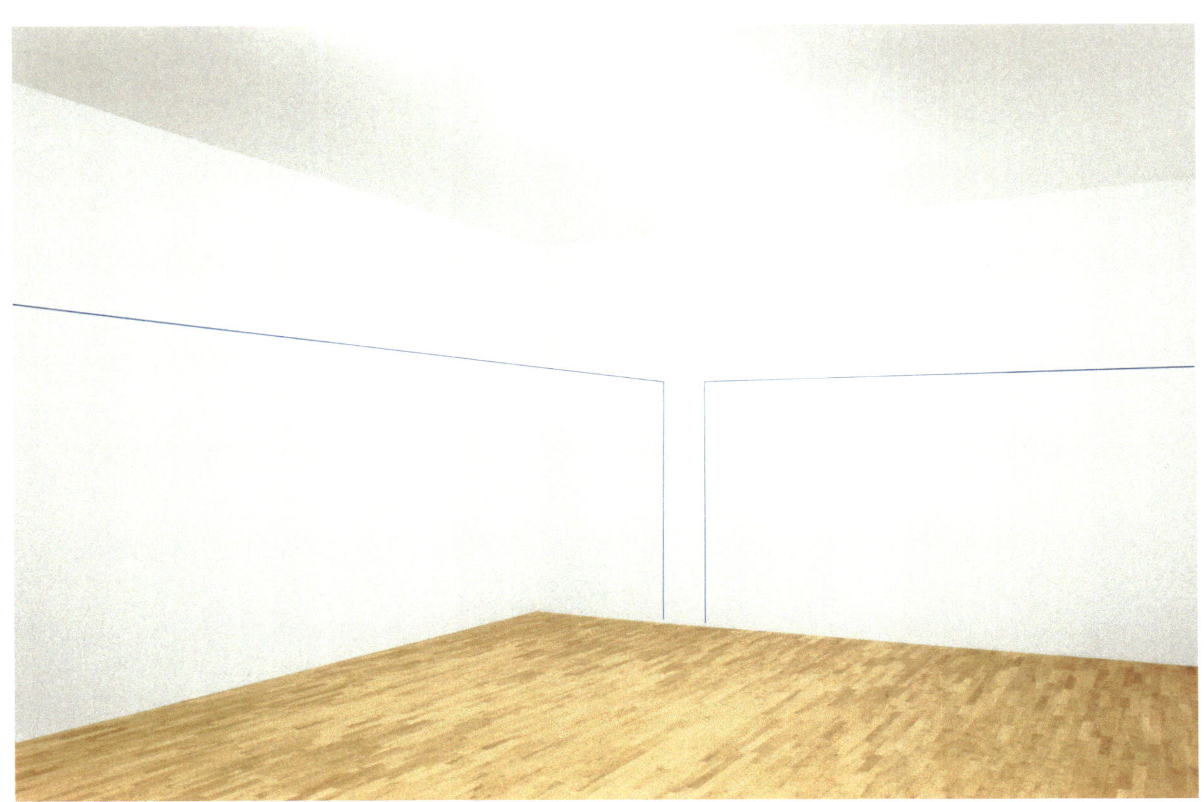

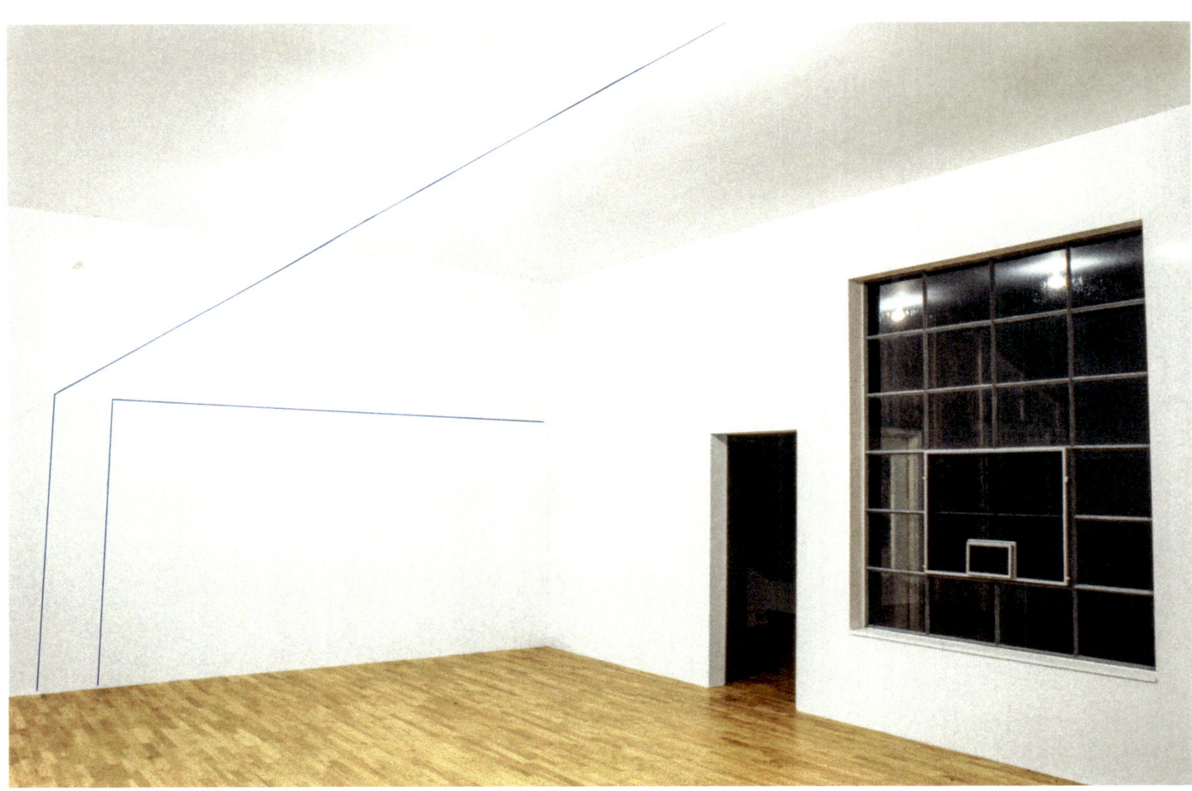

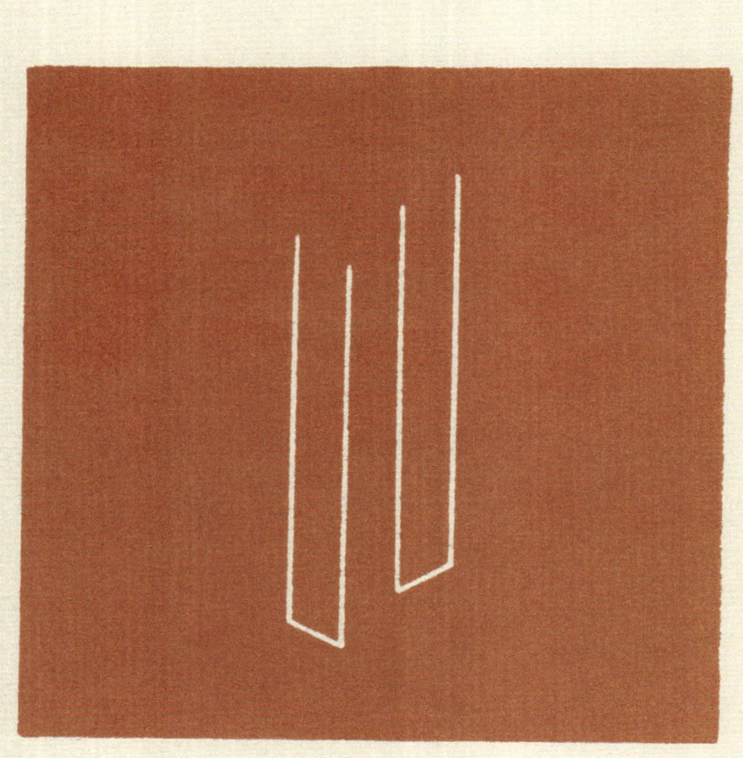

74 Front Street: The Fred Sandback Museum,
sixteen-page booklet published by Dia Art Foundation,
New York, 1982

Existing, Not Existing
Sculpture's Spaces in the Fred Sandback Museum

Edward A. Vazquez

I.

In 1982, the Fred Sandback Museum published a small pamphlet as a manner of introduction. The slim, staple-bound booklet features a linoleum print of perpendicular U-shaped forms figured in white against a square of rust brown with the details "74 Front Street / The Fred Sandback Museum / Winchendon, Massachusetts / June 20, 1981–October 31, 1982" centered below. This information, giving the museum's inaugural exhibition dates, repeats on the interior cover, broken up by a smaller U-shape motif and anchored by one line of additional text in bold: "The Dia Art Foundation." The booklet includes a brief prelude, set above a street-level view of the museum's exterior facade, that describes the current survey of Sandback's work from 1967 to 1981 and shares a few facts about the building's history, notes that access to Sandback's nearby studio is possible via appointment, and finally acknowledges the work of Jean Fincke, as well as the support of Dia. To contextualize the thirteen reproduced artworks—a mix of sculptures, drawings, and prints—Sandback's short, manifesto-like text "Notes," from 1973, precedes the illustrations, followed by a condensed education and exhibition history.

As Sandback writes in "Notes," acknowledging the use value of photography and at the same time voicing a critical view of the fixity imposed on his sculptural constructions by the still image, "The photographs of the work provide one sort of knowledge about the work—a sort of schema of what it is. Beyond that, the pieces are totally contextual and the photographs are of no interest with regard to that."[1] The black-and-white reproductions, nearly all images of art installed in the museum's inaugural exhibition, provide a sense of the objects on view, and the double-page spread of an untitled construction—with two opposing L-shapes set on the diagonal through the museum's main first-floor gallery space—suggests the complex interrelationship of architecture, form, and space that Sandback's spare installations sought to materialize. It is hard, after all, even in such a photo, to see where the sculpture

1. Fred Sandback, "Notes," in *74 Front Street: The Fred Sandback Museum* (New York: Dia Art Foundation, 1982), 4. This text was first published in English and Italian in *Flash Art*, no. 40 (March–May 1973): 14; it is accessible along with all other published writings by Fred Sandback online at https://www.fred sandbackarchive.org/publications.

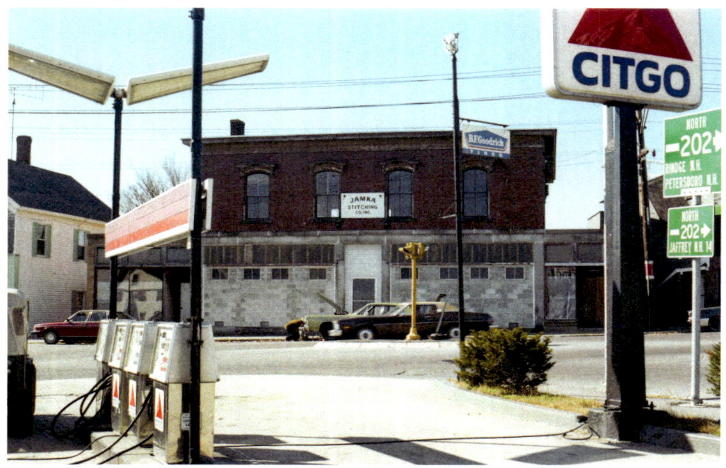

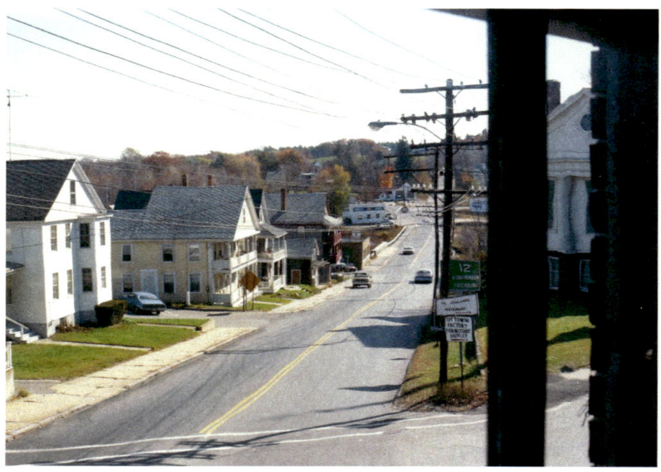

74 **Front Street, Winchendon, Massachusetts**

View from 74 Front Street, Winchendon, Massachusetts

2. Donald and Edward Waisnis, "Fred Sandback Sculpture (in the Context of the Fred Sandback Museum)," *ARTextreme*, no. 2 (1982): 18.

3. In what follows, I use *public* and *private* in a self-consciously simple, workaday way. In doing so, I hope that the entangling of studio and museum in Sandback's case can stand as an instance of the complex conceptual overlaps of each, and the ways that such instabilities echo in the reversals in Sandback's sculptural forms. As Michael Warner writes, "Public and private are not always simple enough that one could code them on a map with different colors—pink for public and blue for private." Michael Warner, *Publics and Counterpublics* (New York: Zone Books, 2002), 27.

starts and where it ends. At a minimum, the reproduced imagery forcefully asserts, as a contemporary review in a local publication had it, with a nod to the gleaming new exterior of the museum and former bank building, "that something uniquely different, from mainstream small-town life, is going on inside."[2] Yet a division between inside and outside—and thus between private and public—finds form in these images in a different way. Of the nine sculptural works photographed, eight document the original installations at the Fred Sandback Museum; one is taken from the artist's studio in Rindge, New Hampshire. Apart from a different-seeming pattern to the wood flooring, the space that houses *First Construction for the Rindge Studio* (1979) looks like many of the others reproduced. While certain similarities in the construction of these relatively simple interiors can be chalked up to the artist's (often literal) hand in the renovation of both spaces, the architectural resonance, and thus the implied spatial continuity, marks the hoped-for porousness between Sandback's studio and museum, collapsing into each other across the selfsame gap of private and public that Sandback's sculptures attempt to unravel in their dissolution of the discrete and internally consistent specific object.[3]

This is to say, during its fifteen-year existence, the Fred Sandback Museum responded to needs and desires rooted in Sandback's artistic practice, a number of which revolved around this tension between public and private. Most concretely, the museum existed so that the site-aware and context-dependent work that Sandback had been making since the late 1960s—itself fully contingent on the availability of space in galleries and museums—could stand in more extended duration. It did this, via the patronage of Dia Art Foundation, as an arts institution open to all; located in a small town neighboring Sandback's own home and studio, the Fred Sandback Museum was, however, most accessible to the artist. In this way, it served as a site of physical exploration and sculptural experiment. Indeed, if among Sandback's most apt descriptors of his practice is that his art functions in "pedestrian space," which he described as "literal, flat-footed, and everyday. The idea was to have the work right there along with everything else in the world, not up on a spatial pedestal,"[4] then the Fred Sandback Museum, even with its white-cube interior, is precisely such a space: one where art and life intermix, each opening onto the needs and aspirations of the other.

II.

The primary motivations for the creation of the museum were none other than the transcendentals of time and space. By the mid-1970s, Sandback's work in yarn had increasingly expanded in scale and often made use of strategies of permutation and variation, as exhibition schedules allowed for only short, punctuated windows of viewing and creating. Recognizing these limitations, Sandback's experience creating work in the newly opened P.S. 1 in 1978 was a watershed. As the artist explained in "Remarks on My Sculpture 1966–86," written on the occasion of a career-spanning exhibition at the Kunsthalle Mannheim in Germany:

> In the summer of 1977, I had the opportunity to use about 10,000 square feet of space at P.S. 1 in Long Island City, as a studio for a month. I had developed a need in the years prior to this for increasingly large and unwieldy formats, and this had led inevitably to the result that I could only build one piece at a time in my studio. Exhibitions, too, often consisted of only one image. Hence it was difficult for me to correlate my experiences, and almost impossible for a spectator to see enough to get what I was up to.
>
> Having these seven huge rooms to work in was a small revelation, in that I was able for the first time to see how these pieces acted together and to work with them simultaneously. It was a chance to crystallize some of the things that I had been pecking away at one at a time, but more than anything, a chance just to do a lot of work in the same place. A usual consequence of my work is that not too much of it can exist in any one place for too long.[5]

Here Sandback describes how the regular venues where he would make and display work—the Annemarie Verna Galerie in Zurich, for example, and Heiner Friedrich's various galleries in New York, Munich, and Cologne—typically had one or two rooms of large exhibition space and would often accommodate placement of only a single sculptural construction, as seen, for example, in Sandback's solo exhibitions at Heiner

4. Fred Sandback, "Remarks on My Sculpture 1966–86," in *Fred Sandback: Sculpture 1966–1986* (Mannheim, Germany: Kunsthalle Mannheim, 1986), 13.

5. Ibid., 14.

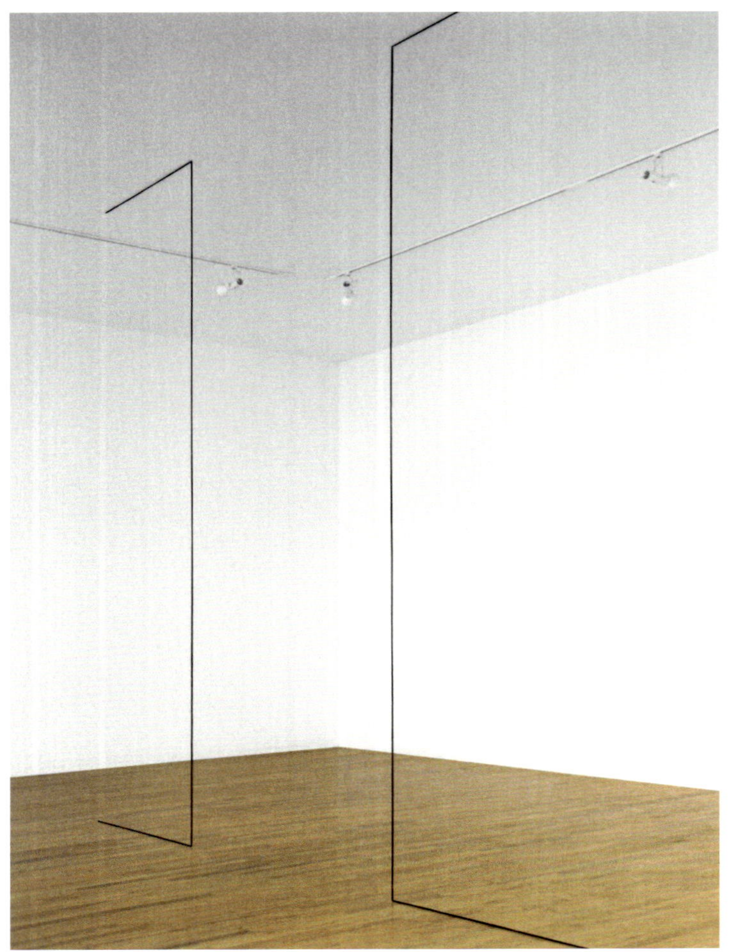

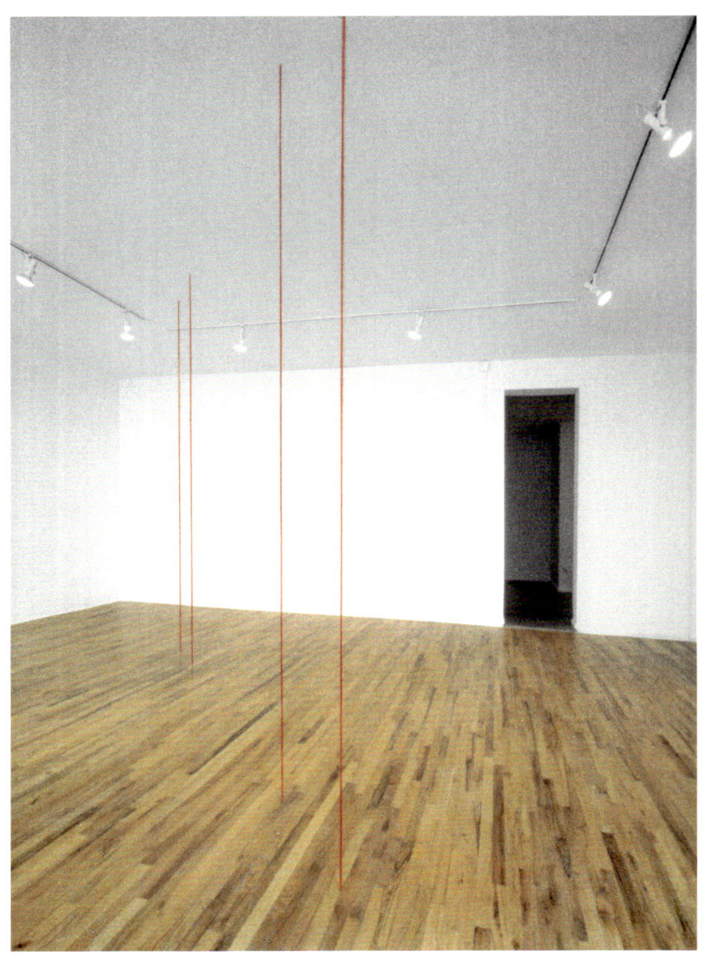

Untitled, 1977. Acrylic yarn (black), situational dimensions, overall dimensions vary with each installation using spatial relationships established by the artist. Installation view, Institute for Art and Urban Resources, P.S. 1, Long Island City, New York, 1978

Untitled, 1978. Acrylic yarn (Venetian red), situational dimensions, overall dimensions vary with each installation using spatial relationships established by the artist. Installation view, Institute for Art and Urban Resources, P.S. 1, Long Island City, New York, 1978

Friedrich, Inc., in New York in 1976 and 1978. The spaces, of course, had not gotten smaller, but Sandback's work, especially as he explored the possibilities of related L- and U-shaped forms, could expand or contract in relation to the discrete parts of each construction and often tended toward the larger. The limits of architecture foreclosed Sandback's ability to explore the interrelationships across these forms in real time, capping not only the artist's capacity to broaden his engagement with these motifs but also the experiential possibilities available to his audience.

Sandback undertook the creation of his museum to address some of the complexities of his increasingly larger-scale, but always site-dependent and ephemeral, sculptural production. In "Remarks on My Sculpture," his discussion of the museum immediately follows that of the installations at P.S. 1, though the tone shifts away from the power of simultaneous sculptural installation and toward the nuances of the evanescent nature of his sculptural production.

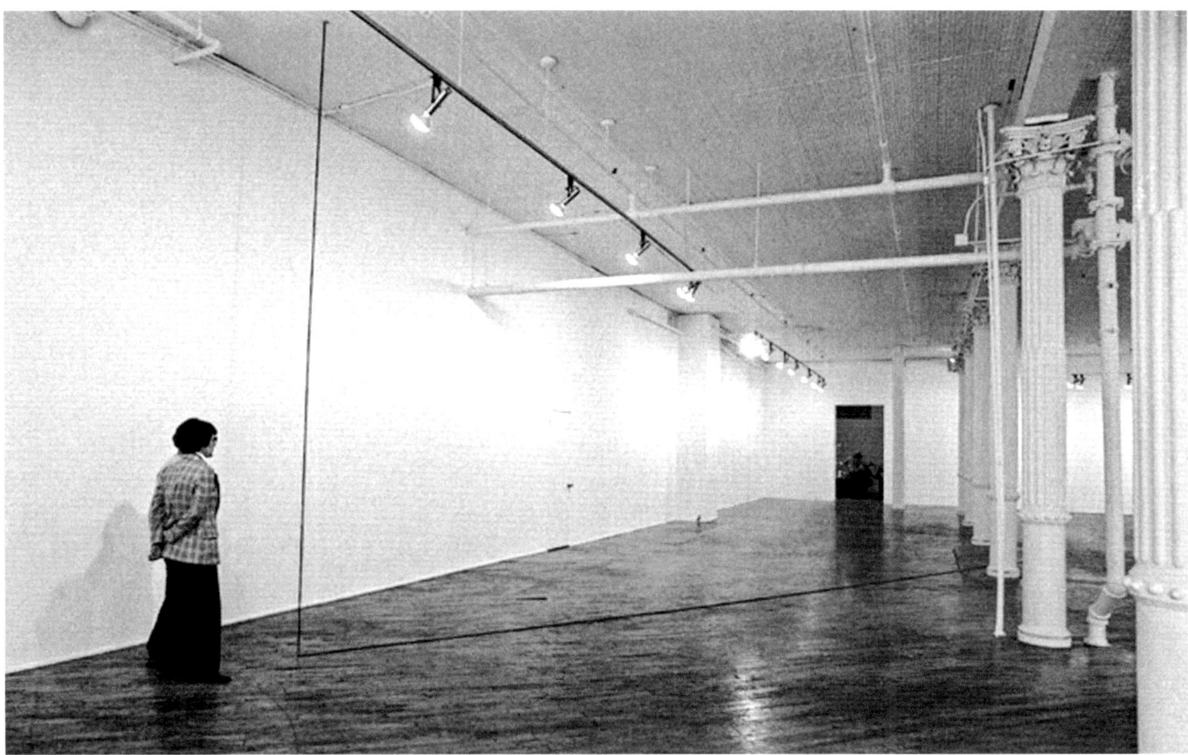

The Museum in Winchendon, which began renovation in 1978 with the caring patronage of the Dia Art Foundation, offered some remedy to my feeling that things were just too diaphanous. I'd been building work for twelve years that had almost completely ceased to exist. I was not producing a product that could be easily acquired or preserved, and I felt a great need for a sense of material continuity and permanence. The idea of having one's own museum is quirky and amusing, but I did feel that the work ought to exist somewhere in a reasonably dense and permanent grouping, outside of the "three week stands" that were the approximate limit in galleries.[6]

In noting the delicate, overly diaphanous reality of his work, Sandback describes an understandable feeling: as an artist committed to exploring the materiality of the world in a variety of complex, if materially limited, sculptural ways, he looked up at a certain moment in his life—a mature artist with a set mode of working—and could point to no "body" of work in a traditional sense.

At the same time, such an awareness points to a material paradox at the core of his practice that runs through every three-dimensional object he had made since 1967, beginning with *Untitled (Red Floor Piece)* (1967), a roughly 2 × 4-inch × 22-foot-long

6. Ibid.

7. The dimensions of Sandback's object in relation to a piece of wood are a little more complicated than described. For a more thorough analysis of the object in relation to Minimalist precedent, see Edward A. Vazquez, *Aspects: Fred Sandback's Sculpture* (Chicago: University of Chicago Press, 2017), 19–27.

8. Sandback, "Remarks on My Sculpture 1966–86," 12.

9. Sandback, "Notes," 4.

10. Sandback's use of "actuality" in this context has a variety of deep, embedded meanings; see Vazquez, *Aspects*, 35–39, for a more thorough discussion of the term.

11. Fred Sandback, conversation with Joan Simon, "Lines of Inquiry," *Art in America* 85, no. 5 (May 1997): 92.

12. Jessica Morgan, introduction to *Dia: An Introduction to Dia's Locations and Sites*, ed. Kamilah N. Foreman, Matilde Guidelli-Guidi, and Sophia Larigakis (New York: Dia Art Foundation, 2021), 11.

13. Founding document, 1974, typescript of archive materials, DIAR.001, Early History records, 1974–1986, Dia Art Foundation Archives, Beacon, New York, quoted in Morgan, introduction to *Dia: An Introduction to Dia's Locations and Sites*, 12.

construction in red wire and elastic cord that can be fairly thumbnailed as the outline of a standard piece of construction lumber.[7] Describing the origin of his sculptural practice, again from "Remarks on My Sculpture," with an analysis of *Untitled (Red Floor Piece)*, Sandback wrote: "I think my first attraction to this situation was to the way it allowed me to play with something both existing and not existing at the same time. The thing itself—2" × 4"—was just as material as it could be—a volume of air and light above the surface of the floor. Yet my forming of it, the shape and dimension of that figure, had an ambiguous and transient quality."[8] In framing a working sculptural practice, this interlacing of the presence and absence in a work with potentially porous and ambiguous boundaries was immensely generative for Sandback, especially as he dispensed with the referential echo internal to *Untitled (Red Floor Piece)*. From the perspective of a working artist engaged in the creation of objects and situations over a series of years, the description of an oeuvre as "both existing and not existing at the same time" lacked a tangible physicality and permanence that, as a general statement, sat uneasily with Sandback in the late 1970s. Sandback concludes "Notes," the text reproduced in the Sandback Museum brochure, with a terse statement of purpose, explaining "there isn't an idea which transcends the actuality of the pieces. The actuality is the idea,"[9] and the expansion of this actuality into increasingly extended durations became possible via the real, physical conditions of the Fred Sandback Museum.[10]

III.

Sandback described the genesis of the museum as a casual development that he proposed to Dia. In a conversation with Joan Simon, Sandback explained, "I presented the notion [to Dia]. There was a small building in Winchendon—a former bank—that was very cheap and derelict. And I needed a place to work. Very rapidly, spontaneously, the idea grew."[11] Such a proposal aligned with Dia's focus on "individual artists' visions and the realization of works wherever they may be constituted."[12] It was the view of Dia's founders—Helen Winkler Fosdick, Heiner Friedrich, and Philippa de Menil (now Fariha al-Jerrahi), that "such active and ongoing endeavors to achieve the construction and public presentation of each single work will result in lasting qualities which people will want to experience in single and repeated visits."[13] While Dia is perhaps most associated with certain sites in New York City, like Walter De Maria's *The New York Earth Room* (1977), and complex works of Land art in the American West, including De Maria's *The Lightning Field* (1977) and James Turrell's *Roden Crater* (1977–present), or even for its initial support of Donald Judd's varied projects in Marfa, Texas, the foundation also acquired numerous other properties "to establish singular sites, each dedicated to an individual artist or work."[14] These included buildings in and around New York City dedicated to the performative work of Robert Whitman, Robert Whitman Projects, which occupied a former Chelsea soundstage (1979–85); a disused mercantile exchange building in Tribeca dedicated to La Monte Young and Marian Zazeela's sound and light environments, as well as their collaborations with Pandit Pran Nath, known as *Dream House* (1979–85); and the permanent installation of Dan Flavin's work at the Dan Flavin Art Institute, a former volunteer firehouse and deconsecrated church on Long Island, now known as Dia Bridgehampton (inaugurated in 1983).[15] Set alongside sites like these, with their mixed use as studios and exhibition and performance spaces, the former bank renovated into Sandback's museum fits right in, even if its location on the Massachusetts–New Hampshire border marks it as something of an outlier.

An undated disclosure statement for the Fred Sandback Museum, which seemingly coincides with its inaugural exhibition in 1981, offers a clear sense of the institution's structure, collections, and aims:

> The Fred Sandback Museum of Winchendon, Massachusetts is privately funded by the Dia Art Foundation of New York City. The museum is a 10,000 square foot building devoted to the permanent exhibition of the three dimensional and graphic work by the artist Fred Sandback. We house an extensive collection of the artist's work dating from 1966 to the present. The basement floor is the print and graphic gallery. The top two floors display the artist's three dimensional constructions. We are open to the public two afternoons a week, and by appointment, through the office, anytime.
>
> We have thirteen sculptures on display at this time. There are also 46 prints and graphics on display with others in storage on the premises for future display.
>
> The building also includes an archive reading room that is in the process of becoming fully utilized as a place to study and learn about the artist's work and it's [*sic*] place in the contemporary art world.
>
> The museum also includes the artist's studio in the neighboring town of Rindge, New Hampshire, where a series of nine constructions for that space is being presented.
>
> Our purpose is twofold. We are interested in maintaining an on-going presentation of the work of Frederick Lane Sandback to the public for interpretation and study in a framework that is not possible in a gallery or museum setting because of the nature of the work.

14. Morgan, introduction to *Dia: An Introduction to Dia's Locations and Sites*, 12.

15. For discussion of each of Dia's sites, see the wider context and documentary materials in *Dia: An Introduction to Dia's Locations and Sites*.

We are also interested in formally documenting the information available about the artist and his work in an archives [*sic*] that presently includes press clippings, catalogues, photos and slides of the work, a card catalogue file of the sculpture and an up to date documentation of pieces on exhibit at the museum and studio. We will expand the archives to include more detailed information on previous exhibitions. The archives are available to the public and other institutions.

We are hoping to make the work not only available to the art viewing population based on Mr. Sandback's international reputation but also to present the work on a specific local level to the immediate community and surrounding towns. We see the museum as a local public resource as well as an international one.

We are a vehicle for furthering exposure to the artist's work, and hopefully from that exposure, people will increase their knowledge and understanding of the artist's work.

We are interested in creating and maintaining a viable cultural institution in a place where there are very few cultural institutions.

We hope to encourage further exhibits of the artist's work by making museums aware of our collections and arranging loan exhibitions.[16]

Many elements of this text bear mention. Though the clear commitment to Sandback's work and to the documentation of his practice stand as the core motivators for the museum, it equally saw itself as functioning for the public good and as a potential bridge between an international, cosmopolitan arts community and a more locally rooted population; the repeated invocations of the audience range between the general ("open to the public") and specific ("creating and maintaining a viable cultural institution in a place where there are very few cultural institutions"). Not only was the Fred Sandback Museum a space of experimentation and exhibition for the artist, but it was also an archive, repository, and community-minded venue. Sandback's twinned ideas that the museum house a print workshop and library, while seemingly never realized, emphasized such intentions. In a fall 1979 letter to the Lone Star Foundation, the sister entity of Dia, Sandback suggested that

a possible function of the Fred Sandback Museum with a very immediate sort of local public resonance would be the establishment of a small library. . . . There seems to be no adequate source of printed matter dealing with the arts in the area. Bookstores are virtually nonexistent, and library facilities are minimal. A very modest collection of good texts might yield a very positive public service for the energy involved in establishing it.[17]

16. "Fred Sandback Museum Disclosure Statement," n.d. Fred Sandback Archive, New York.

17. Fred Sandback, letter to the Lone Star Foundation, September 6, 1979. Fred Sandback Archive, New York.

Subsequent documents imply that this laudable idea, perhaps beyond a few volumes sourced by the artist alongside the archival reading room of press clippings, slides, and the card catalogue of sculptures mentioned above, never came to full fruition.

As per the disclosure, the museum owned an "extensive collection" of Sandback's art, as befits an institution dedicated to the work of a single individual. The process of building this collection was likely an organic one, though Sandback formally recommended specific acquisitions and commissions for the museum in multiple letters addressed to the Lone Star Foundation. In one, dated June 8, 1979, Sandback urged the museum to acquire a series of seven early works from 1967, all of which mark the origins of his mature sculptural production.[18] In another letter, written the same day, Sandback offered to execute a series of drawings for the museum, which would "establish a comprehensive visual record of the public life" of his work.[19] Sandback proposed two discrete suites of drawings as a mode of archival documentation: one of the complete "situational" pieces he had made, with attention to the context of each piece, and a second that would stand as a record of his one-person gallery shows and museum exhibitions. In making his case, Sandback explained, "I feel that this body of drawings is quite important as a form of documentation, but perhaps more so because there is so little visual overview of my work, photography being often inadequate and sometimes irrelevant."[20] In concluding his proposal, Sandback described the dimensions these drawings would take and their individual cost to the foundation.

Artists, just like anyone else, should receive payment for their work. Yet it is a third letter, also dated June 8, 1979, that most directly marks the complex intertwinement of public and private in the Fred Sandback Museum. In this letter, Sandback not only suggests the creation and purchase of a series of nine sculptural constructions, executed and exhibited on a rotating basis in his studio in Rindge, but further puts forth "that the studio on Old New Ipswich Road be maintained as a public space and as an extension of the Winchendor Museum."[21] Dia adopted this proposition in some form, as the disclosure states that "the museum also includes the artist's studio in the neighboring town of Rindge, New Hampshire, where a series of nine constructions for that space is being presented." In a hearing in November 1979, the Board of Adjustment of the Town of Rindge formally acknowledged the arrangement by approving a special exemption proposed by both Sandback and Dia Art Foundation that public, noncommercial access be granted to the artist's studio.[22]

It is unclear from the extant archival documentation whether Dia ultimately assumed ownership of Sandback's studio or simply provided funding to maintain the space as a satellite of the museum. It is equally unclear—and mostly inconsequential—

18. Fred Sandback, letter to the Lone Star Foundation, June 8, 1979. Fred Sandback Archive, New York. Sandback notes additional works in the letter, already in the collection of the Lone Star Foundation, which further suggests these works were proposed for purchase.

19. Fred Sandback, letter to the Lone Star Foundation, June 8, 1979. Fred Sandback Archive, New York.

20. Ibid.

21. Fred Sandback, letter to the Lone Star Foundation, June 8, 1979. Fred Sandback Archive, New York.

22. Notice of Decision, November 13, 1979, Town of Rindge, Board of Adjustment, held in the Fred Sandback Archive, New York. Ever practical, the board agreed to the exemption, noting that "it will not create excessive traffic congestion, noise, odors, nor tend to reduce the value of surrounding properties."

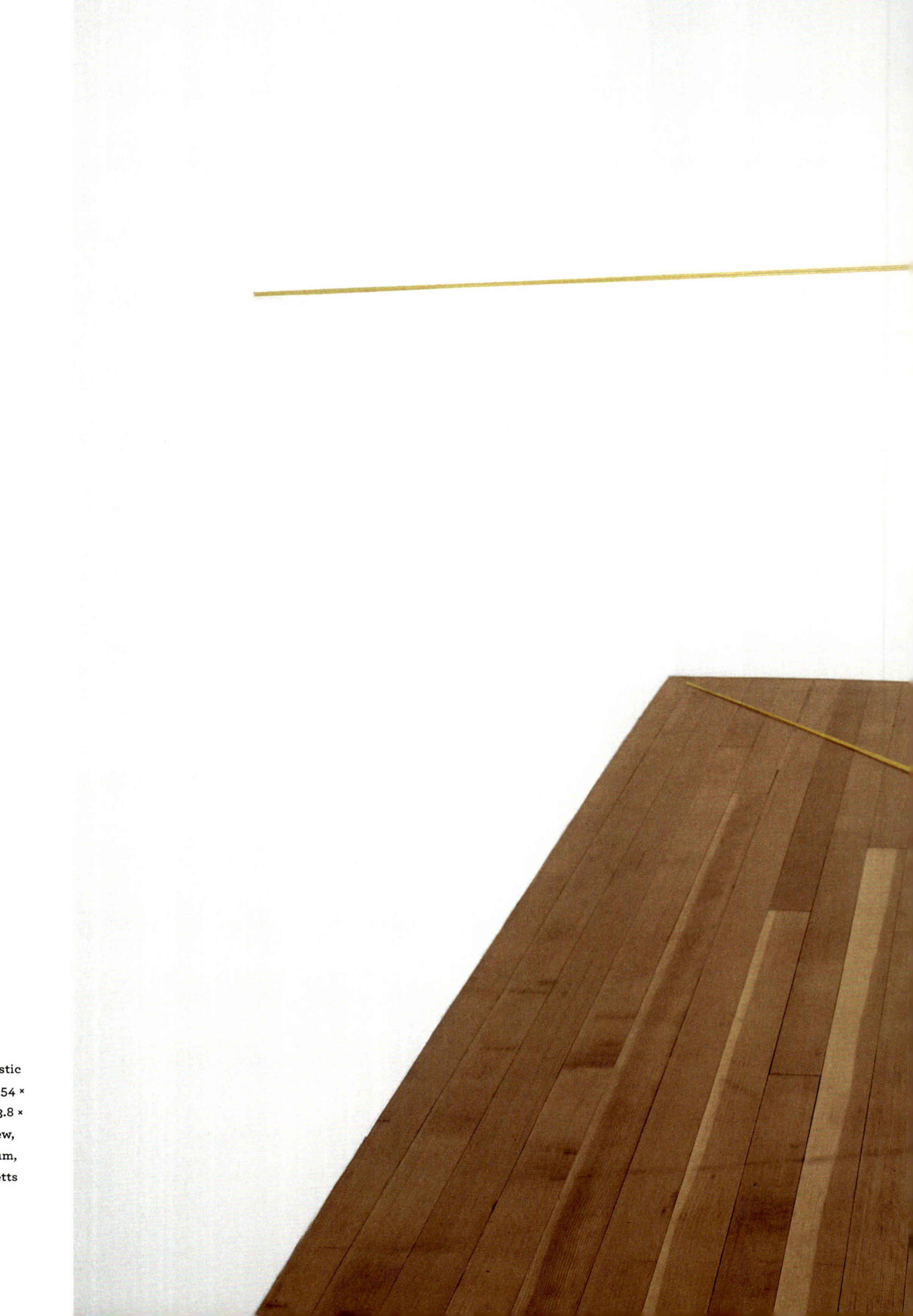

Untitled, 1970. ⅛-inch elastic cord (school-bus yellow), 54 × 96 × 96 inches (137.2 × 243.8 × 243.8 cm). Installation view, The Fred Sandback Museum, Winchendon, Massachusetts

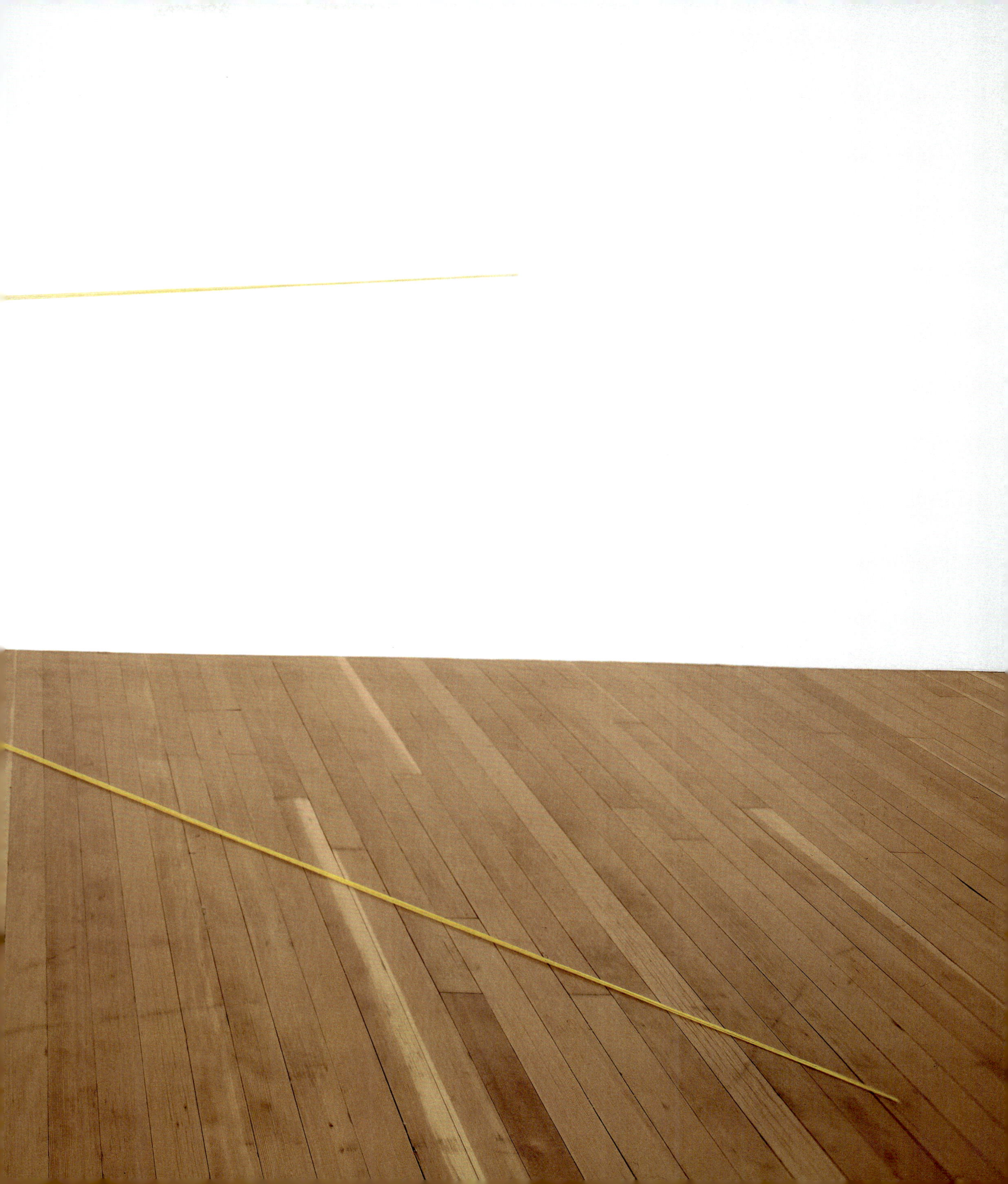

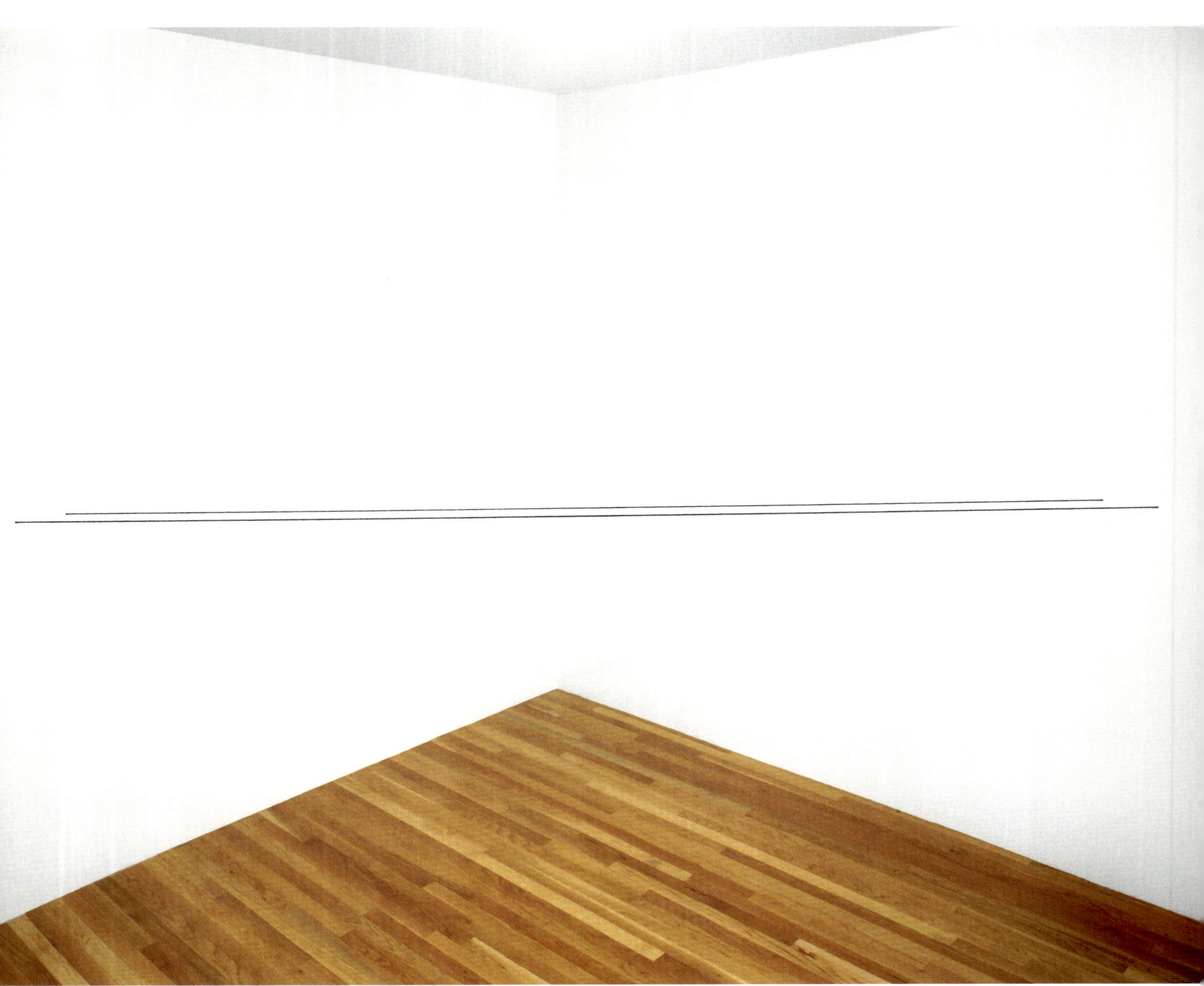

Untitled, 1971. ¼-inch elastic cord (black), 54 × 96 × 96 inches (137.2 × 243.8 × 243.8 cm). Installation view, The Fred Sandback Museum, Winchendon, Massachusetts

Untitled, 1974. Acrylic yarn (black), 144 × 2 × 6 inches (365.8 × 5.1 × 15.2 cm). Installation view, The Fred Sandback Museum, Winchendon, Massachusetts

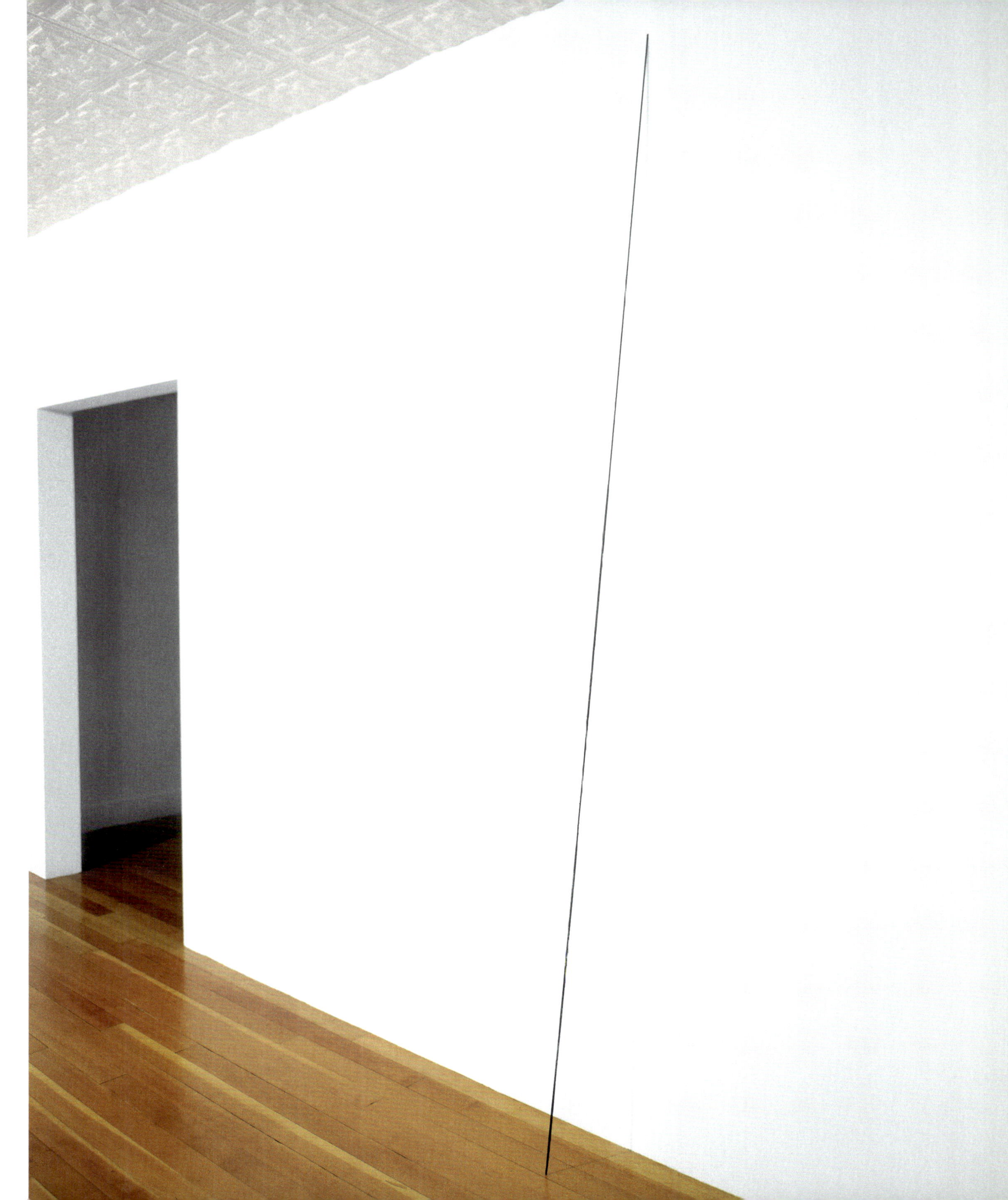

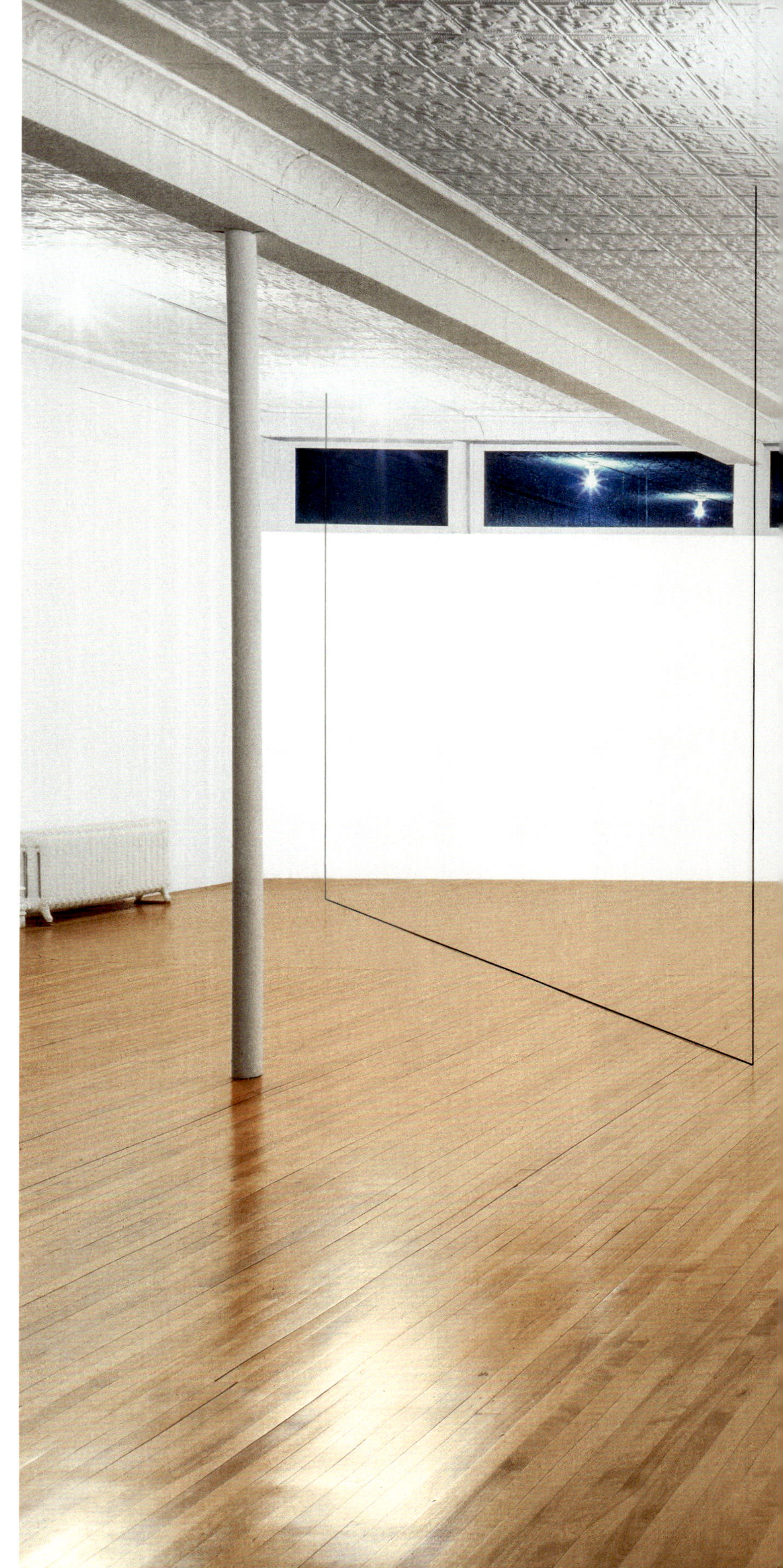

Untitled (from Ten Vertical Constructions),
1977–79. Acrylic yarn (black), situational
dimensions, overall dimensions vary with
each installation using spatial relationships
established by the artist. Installation view,
The Fred Sandback Museum, Winchendon,
Massachusetts

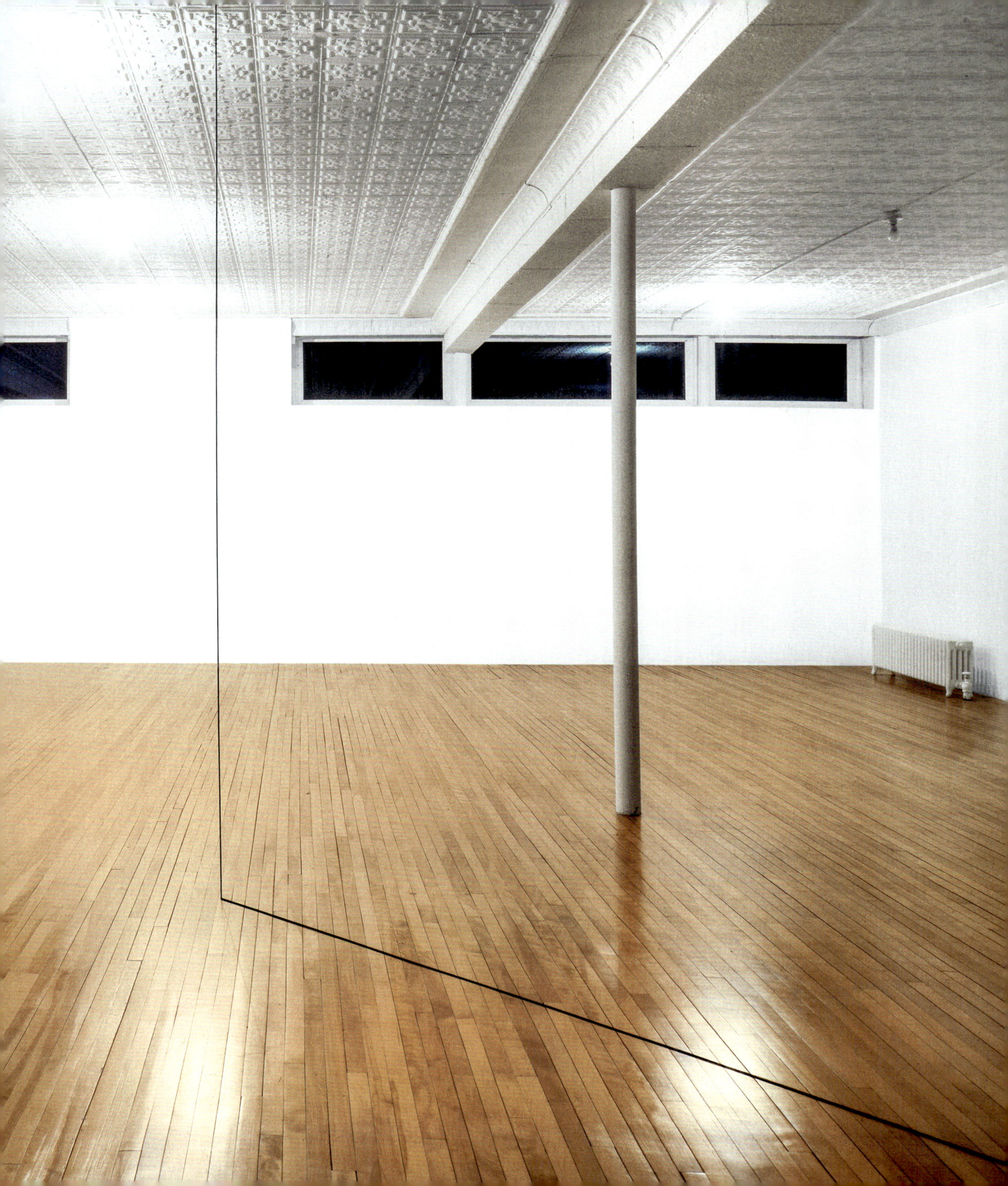

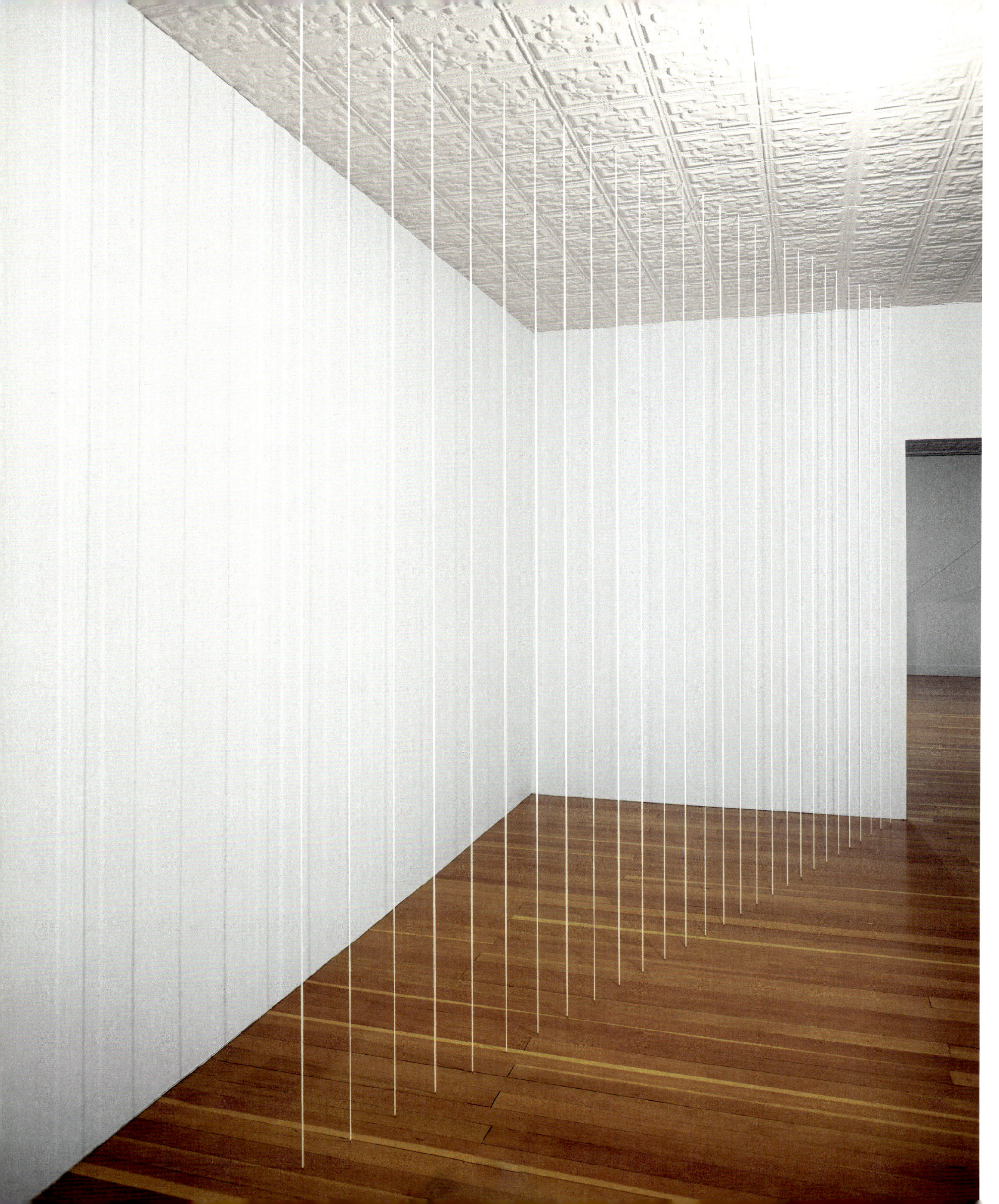

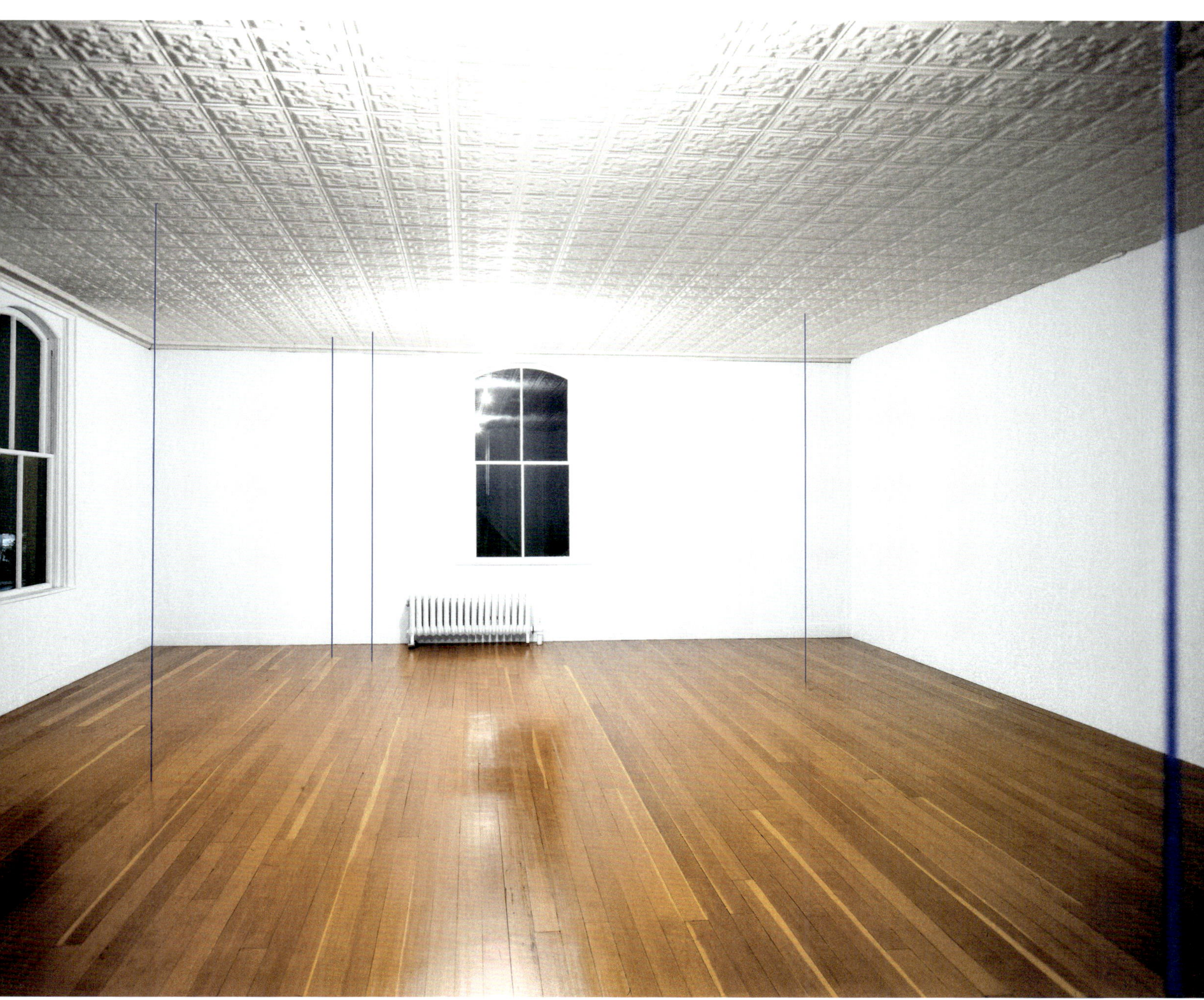

Untitled, 1983. Acrylic yarn (off-white), situational dimensions, overall dimensions vary with each installation using spatial relationships established by the artist. Installation view, The Fred Sandback Museum, Winchendon, Massachusetts

Untitled, 1983. Acrylic yarn (ultramarine), situational dimensions, overall dimensions vary with each installation using spatial relationships established by the artist. Installation view, The Fred Sandback Museum, Winchendon, Massachusetts

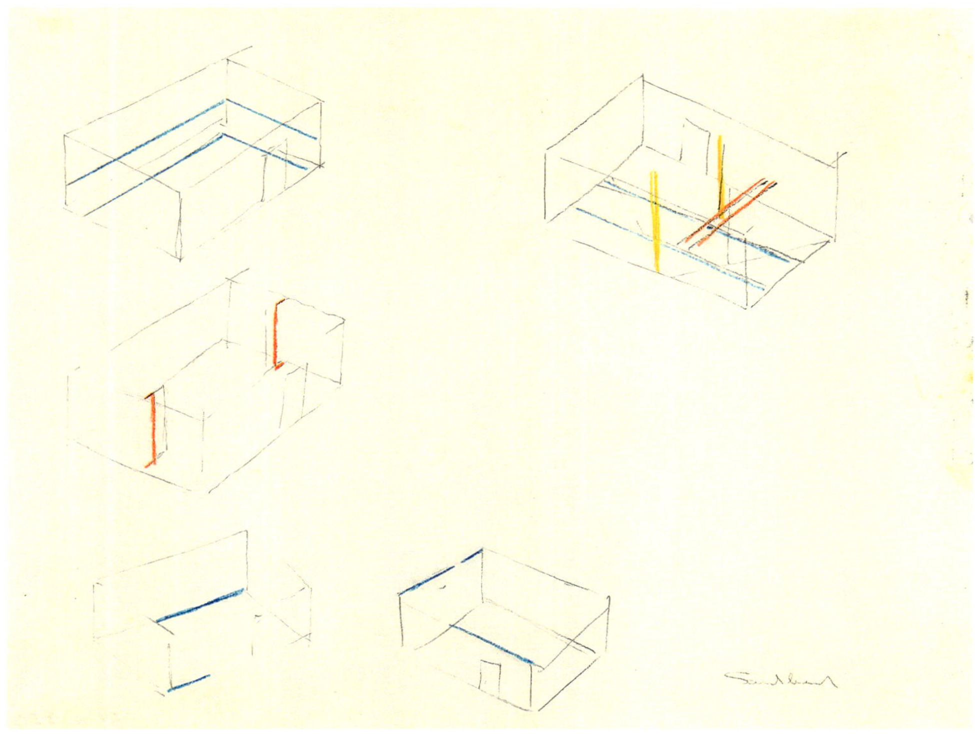

Untitled, c. 1978. Pencil and colored pencil on paper, 8½ × 11 inches (21.6 × 27.9 cm)

23. Fred Sandback, interview by Stephen Prokopoff, in *The Art of Fred Sandback: A Survey* (Champaign-Urbana, IL: Krannert Art Museum, University of Illinois, 1985), n.p.

how many visitors to the museum in Winchendon would have taken the short drive to Rindge to visit the artist's private studio, which here functioned as an annex to his public museum. What matters is the way that Sandback—for a variety of reasons, to be sure—asserted an equivalence between the private space of the studio, itself often a site of provisional actuality for a contextually driven, poststudio artist, and the public space of the museum, which, in the context of Sandback's working methods, was itself something of a studio once it had become his own institution. Such an entwining provides another way to read the complex materiality of Sandback's work, whether *First Construction for the Rindge Studio* or *Untitled (from Ten Vertical Constructions)* (1977–79), as it found form in the Fred Sandback Museum. In both cases, Sandback's linear forms exploit and undo our fundamental understanding of boundaries, defining shapes and opening up to their dissolution at the same time. If a consistent critical topos of the Sandback literature turns on the undecidability of surface and material in Sandback's work—as Sandback put it in a 1985 interview, the phenomenological acknowledgment "that the sculptures didn't stop where the lines did"[23]—then this indeterminacy between material and immaterial, between line and plane, between inside and outside, also threads through the boundaries of private studio and public museum.

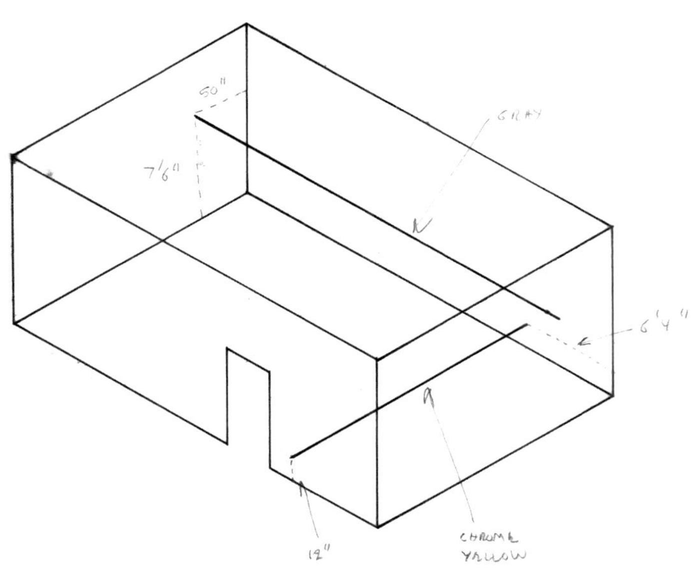

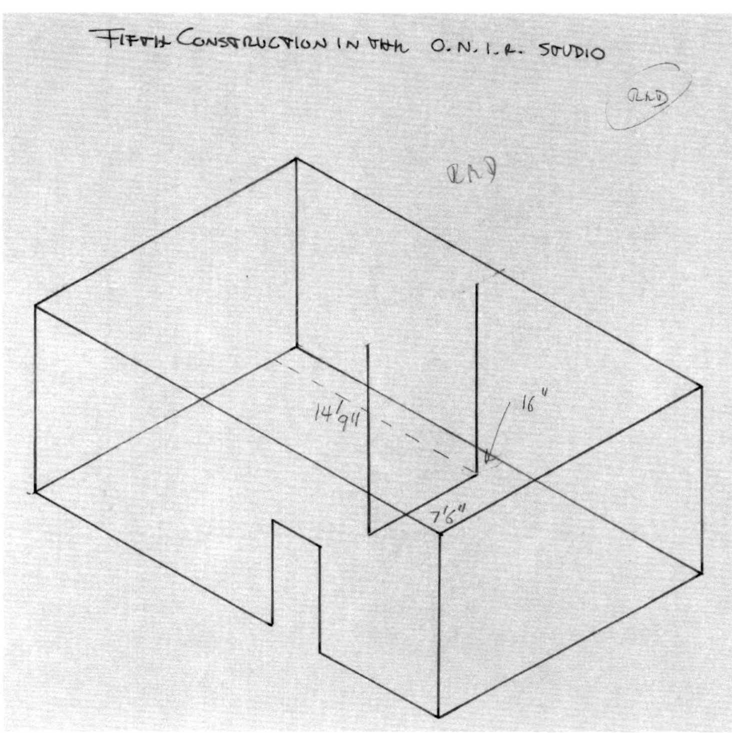

Sketches for *Fourth Construction for the Rindge Studio* (1979) and *Fifth Construction for the Rindge Studio* (1979)

24. Sandback, "Notes," 4.

25. Letters in the Fred Sandback Archive from Dia's executive director Charles Wright suggest that plans for closing the Fred Sandback Museum were circulating in the late 1980s, as per a letter to Sandback dated September 8, 1989. An internal Dia memorandum from Margaret Thatcher to Wright, from February 26, 1986, details the precarious situation of the museum from Dia's perspective, noting that "for some time now the Museum has been in a 'holding' pattern. It would not be possible to consider the current situation of marginal care, limited public access, and extremely limited public exposure as sufficient for the long term."

Responding to the tension between the "real" and the "imagined" in his work in "Notes," as reproduced in the museum brochure, Sandback would explain, "In no way is my work illusionistic. Illusionistic art refers you away from its factual existence toward something else. My work is full of illusions, but they don't refer to anything. Fact and illusion are equivalents. Trying to weed one out in favor of the other is dealing with an incomplete situation."[24] This statement may read as materially driven, which is to say as being about Sandback's sculpture. Yet, in the context of the Fred Sandback Museum, it also may mark the facts and illusions of a private, personal artistic practice as it interfaces with the world, with its publics, and with meaning making. To consider one without the other—without all the weight, baggage, and requirements of each—is an incomplete situation indeed.

IV.

The Fred Sandback Museum closed in 1996 after a run of fifteen years. During that time, Sandback mounted four discrete exhibitions, the last of which opened in May 1987. In closing the museum, there were conversations with Dia about money, the viability of the institution, and about visitors.[25] Perhaps concerns about its limited audience can be encapsulated in an anecdote shared by the artist Mary Walling

Blackburn, who, in a short essay that explores issues of class through the metaphor of the Fred Sandback Museum, recalls, "After a screening at MoMA, I am introduced to another attendee—a filmmaker who was raised in Winchendon, Massachusetts. Like me, the person might be lumpen, queer, and brainy. I ask: 'As a kid, did you ever go to the Fred Sandback Museum?' The filmmaker laughs: 'IF ONLY! What an opportunity that would have been, eh?! Never was open.'"[26]

However true this may have been, even if just for the filmmaker in question, Sandback's own remarks about the closing of the museum were driven by his experience of the work installed there. As he described it in the concluding sentences of "Remarks on My Sculpture," holding open such a location to make work served only to alienate him from his own objects; they became more separate, singular forms the longer they held space, even though the process of working in the building was deeply generative.

> This permanence, once established with the opening of the Museum in 1981, did indeed produce the necessary sense of having some ballast, and designing the interior space and the work was a source of great pleasure. But it was a surprise to see how quickly it became something on its own, not necessarily connected to me. Once the work was done, it was done, whereas I had a continuing need to disrupt that permanence that I had wanted. Perhaps indeed, I have nomadicized my existence.[27]

Writing in 1986, just before the opening of the final exhibition at the Fred Sandback Museum the following year, Sandback recognized the separation between in-process work, with its spark of creative plasticity and its seeming calcification into a self-sufficient completeness that almost turned away from the artist, suggesting both the power and the limitations of the project and institution for him. Though Sandback returned to discrete spaces many times over the years, calibrating his work for each new spatiotemporal situation, his work sought the sparkle of newness, coalescence, and a feeling of integration of place, object, and, equally, the artist.[28] Sandback spoke publicly about Winchendon for the last time, in more casual terms, during a conversation at the Chinati Foundation in Marfa, Texas, in 2002 with Dia Art Foundation director Michael Govan, Chinati Foundation director Marianne Stockebrand, and Sandback's longtime gallerist Gianfranco Verna. Responding to a question from Govan about Dia's historical interest in permanence relative to the establishment of the museum, Sandback offered:

26. Mary Walling Blackburn, "A Lumpen Line through the Fred Sandback Museum," *e-flux*, no. 127 (May 2022), https://www.e-flux.com/journal/127/466023/a-lumpen-line-through-the-fred-sandback-museum.

27. Sandback, "Remarks on My Sculpture 1966–86," 14.

28. As Sandback would write, "My intrusions are usually modest, perhaps because it seems like it's that first moment when things start to coalesce that is interesting. Most of my work now is executed in and for a particular place. It's always been conceived with at least a generalized sort of place in mind, but these pieces are now bound to one site. This doesn't mean that I won't redo a piece in a new location, but it will be a whole new kettle of fish. There are things that I want to do, but until they have a place they remain necessarily vague and indeterminate. The work is 'about' any number of things, but, 'being in a place,' would be right up there on the list." Sandback, "Remarks on My Sculpture 1966–86," 13.

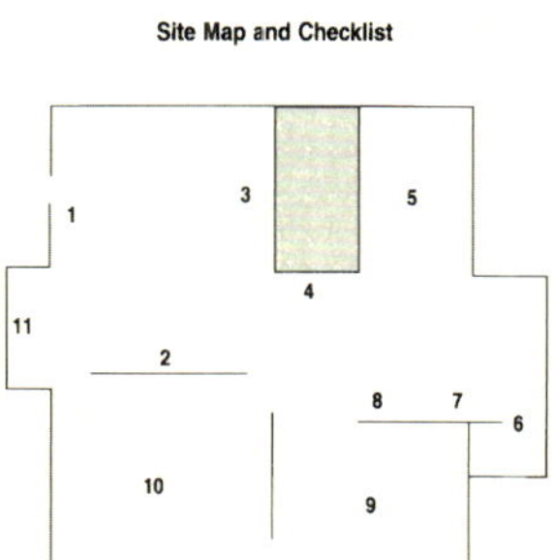

1. **Untitled** 1992
   Acrylic yarn (terra cotta)
   Collection of the artist
2. **Untitled** 1977/1996
   Acrylic yarn (light blue)
   Collection of the artist
3. **Untitled** 1996
   Six-part vertical construction
   Acrylic yarn (white)
   Collection of the artist
4. **Untitled** 1996
   Bas relief, diptych
   Acrylic housepaint on wood panel
   Collection of the artist
5. **Untitled** 1977
   Four-part vertical construction
   Acrylic yarn (black)
   Collection Dia Center for the Arts
6. **Untitled** 1996
   Acrylic yarn (light brown, dark gray)
   Collection of the artist

7. **Untitled** 1996
   Bas relief
   Acrylic housepaint on wood panel
   Collection of the artist
8. **Untitled** 1992/96
   Two-part vertical construction
   Acrylic yarn (pink)
   Collection of the artist
9. **Untitled, diagonal (one of four)**
   1970/96
   Acrylic yarn (cardinal red)
   Collection of the artist
10. **Untitled** 1977
    Two-part vertical construction
    Acrylic yarn (black)
    Collection Dia Center for the Arts
11. **Untitled** 1996
    Bas relief, diptych
    Acrylic housepaint on wood panel
    Collection of the artist

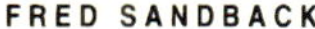

Sculpture

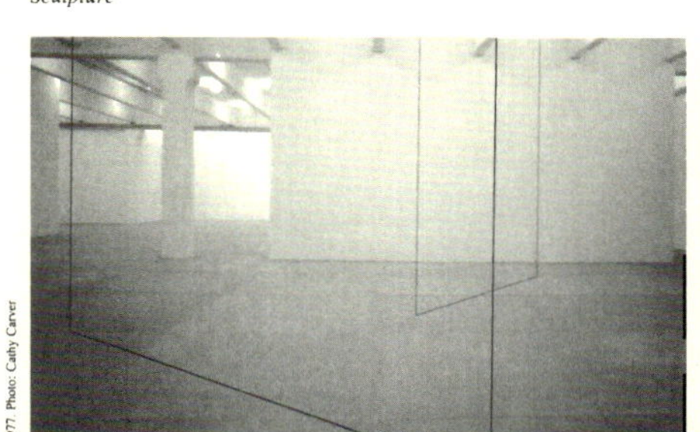

September 12, 1996–June 29, 1997

548 West 22nd Street, New York City

Brochure for *Fred Sandback: Sculpture*. Dia Center for the Arts, New York, 1996–97

I didn't particularly want to see my piece of string hang forever, but I did want to have control over how I could play one sculpture against the other and learn from that. So the project with Dia that lasted for fifteen years in Winchendon, Massachusetts, left me with about ten thousand square feet to think in. Things could recede; they could go away over slower periods of time. That was tremendously useful to me, but I had a little skepticism about Heiner Friedrich's need to think about forever. It's just too long.[29]

This retrospective statement, which describes the museum as something of a spatialized thought experiment—or maybe just as a 10,000-square-foot studio—suggests that the building and institution of the Fred Sandback Museum were never permanent in the mind of the artist. Sandback's reflection that his experience of thinking in the space was one where "things could recede" conjures an image of emergent sculptural problems—indeed of a form of coalescence—and then of an eventual settling down, like dust.

29. Fred Sandback, in conversation with Michael Govan, Marianne Stockebrand, and Gianfranco Verna, in *Chinati Foundation Newsletter*, no. 7 (October 2002): 30.

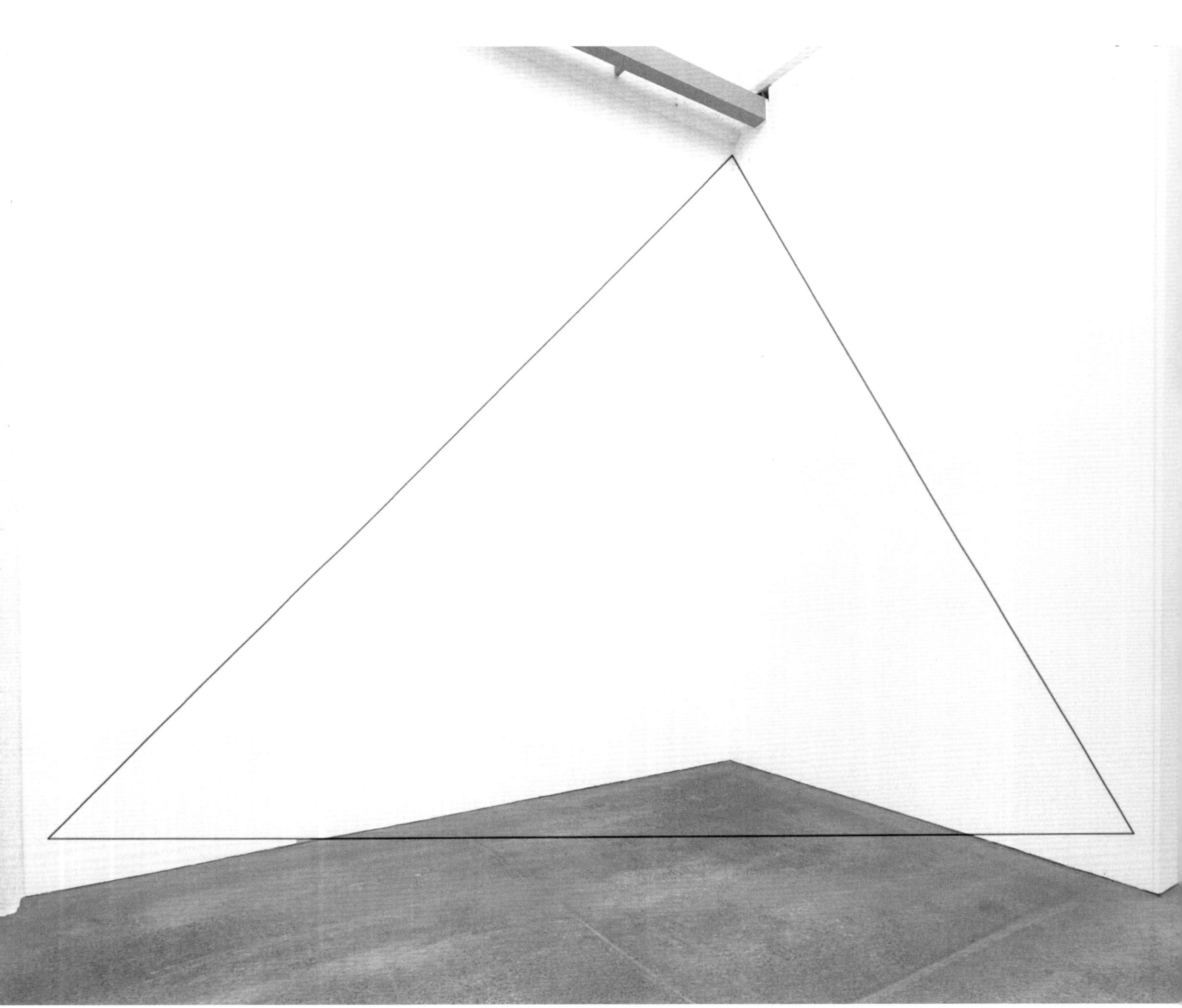

Untitled, 1996 (details). Acrylic yarn (light brown and dark gray), situational dimensions, overall dimensions vary with each installation using spatial relationships established by the artist. Installation view, Dia Center for the Arts, New York, 1996

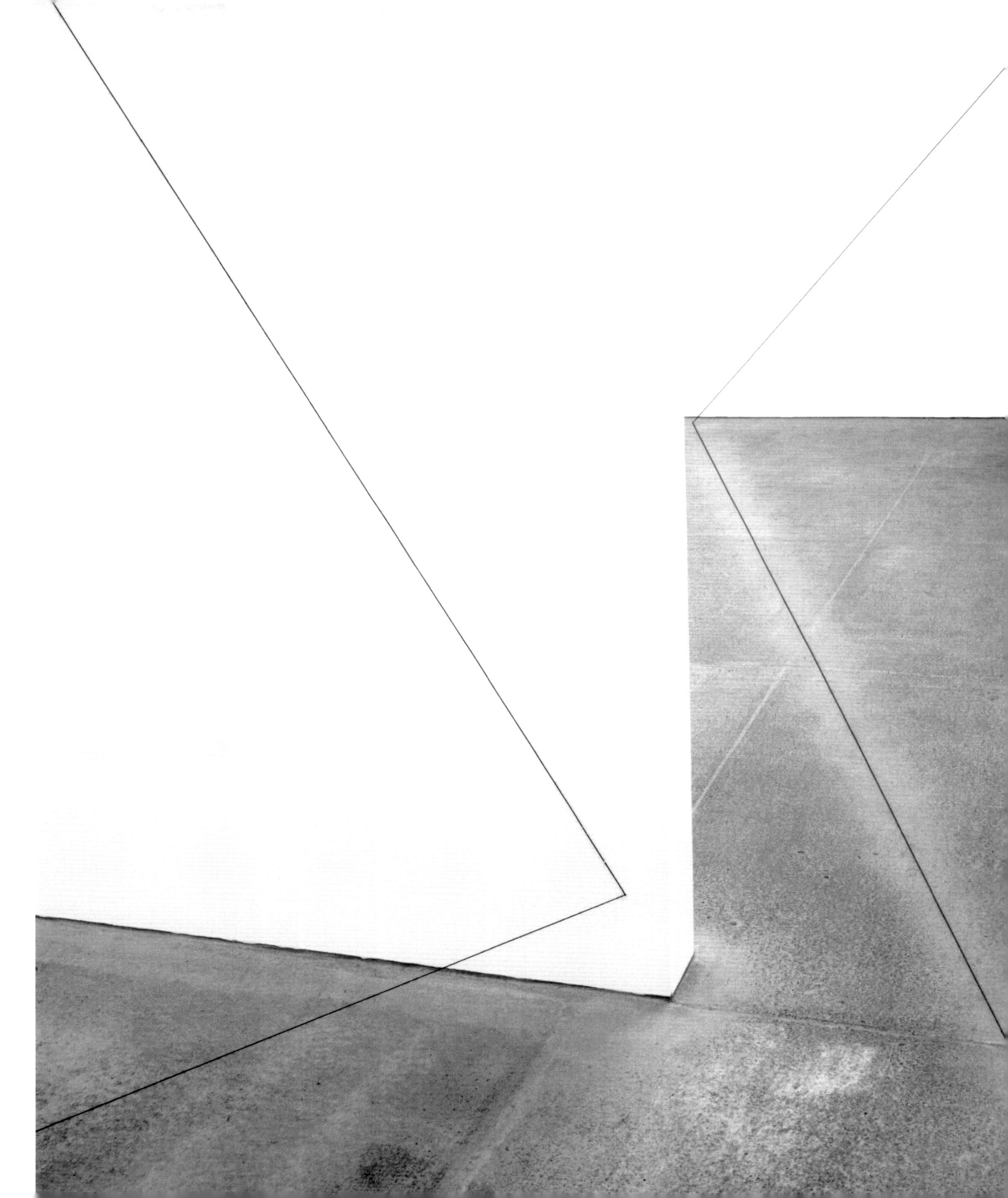

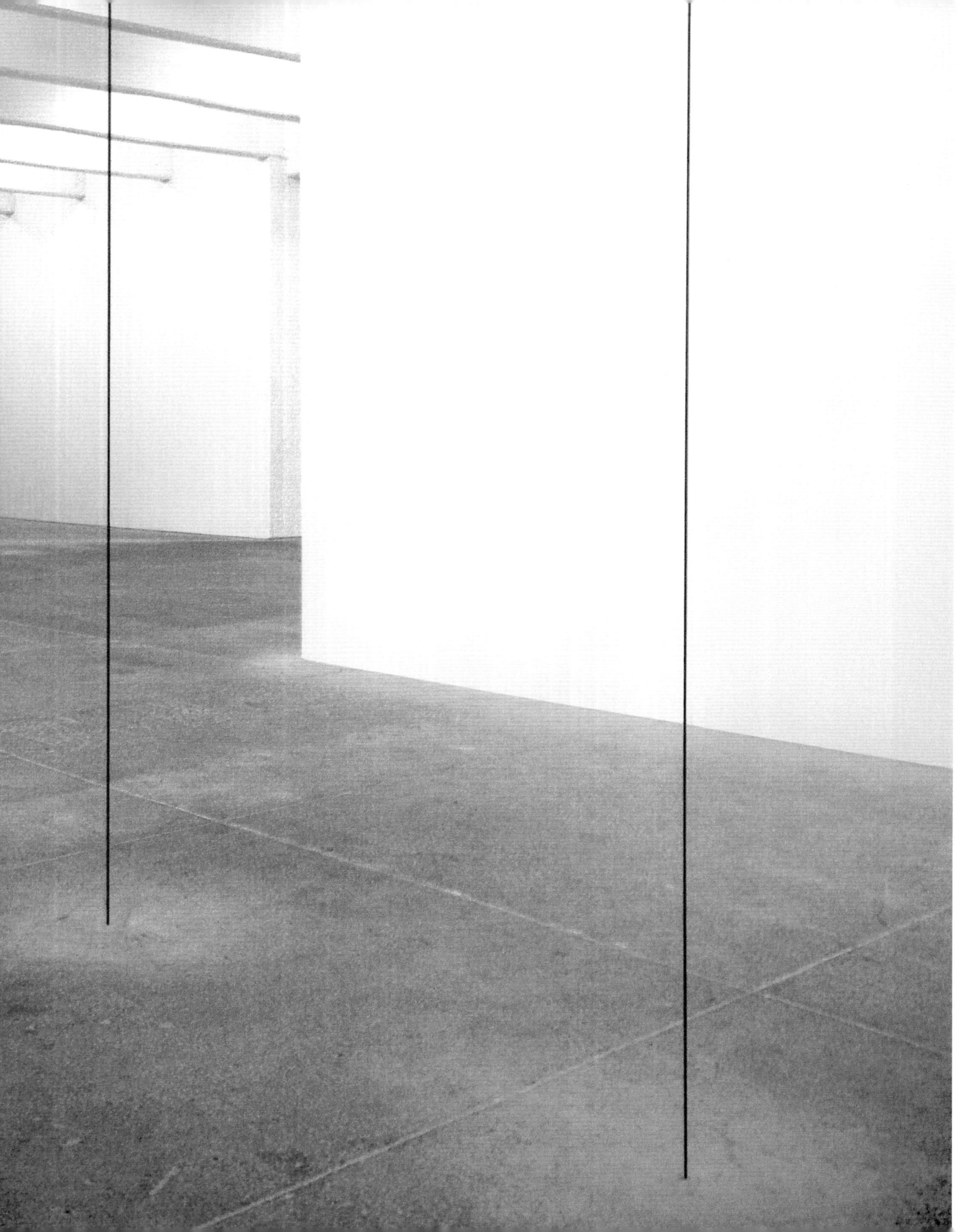

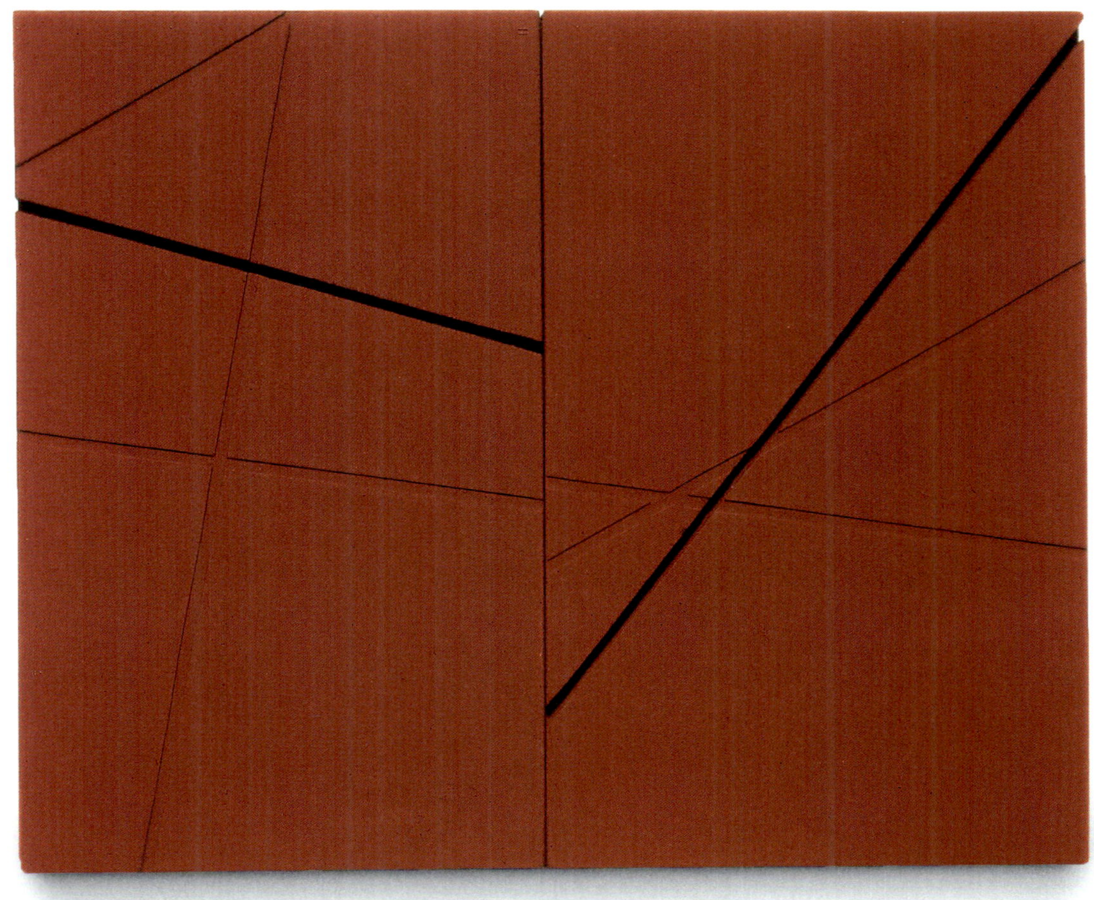

Untitled (from Ten Vertical Constructions), 1977–79
(detail). Acrylic yarn (black), situational dimensions, overall dimensions vary with each installation using
spatial relationships established by the artist. Installation
view, Dia Center for the Arts, New York, 1996

Untitled, 1996. Acrylic on wood, two parts: 9⅞ × 11¾ inches
overall (25 × 29.8 cm)

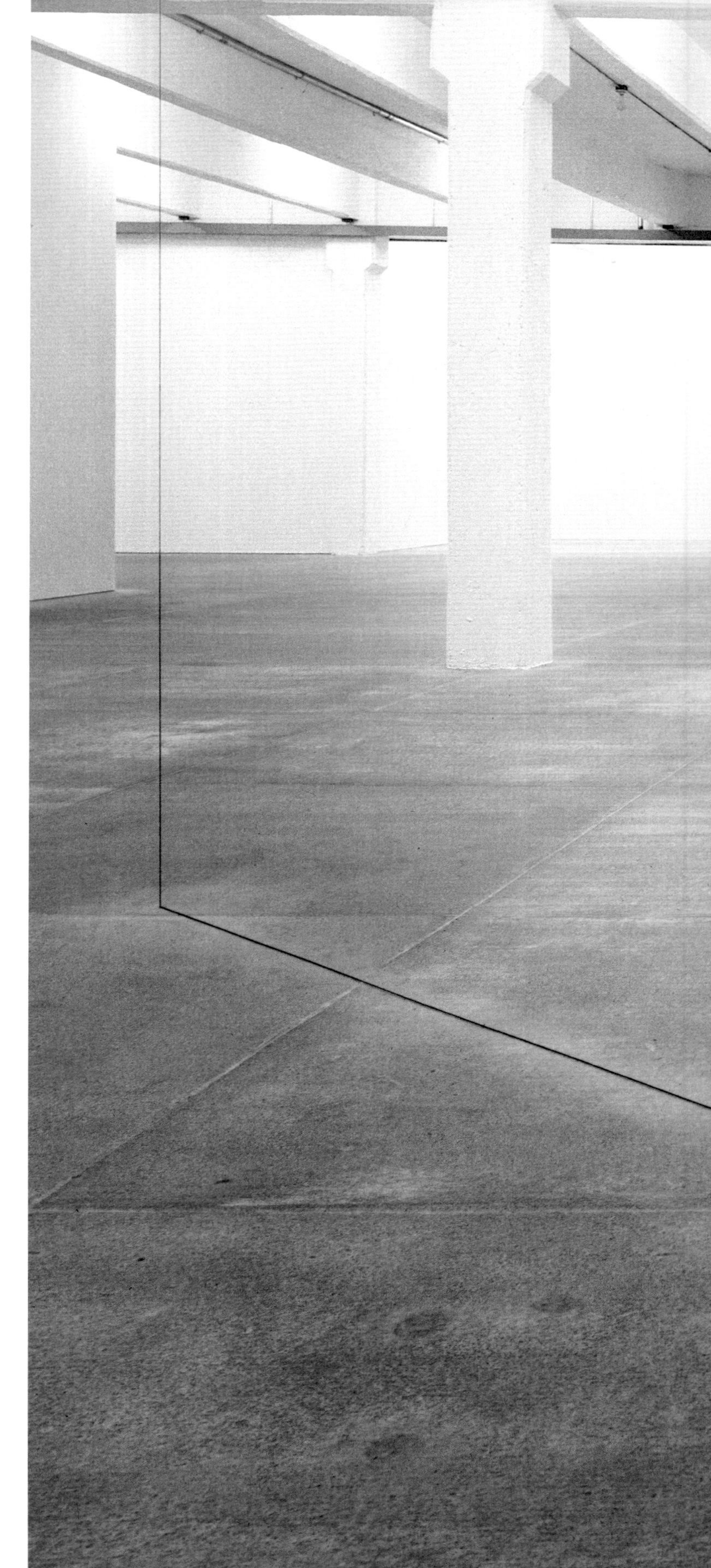

Untitled (from Ten Vertical Constructions), 1977–79.
Acrylic yarn (black), situational dimensions, overall
dimensions vary with each installation using spatial
relationships established by the artist. Installation
view, Dia Center for the Arts, New York, 1996

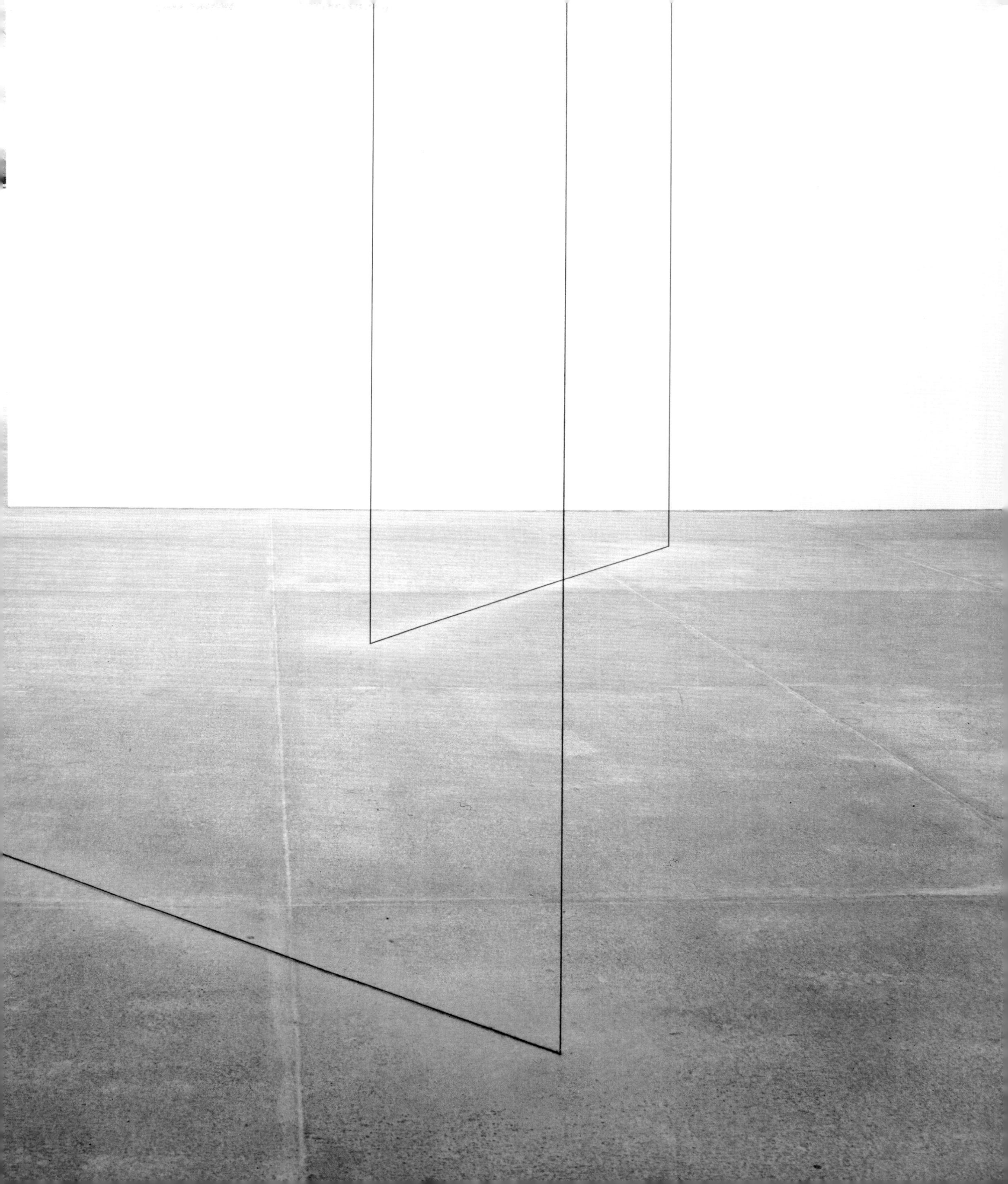

The decision to close the museum was finally put into process in 1996, coinciding with a major, more than yearlong exhibition of Sandback's work at Dia Center for the Arts in Manhattan's Chelsea neighborhood, which offered a new, large space in which to think. In this exhibition, Sandback presented eleven objects, with eight yarn constructions capturing a range of the artist's primary vocabularies and forms. The additional three pieces represented a new body of work: small wooden reliefs simply cut with linear motifs that reverse the materiality of Sandback's line—cuts referencing the fuzzy draw of yarn and the planarity of wood cuing the materiality of space caught between the lines of Sandback's forms. With these works, Sandback found a model for a studio-based practice that complemented the site-dependent nature of his yarn constructions. As he explained to Joan Simon around the time of the Dia show, "It's a big burst of fresh air for me to work with my whole concentration in the studio. One of my frustrations is that I got myself into always using the dynamics of the buildings I worked in, and so became bound temporally to the specific site. The new pieces extricate me from that segmentation of experience."[30] One way to understand the temporal concurrence of the closure of the Fred Sandback Museum and the advent of this new sculptural vocabulary is that Sandback found a different genre of ballast, one that allowed him to work and think in a way that approximated his experience of engaging with existing architecture but that did so at variable scale and in a fixed structure. He found another mode of actuality.[31]

V.

When I began research on Fred Sandback's work as a graduate student in 2005, a book recommended to me as one that mattered to the artist was the New York–based psychologist Mark Epstein's *Thoughts without a Thinker: Psychotherapy from a Buddhist Perspective*, first published in 1995, perhaps as decisions to finalize the closure of the Fred Sandback Museum were being made. I had always meant to engage with the book but never did. It felt more important to me, at that time, to work through other texts, ones with a much less concrete connection to the artist but that seemed more useful as models of theory, whatever that meant. In the course of Epstein's book, whose subtitle makes plain the overall drift of his analysis, he recounts a visit to a forest monastery in northeastern Thailand, Wat Ba Pong. Epstein was there in 1978 with his meditation teacher, Jack Kornfield, to seek an audience with Achaan Chaa, his teacher's teacher, the monk who ran the monastery and who was known as a "meditation master of the first order."[32] Epstein shares the story while detailing Buddhism's Third Noble Truth, which explains how to end suffering by abandoning urges and yearnings. When Epstein and

30. Sandback, conversation with Joan Simon, "Lines of Inquiry," 143.

31. Sandback's relief sculpture is a varied and complex body of work that cannot be treated fully here. For a deeper analysis that explores the context of these works in relation to the closure of the Fred Sandback Museum, see Vazquez, *Aspects*, 135–61.

32. Mark Epstein, *Thoughts without a Thinker: Psychotherapy from a Buddhist Perspective* (New York: Basic Books, 1995), 79.

Kornfield asked the monk about an end to cravings in direct terms, hoping to glean understanding from the master, he responded with a parable. As Epstein writes:

> Achaan Chaa looked down and smiled faintly. He picked up the glass of drinking water to his left. Holding it up to us, he spoke in the chirpy Lao dialect that was his native tongue: "You see this goblet? For me, this glass is already broken. I enjoy it; I drink out of it. It holds my water admirably, sometimes even reflecting the sun in beautiful patterns. If I should tap it, it has a lovely ring to it. But when I put this glass on a shelf and the wind knocks it over or my elbow brushes it off the table and it falls to the ground and shatters, I say, 'Of course.' But when I understand that this glass is already broken, every moment with it is precious." Achaan Chaa was not just talking about the glass, of course, nor was he speaking merely of the phenomenal world, the forest monastery, the body, or the inevitability of death. He was also speaking to each of us about the self. This self that you take to be so real, he was saying, is already broken.[33]

For Epstein, this story solidified his understanding of a fractured self, of an ego always striving to return to an impossible prior moment of imagined perfection and wholeness. "It is this wish that, in the Buddhist view, drives us to see self and other as fixed, immobile, and permanent *objects* that can be possessed or controlled and that in some way contain a piece of that original security."[34] Many of our base desires feed this illusion, and if we are able to unmask them for the illusions they are, we can begin to see the world otherwise, through the cultivation of bare attention, emptiness, and other modes of mindfulness.

I do not know if Achaan Chaa's parable of the broken cup or the invocation of an illusory fixity, objecthood, and completeness at the core of ourselves struck Fred Sandback as he read these words. Perhaps Sandback intuitively understood the language of impermanence used in the story. Considering it in relation to the Fred Sandback Museum, I cannot help but read the museum itself as a broken cup mistaken for whole, at least for a time. If it provided a center of gravity for years, which it most certainly did, it did so in service of the illusion of the potential stability and completeness of the artwork and perhaps the artist too. Yet Sandback understood his work too well to let the pretense stand—or stand incompletely—alongside all the other facts and illusions comprised by his work and so much else.

Another way to end: Dia, from the Greek δια, means "through." For Sandback and the Fred Sandback Museum, it marks a movement from diaphanous to ballast and back again.[35]

33. Ibid., 80–81.

34. Ibid., 86–87, emphasis in original.

35. Jessica Morgan discusses this original meaning and its implications for Dia's varied understandings of temporality as well. See Morgan, introduction to *Dia: An Introduction to Dia's Locations and Sites*, 11.

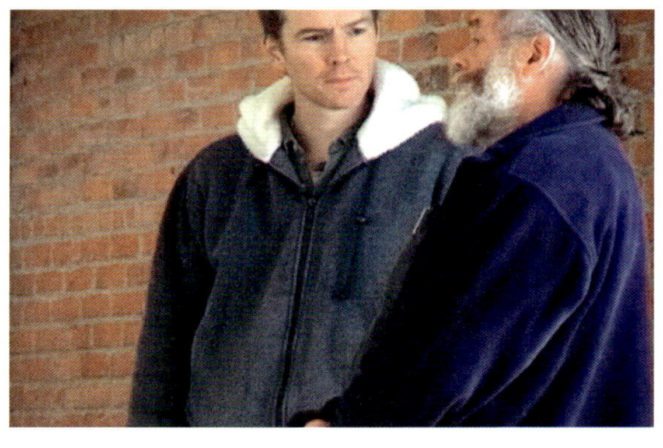
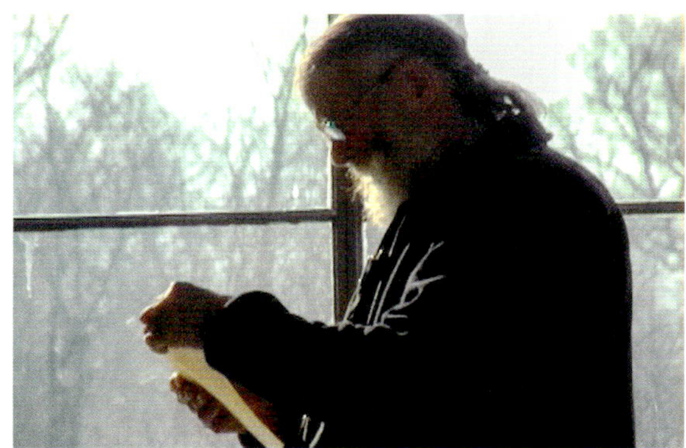
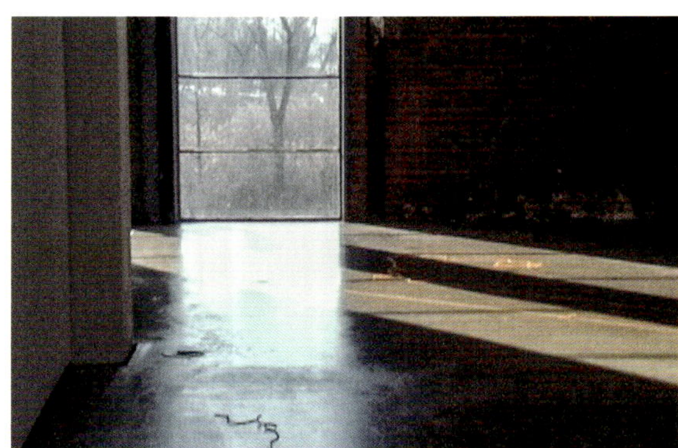
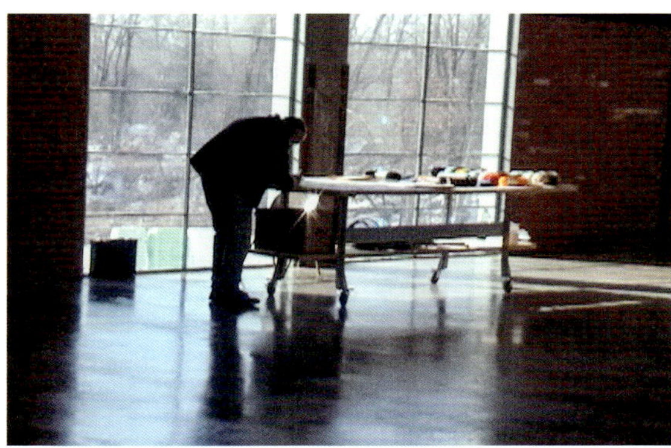
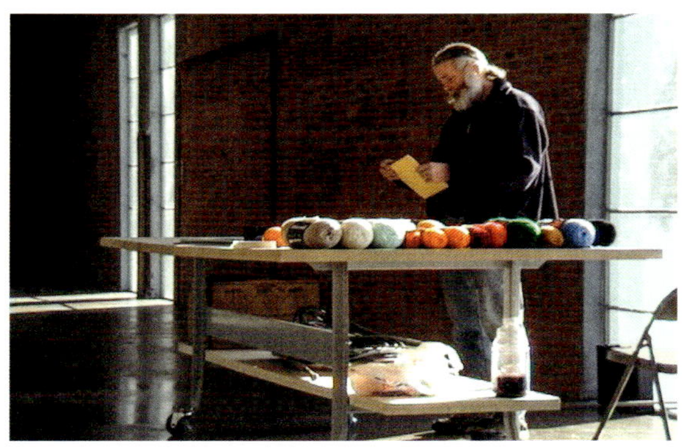
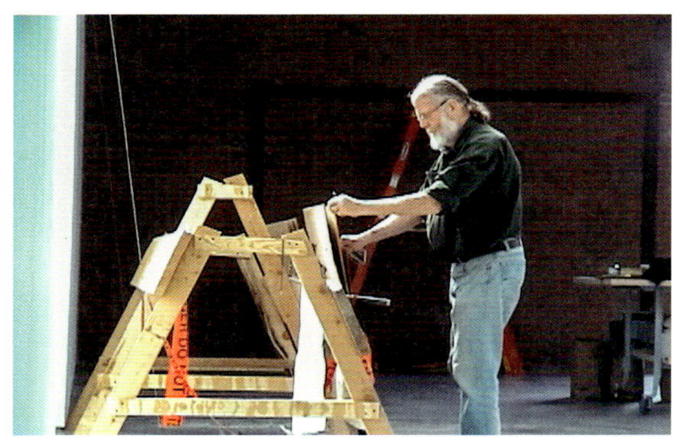
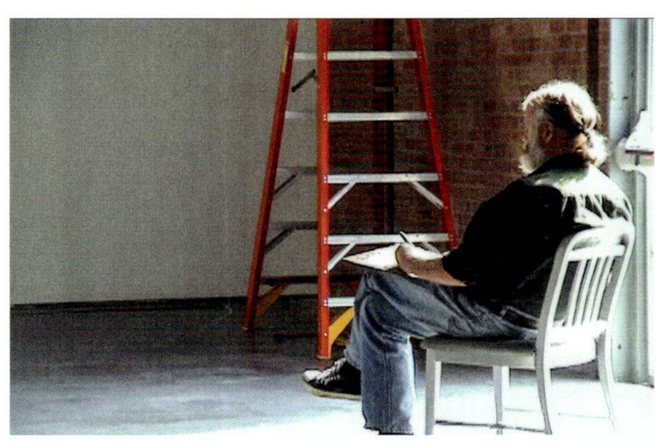
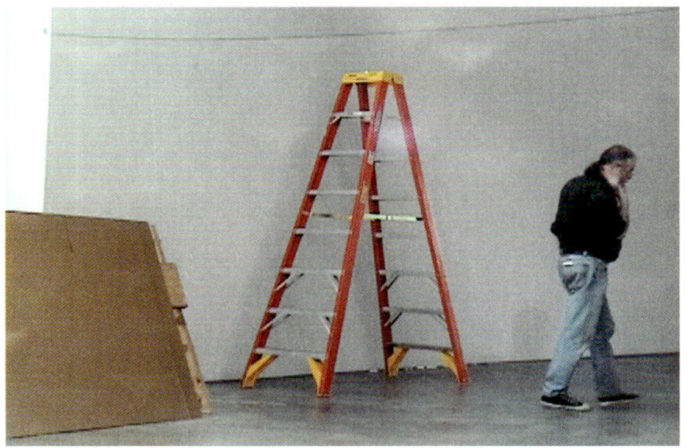

Fred Sandback installing his work at Dia
Beacon, Beacon, New York, 2003 (video stills)

Fred Sandback and Dia Art Foundation

Matilde Guidelli-Guidi
in conversation with Curtis Harvey, August 2023

Matilde Guidelli-Guidi, Curator and Curatorial Department Cohead, Dia Art Foundation

Curtis Harvey, Director of Exhibitions, Dia Art Foundation

Matilde: I have been diving into the archives to learn more about Dia's relationships with artists from the mid-1970s to the mid-1980s—that is, during its first decade. The documents reveal the ways in which Dia supported artists over many years through acquisitions and project development, leading not only to ambitious works of art but also to the idea of devoting whole museums to the work of individual artists, including Fred Sandback. The nature of these relationships was idiosyncratic—tailored, that is, to personalities and temperaments.

Curtis: Dia's most recent engagement with Sandback's work is its current installation at Dia Beacon, which you and I managed in 2021,[1] but Dia cofounder Heiner Friedrich's relationship with Sandback goes back to even before the institution was established, right?

Matilde: Fred's second solo show was at Heiner's gallery in Munich in 1968, when he was still at Yale.[2] Donald Judd had invited him to stage a presentation in his Manhattan studio in January 1968; it is possible that Fred met Heiner there. I'd add his first solo show in the United States was at Dwan Gallery, New York, in 1969, which served as his master's presentation. Heiner went on to mount several Sandback shows in his Munich and Cologne galleries, as well as three at his New York gallery. When, in 1974, Heiner, Helen Winkler Fosdick, and Philippa de Menil [now Fariha al-Jerrahi] founded Dia, dialogues with the artists began around the idea of these single-artist museums. With Fred, the conversation developed in two ways: on the one hand, it led to the purchase of a building in the small town of Winchendon, Massachusetts; and on the other hand, Dia agreed to help him build his nearby studio in Rindge, New

1. Fred Sandback's work in Dia Beacon was first on view from May 18, 2003, to March 10, 2019. It was reinstalled for long-term presentation in December 2021.

2. *Fred Sandback*, Galerie Heiner Friedrich, Munich, October 24–November 17, 1968. Sandback's first solo exhibition, *Fred Sandback: Plastische Konstruktionen*, was held at Konrad Fischer Galerie, Düsseldorf, May 18–June 11, 1968.

Hampshire. In addition, Dia built its collection of Sandback works through extending a stipend to Fred in exchange for the creation of proposals for new pieces.

Curtis: At that point, were these agreements made over a handshake with Heiner?

Matilde: No, It's all laid out in a paper trail, though some documents were retroactive. The negotiations around the Winchendon museum started in mid-1978. Philippa was his main interlocutor—not Heiner—especially regarding the real-estate and renovation budgets. Their correspondence was about renovating the building, which had been a bank and, earlier, a stitching company, with the studio developing more slowly. The beautiful thing that comes up in these documents is all the ideas that Fred had about the kind of single-artist museum he envisioned. While Donald Judd wanted Fort D. A. Russell military base in Marfa, Texas, and Dan Flavin found a former church in Bridgehampton, New York, and Dick's Castle in Garrison, New York, Sandback landed on renovating a building for the explicit purpose of installing and documenting his work. After about four years of conversations and construction, Fred's museum opened in Winchendon in 1981. In the following years, he would also propose ancillary projects for the community—for example, a library, because there were no bookstores in town.

The reason I turn to the archive is not only to build some kind of chronology of Fred's relationship with Dia but also to find his voice, to hear how he would negotiate how to make a living and take advantage of this unusual opportunity to present his work as an aspect of his practice. The museum wasn't antithetical to his practice; it gave him both financial compensation and the opportunity to look at the function of his works in a certain space. There are several proposals for making drawings that would document how a work would be installed. Making multiple drawings for a single work, he used the site to think precisely from a conceptual standpoint. The sketches for Winchendon show that he was not thinking of individual works as singular.

Curtis: Fred's work is fluid in that regard. His idea of site-specificity is not the same as what we typically think of it as, rather more akin to site-determining and site-determined. A piece that's 15 feet high in one space can be moved to another gallery and become 8 feet high. It retains its relationship to space but is nevertheless in conversation with each new home. That's unique to his work. I don't know of other sculptures that have that capability.

Matilde: One of his most well-known statements, "Notes" [1975], beautifully clarifies his intention.[3] He says, "My work always exists in an interior space," and "Pieces are conditioned by and bound to a particular place." He thinks of his work like a

3. Fred Sandback, "Notes," in *Fred Sandback* (Munich: Kunstraum München, 1975), 11–12. This text is available online along with all other published texts by Sandback at https://www.fredsandback archive.org/publications.

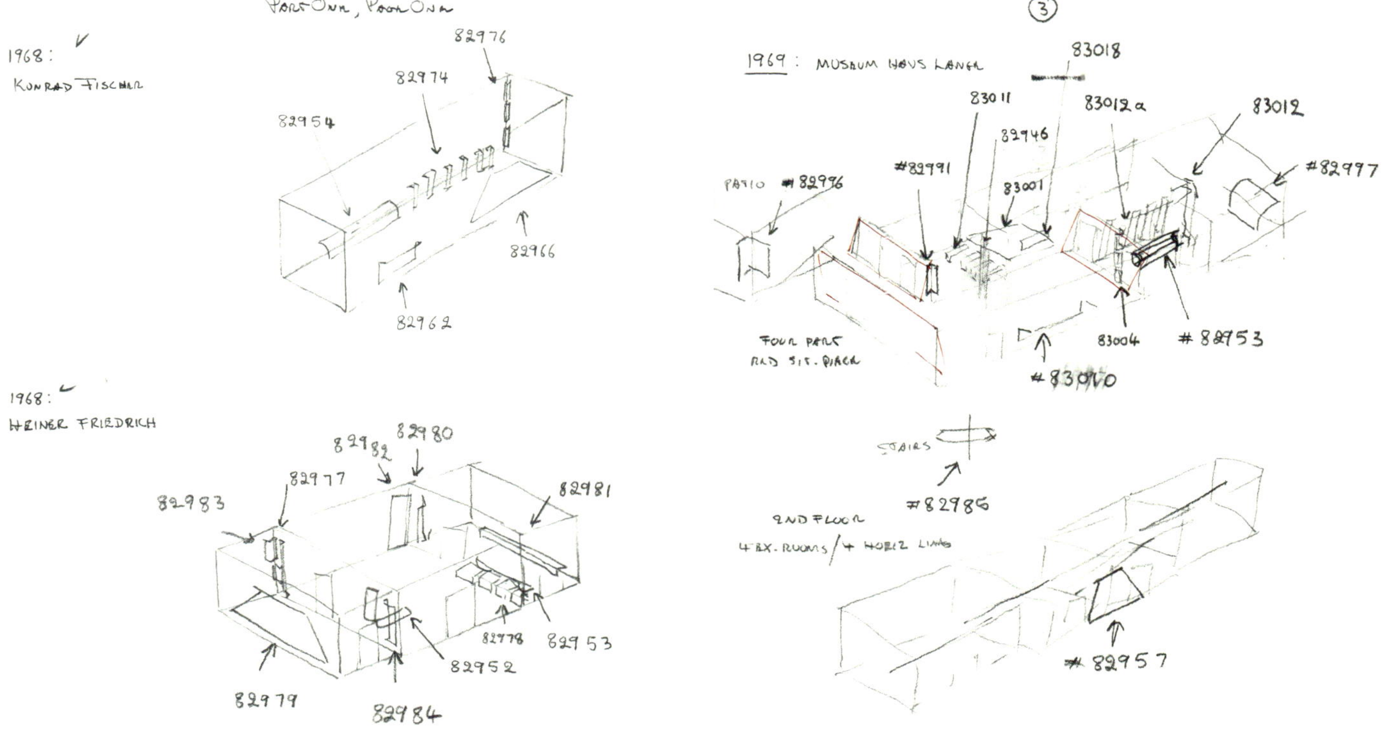

Cataloguing and documentation drawings for 1968–69 exhibitions, c. 1985

performance—as contingent on the time it is presented: "There's an inherent transience to my work. . . . They are in principle always able to come into existence again at a future time, but will then be part of a new situation. If I remake a piece in a new place, it's a different piece." He's thinking about the structure of the practice.

Curtis: The piece doesn't change, but the scale does; in theory, that changes the work, but it still has the same title. There's an example right here at Dia Beacon, *Untitled (Six-part Vertical Construction)*. It's dated 1996, as it was first shown in a variation in Fred's show [1996–97] at the former Dia building on 22nd Street in Manhattan, but the height, width, and depth are different in response to the available wall here in Beacon. I wonder about Fred's comfort level with that. Was that always just part of his process?

Matilde: The proposals in the Dia archive, which he likely made in the seventies, show this idea. But there are also gorgeous drawings in the archive that show how Sandback mapped early exhibitions in Germany. Here is a drawing for shows at Heiner Friedrich's and Konrad Fischer's galleries.

93

Curtis: Even in the simplicity of these little drawings, you see how the works relate to a room.

Matilde: He calls them "situations."

Curtis: Yes—at least largely after 1970—for works that respond, vary, or change according to their spatial circumstances. I use the term *situational* in my music. While there are songs, there are also certain areas in the structure of the music that depend on the vibe in the room and the crowd. In a way, Sandback does that with rooms. His works are in conversation with the architecture.

Matilde: Similar terms are being applied by and to other artists at this time, such as *environmental art*. Sandback was very aware of the dominant discourse of the time and famously distinguished his own work within it: "My work isn't environmental. It's present in pedestrian space, but is not so strong or elaborate that it obscures its context." He also says it is not illusionistic. Nor dematerialized. He really understands the terms that are being applied or assumed and how his work might be differentiated.

Curtis: He says, "I complicate actual situations, and this is as material as anything else."

Matilde: Yes. Though his work is certificate-based, he's pushing back on Lawrence Weiner's concept that the artist may or may not execute an idea, pushing back on the notion that you have a script or a score but it doesn't have to be performed to be a work, if you will. Sandback writes, "I don't have an idea first and then find a way to express it. That happens all at once. That notion of executing an idea is the same as giving form to material, and it's a confusion of terms. Ideas are executions." In other words, he rejects the dichotomy that one thing—an idea or execution—presides over another in favor of all the conditions of a work coming together in an organized space. That's why the word *situation* is interesting—because it is idea *and* execution.

    In 1985–86, Dia closed the door on many spaces in a major restructuring. A lot of real estate was sold. Dia began pulling funds from the Winchendon space in about 1986. For a little while, though, Winchendon was sustained through a seasonal budget. When Charles Wright, the director at the time, suggested, "Perhaps we can close Winchendon," offering Sandback in exchange a floor in a space on Mercer Street in Manhattan that also accommodated performance space and administrative offices so that he might "still have this idea about a permanent installation," Sandback was resistant. "I put a lot into 74 Front Street. The idea of abandoning it is not easy just yet." But he conceded, "The possibility of ending the project is right around the corner, so it offers me a possibility for direct involvement which otherwise doesn't exist."

In 1988, an installation of four works opened on Mercer Street. Meanwhile, Sandback continued to maintain the space in Winchendon at his own expense until the summer of 1996. A show of newer work at Dia Center for the Arts took place in 1996–97. Did you see that exhibition?

Curtis: No. Until my work with him at Dia Beacon, I'd only seen drawings and small wood relief pieces.

Matilde: How did you get to work with Sandback? When did you first see the work, and how did you get to work with him?

Curtis: Jim Schaeufele, Dia's long-time operations director who had a long relationship with Sandback, introduced me to Fred in early spring 2003. I was on-site in Beacon, getting the museum ready to open later that year. I was to be Sandback's go-to in facilitating the installation of his work at Dia Beacon. In installing their works in Beacon, each artist was assigned a preparator. I also spent a lot of time then with Robert Whitman, working on restagings of *Prune Flat* [1965] and *Light Touch* [1976]. I was actually building out those works, so our discussions were very technical. I was there to facilitate Fred's work, but he installed it. My conversations with him, in contrast, generally had nothing to do with art. He was quite reserved, soft-spoken, but I felt comfortable just hanging out with him and getting to know him. We found common ground with music, and we developed quite a friendship around that—Fred had the most eclectic record collection, with almost every genre imaginable, from obscure Tibetan flute music to country artists, rock, and jazz. But when installing, he did all the work himself, without assistants, and spent a lot of time alone in each space, just taking it in, trying to understand how a work might live within it. There was nothing haphazard, nothing he left to chance.

Matilde: That is palpable; the placement, the proportions, and the colors are all very satisfying.

Curtis: He ended up teaching me how to install his work so that when the museum was operational, I could be the caretaker. Since these are all pieces made from yarn, they require attention over the long-term, occasionally needing repairs or complete reconstruction as the yarn wears down in response to certain environmental conditions. Fred made a lovely manual for us. He handed it to me when the installation was over and said, "Everything you need to know is here." Examples of the connections are taped into the book to show the methods he used. Around that time, Fred also told me about drawings he made for a proposed exhibition at the Pinakothek der Moderne in Munich. I casually offered to help install it but worried that I may have overstepped

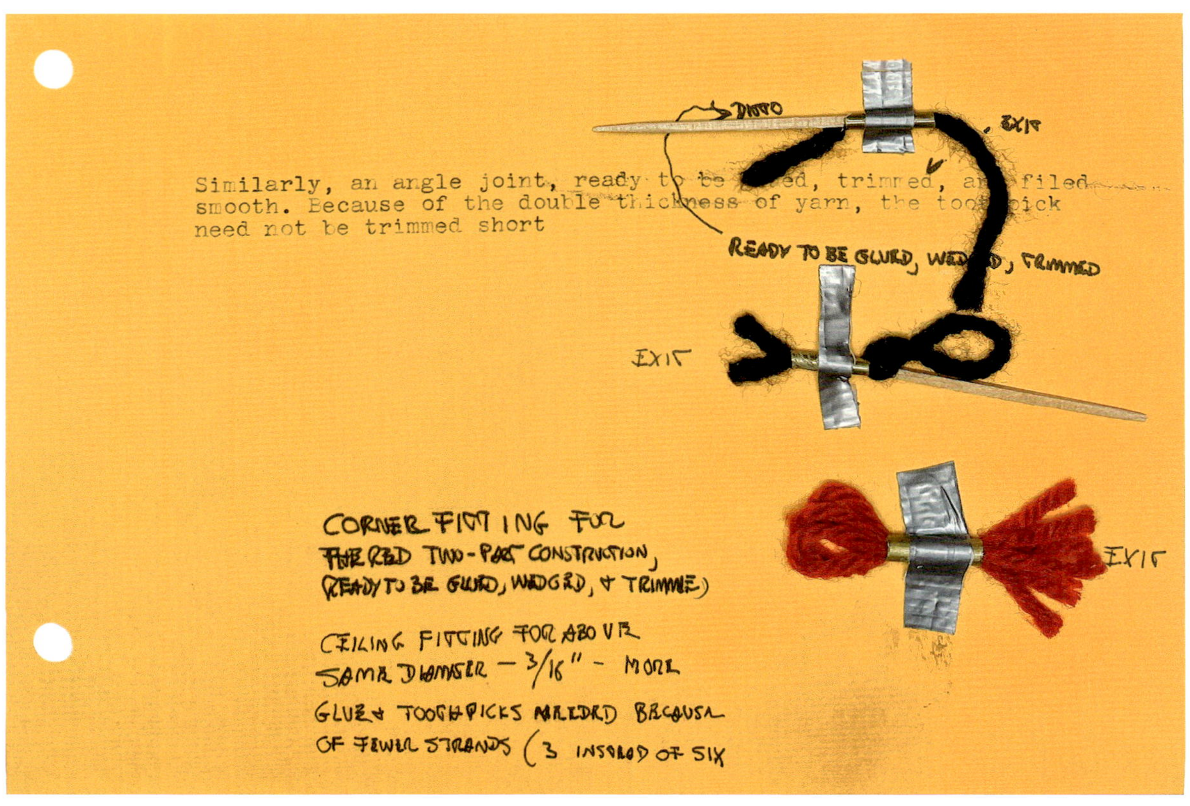

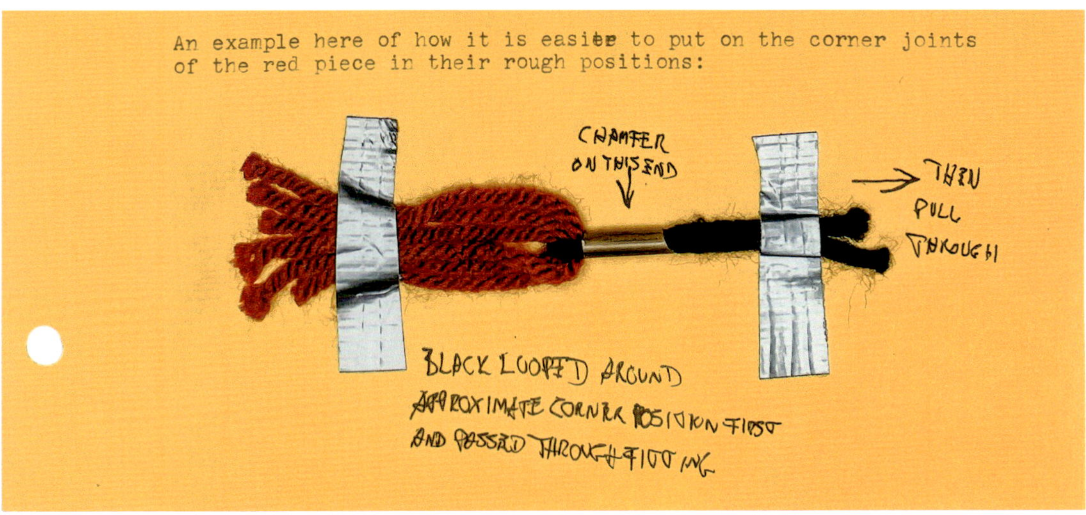

Details from "Provisional Notes for the
Care, Repair, and Maintenance for the
Sandback Sculptures at Dia:Beacon," 2003

my role, considering his work ethic. Sadly, Fred passed away before the exhibition in Munich opened, so Fred's wife, Amy, approached me to install it.

Matilde: Fred's works were up for almost sixteen years in their first presentation in Beacon. At its inception, Dia Beacon was to be the home for Dia's collection, so most of the artists that would be represented there had a long-term relationship with the institution. The curatorial mandate was that, at least for the first years, the museum would show exemplary works from the collection. Some works by additional artists would be brought in to even out the presentation, but those would be contemporaneous with the works in the collection. Originally, the only space that would be devoted to new commissions was the space that ultimately housed Gerhard Richter's *Six Gray Mirrors* [2003].

Curtis: Yes, it was for the most part legacy pieces and pieces that defined early Dia history.

Matilde: As much as possible, the artists were to have a role in how their works would be installed, but they were to choose from preexisting pieces. Lynne Cooke, Dia's curator from 1991 to 2008, and Michael Govan, director from 1994 to 2006, allocated general areas to each artist, but then they worked with the artists to choose the works and install them.

I can see that this proposal might have been difficult for those artists who had been offered space and new commissions, which led to acquisitions that supported their practices in the 1970s and early 1980s. Indeed, Sandback was taken aback that it would not be possible to make a completely new piece for Beacon. He was explicit about this in a fax sent to Cooke, suggesting instead a new work—something he called a "swimming pool piece," like *El baño* [2002], which he'd shown at Museo Tamayo in Mexico City earlier that year. The initial installations in Beacon were an effort to look back and acknowledge Dia's exceptional early history and freeze those works in their time, but unlike with the Fred Sandback Museum and the Dan Flavin Art Institute, for example, the installations at Beacon were never intended to be permanent.

Curtis: Even so, Fred's work in Beacon really became part of the space, not like the other works, which sit in the space. *Untitled (Two-part Vertical Construction, from Ten Vertical Constructions)* [1977–79] is anchored to the floor and the ceiling. For me, it's as if it is a column holding up the roof.

Matilde: Though Sandback did not specifically make the works for Beacon, he calibrated their color, the number of the threads he used, and the length of the threads to fit the space.

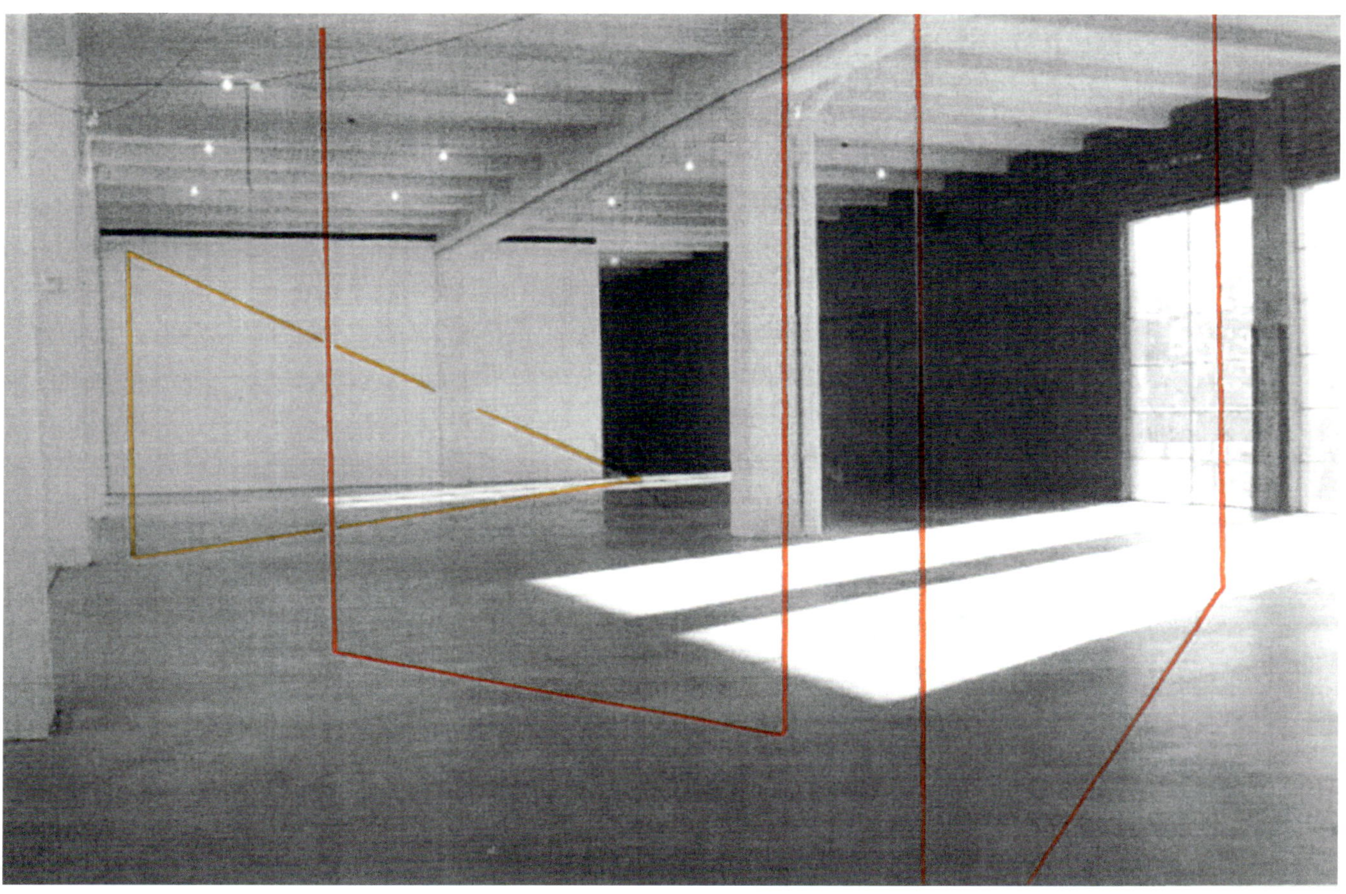

Untitled (Study for Dia:Beacon), c. 2003.
Pastel on photocopy on paper, sheet size:
11 × 8½ inches (27.9 × 21.6 cm)

Curtis: I don't think there's any other sculptor I can name who has done so much with so little. The fact that the material is so common and the technique is so simple truncates the viewer's perception of it. You don't have to spend a lot of time figuring out how it is made. That allows time to open up possibilities for interpretation. He creates a slender column or a massive wall with a handful of yarn. It's as if he sketched in space.

Matilde: Though the material is so simple, the work demands a perceptual focus from the viewer. As I was going through the sketches, I tried to understand the practice that went into creating the spatial relations. It's not a matter of harmony or preconceived proportion. And the fuzziness of the yarn has the effect of making the work exist and disappear at once.

Curtis: I also love the juxtaposition of Fred's work to Michael Heizer's, who has a very different idea of negative space, with his tons of steel! For Sandback, the negative space becomes the "weight" and the volume of the work, and the viewer's mind makes

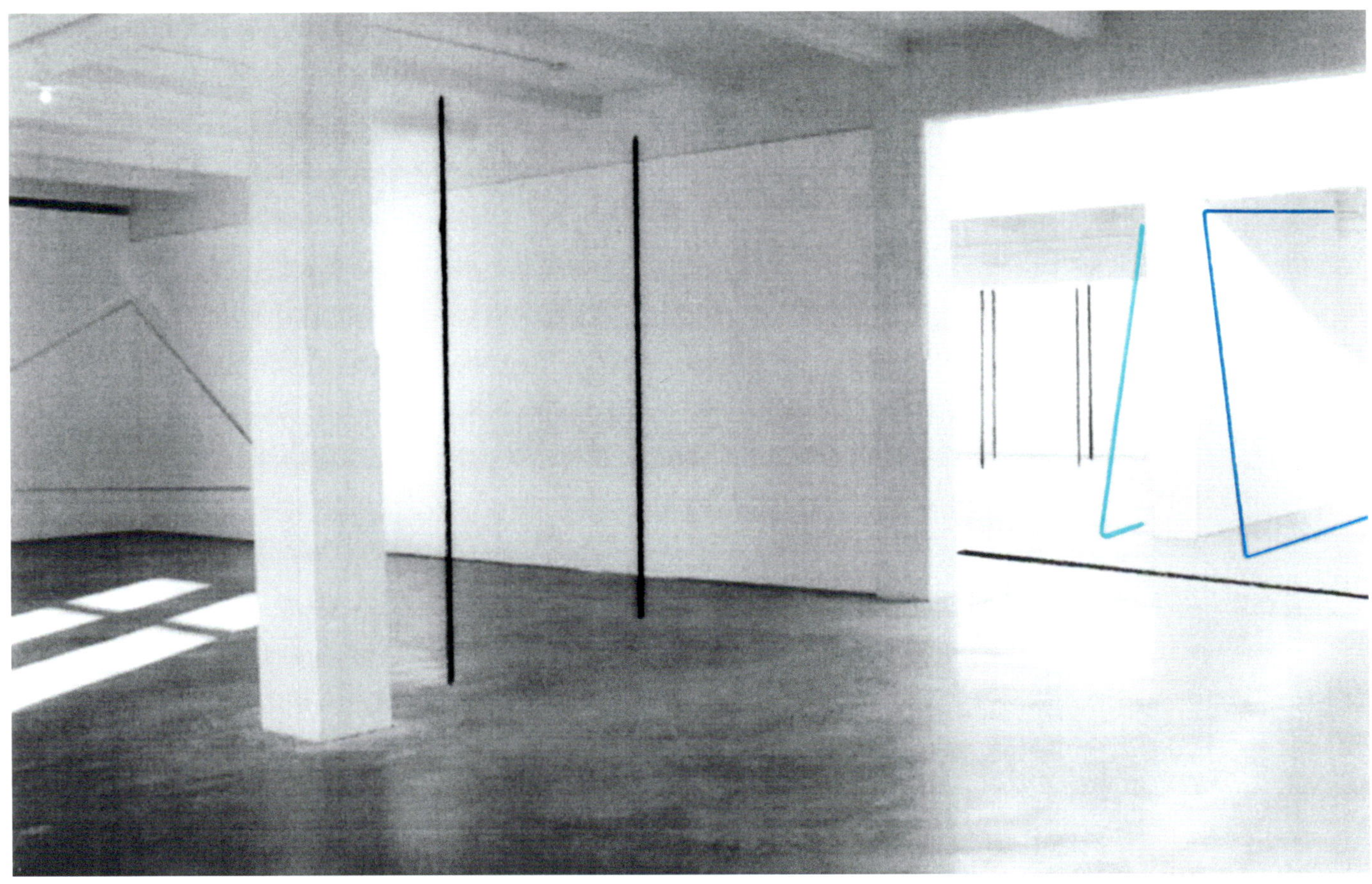

that happen. What's not there, as much as what's there, becomes the sculpture. There is so much beauty in that; it's very moving.

Matilde: In 2004, the year after Dia Beacon opened, Lynne Cooke invited Andrea Fraser, an artist who had worked as a gallery attendant at Dia in Chelsea, to lecture on an artist in Dia's collection. Fraser chose to discuss Sandback because his works, she said, made her cry. She proceeded to articulate her emotional response using Marxist psychoanalytic theory and the sociological-aesthetic ideas of Pierre Bourdieu, positing that Sandback's work refuses to become institutionalized and thus separated from its viewers. This is very intentional, and I think he had alluded to this refusal when he talked about "pedestrian space" in his "Notes." There is a sense of calm that Sandback's work elicits that is missing from so much art of Sandback's peers. Traditionally there is a set of unwritten rules that are imposed on the relationship between you and the artwork. Sandback was interested in undermining those rules and generating an encounter where you would feel more at ease in sharing a space with the sculptural object and, in that way, finding a place within the institution that hosts it.

Sculpture by Fred Sandback in the Collection of Dia Art Foundation

Unless otherwise noted, situational dimensions, overall dimensions vary with each installation using spatial relationships established by the artist.

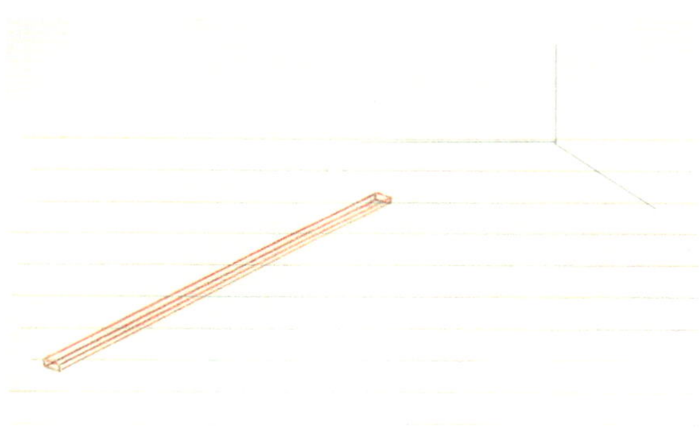

Untitled (Red Floor Piece), 1967
$\frac{1}{32}$-inch elastic cord (red) and acrylic (red) on steel
1⅝ × 4½ × 264 inches (4.1 × 11.4 × 670.6 cm)
1980.558

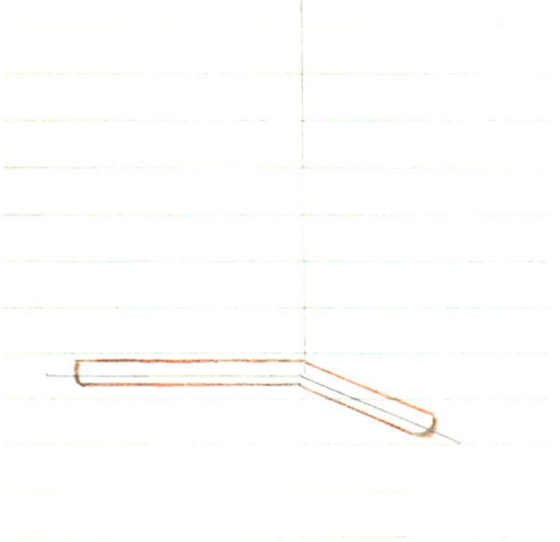

Untitled, 1967
$\frac{1}{32}$-inch elastic cord (fluorescent orange)
4 × 84 × 36 inches (10.2 × 213.4 × 91.4 cm)
1980.561

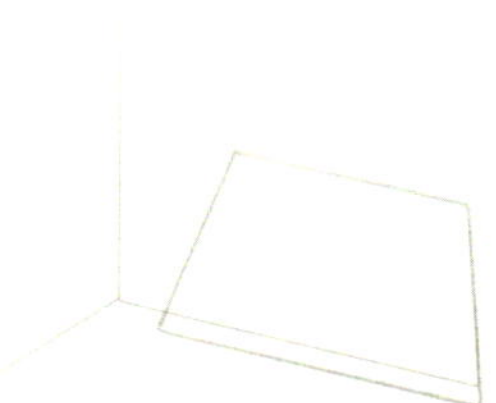

Untitled, 1967
⅛-inch elastic cord (silver-gray)
61 × 115½ × 30 inches (154.9 × 293.4 × 76.2 cm)
1980.098

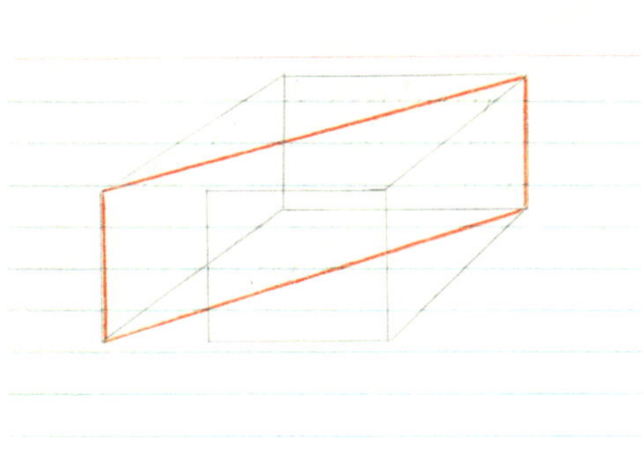

Untitled, 1967
⅜-inch elastic cord (fluorescent orange)
1980.562

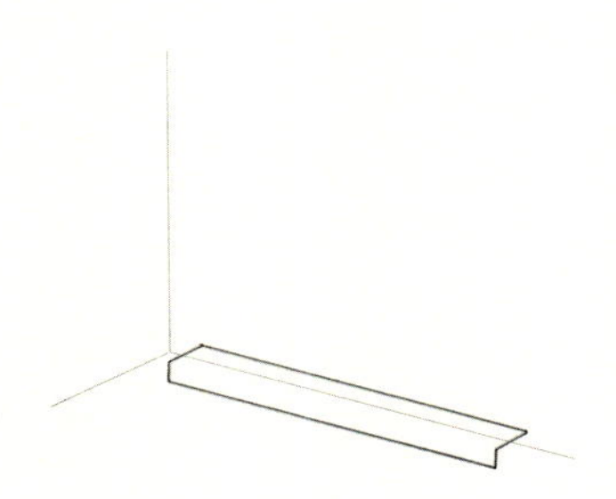

Untitled, 1968
Acrylic (dark gray) on ¼-inch elastic cord and steel
13 × 228 × 27 inches (33 × 579.1 × 68.6 cm)
1994.001

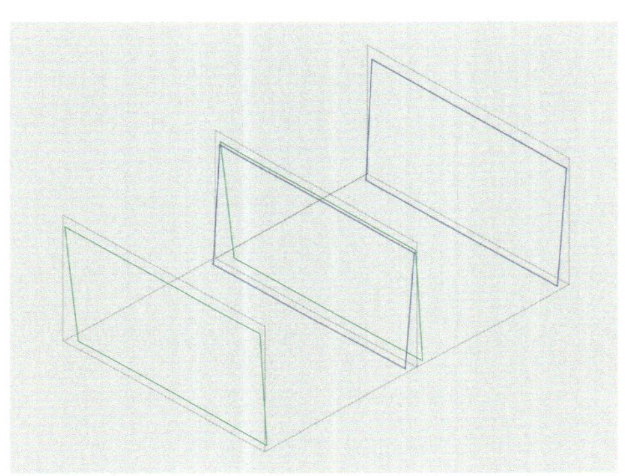

**Construction of Four Parallel Leaning Planes (from
133 Proposals for the Heiner Friedrich Gallery)**, 1969
Acrylic yarn (blue and green)
2003.084.1-4

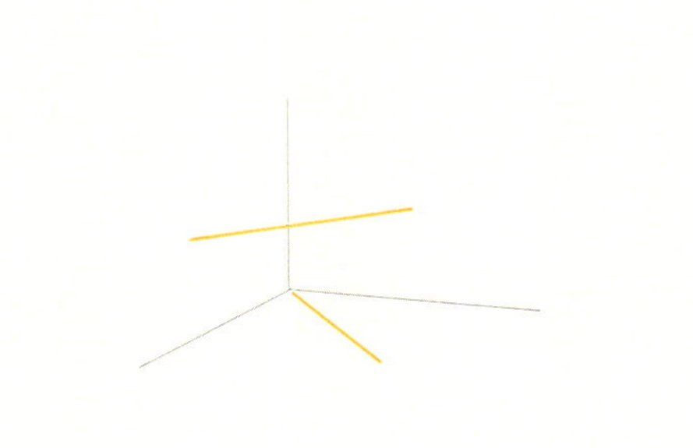

Untitled, 1970
⅛-inch elastic cord (school-bus yellow)
54 × 96 × 96 inches (137.2 × 243.8 × 243.8 cm)
1980.099.1-2

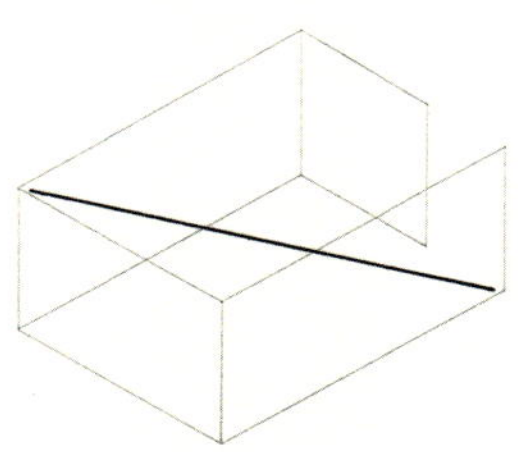

1980.059

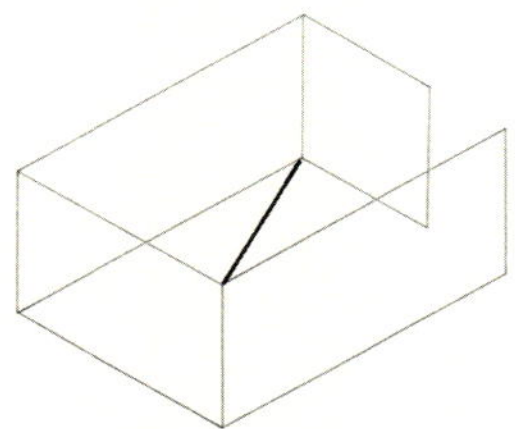

1980.060

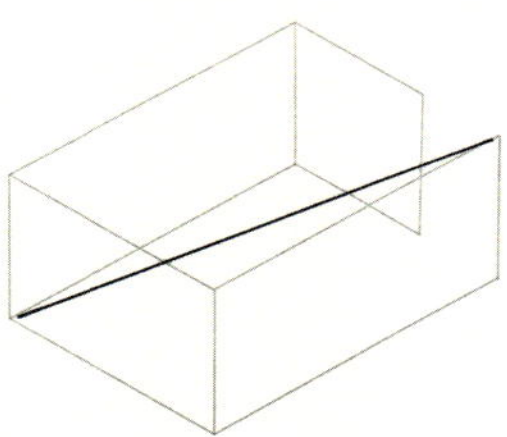

1980.061

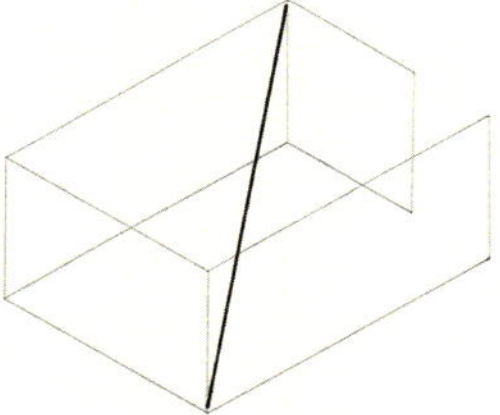

1980.062

Four Black Diagonals (Closed Series), 1970
Acrylic yarn (black)

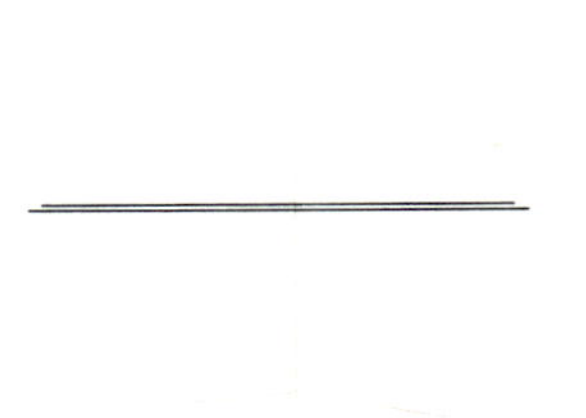

Untitled, 1971
¼-inch elastic cord (black)
54 × 96 × 96 inches (137.2 × 243.8 × 243.8 cm)
1980.100

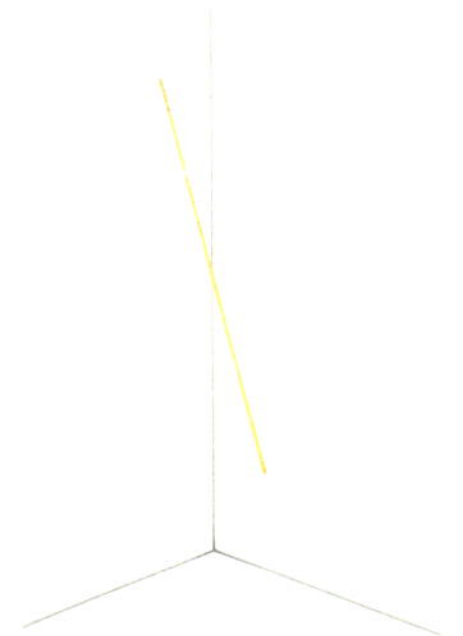

Untitled (Diagonal Cornered Construction), 1974
Acrylic yarn (yellow ocher)
63 × 6½ × 6½ inches (207 × 16.5 × 16.5 cm)
Edition 2/5; 1994.002

Untitled, 1972
Acrylic (red oxide) on ¼-inch elastic cord
123 × 120 × 6 inches (312.4 × 304.8 × 15.2 cm)
1980.101.1-2

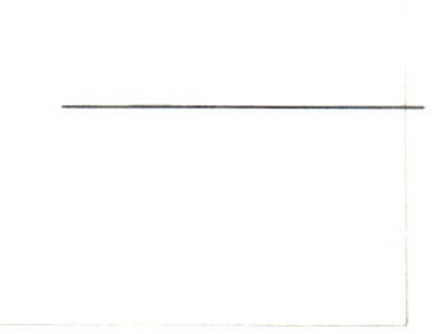

Untitled, 1974
Acrylic yarn (black)
64 × 120 × 6 inches (162.6 × 304.8 × 15.2 cm)
1980.103

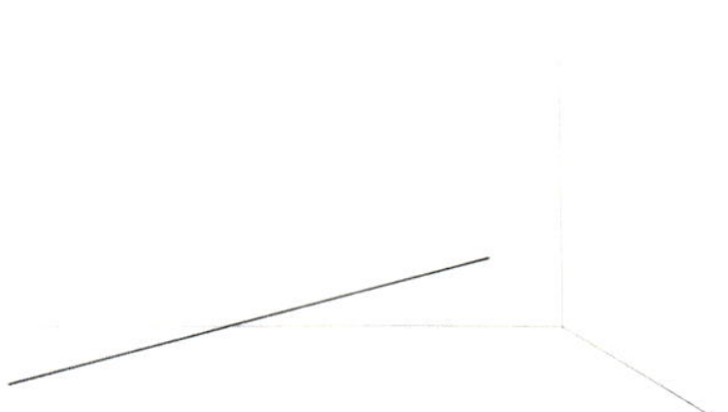

Untitled, 1973
Acrylic yarn (black)
60 × 240 × 60 inches (152.4 × 609.6 × 152.4 cm)
1980.102

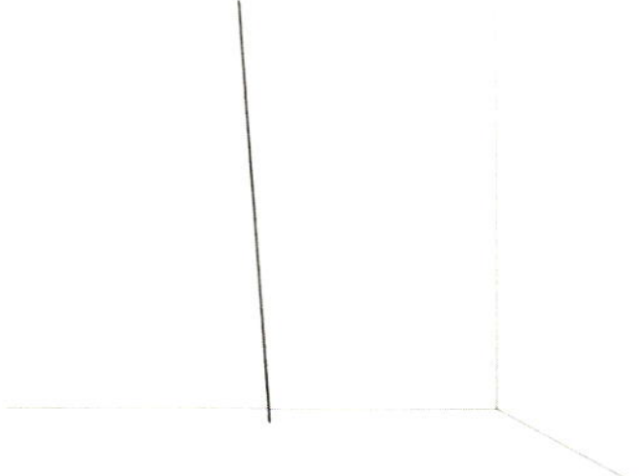

Untitled, 1974
Acrylic yarn (black)
144 × 2 × 6 inches (365.8 × 5.1 × 15.2 cm)
1980.104

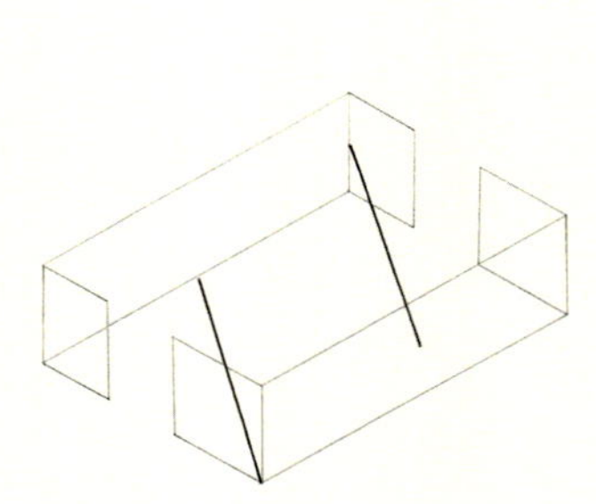

1980.105.1-2

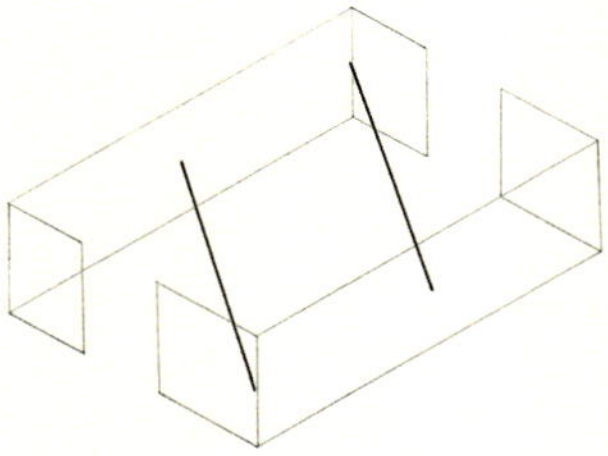

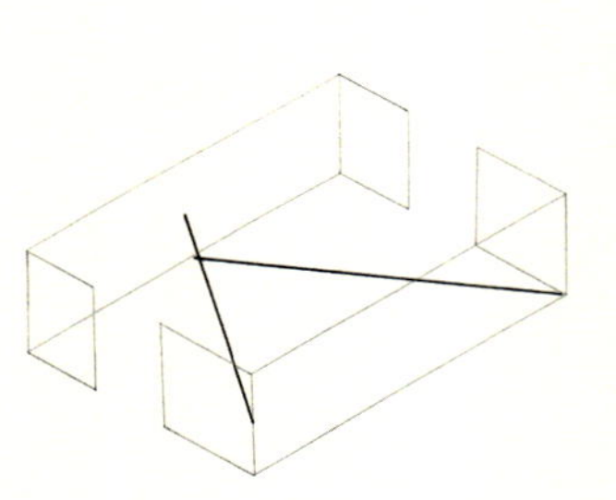

1980.109.1-2

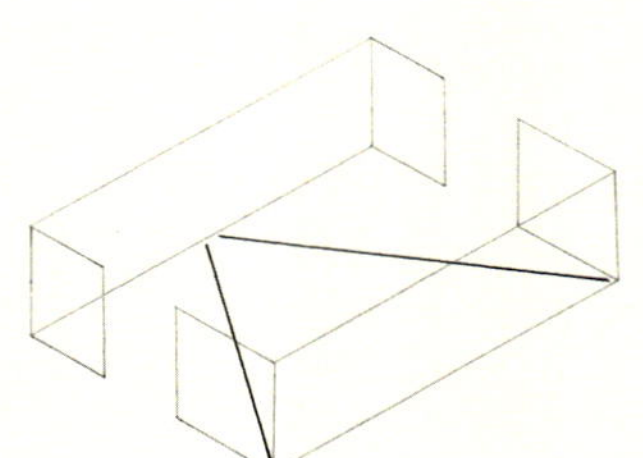

1980.106.1-2

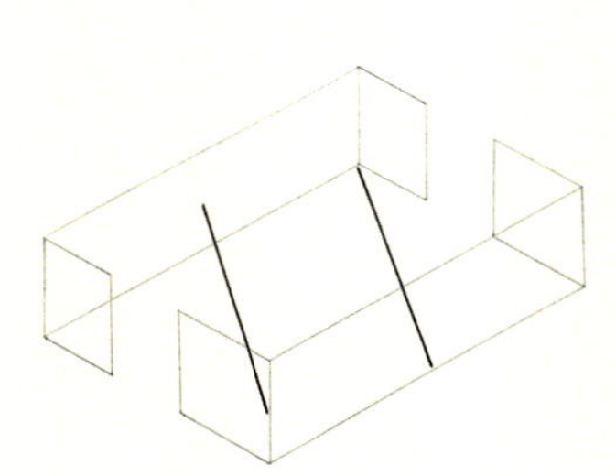

1980.110.1-2

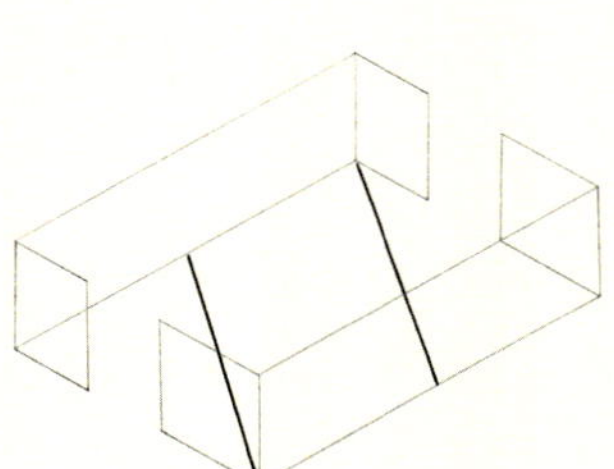

1980.107.1-2

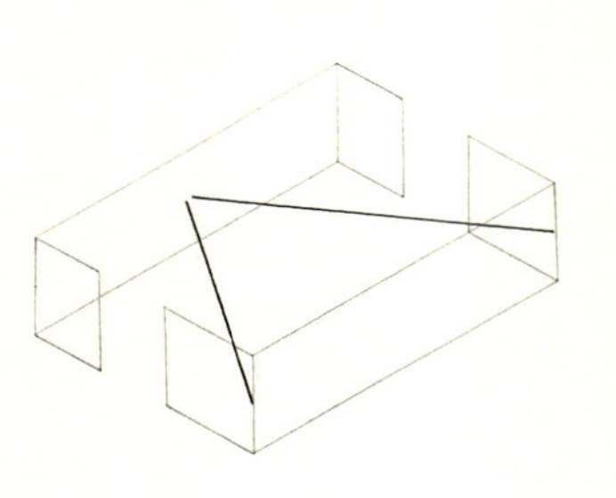

1980.111.1-2

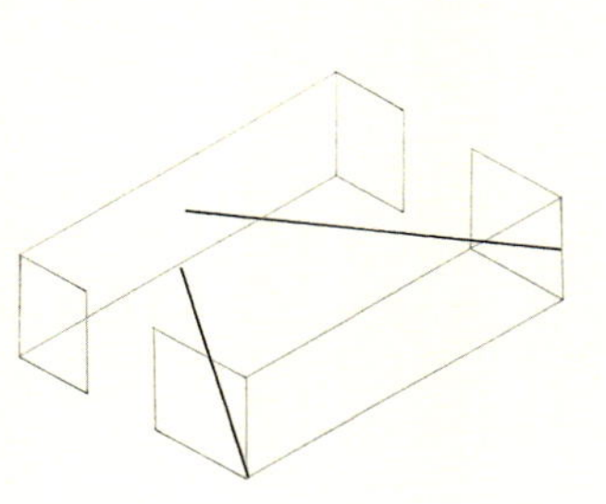

1980.108.1-2

1980.112.1-2

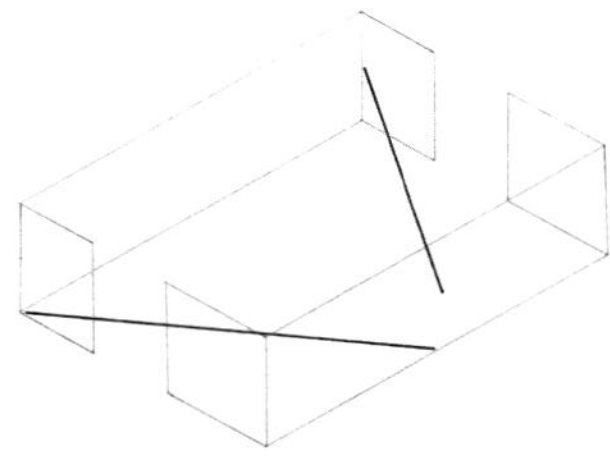

1980.113.1-2

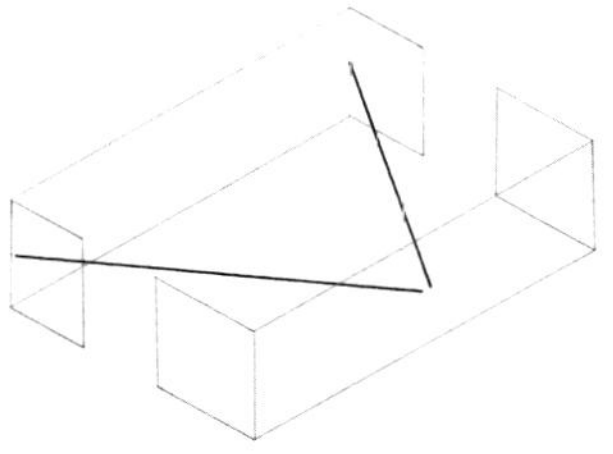

1980.117.1-2

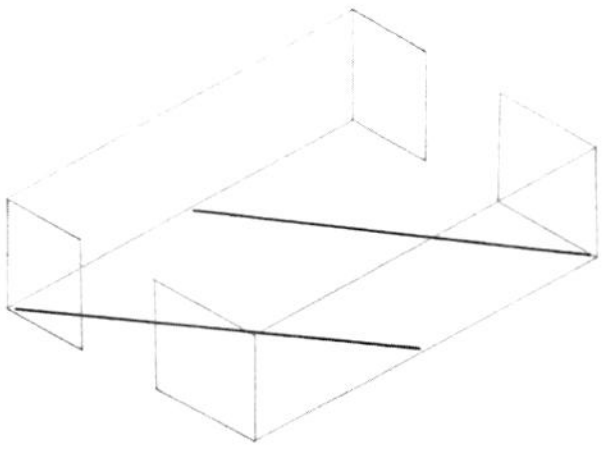

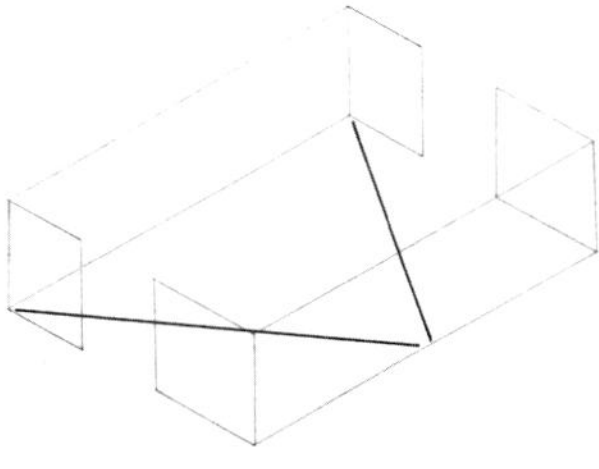

1980.114.1-2

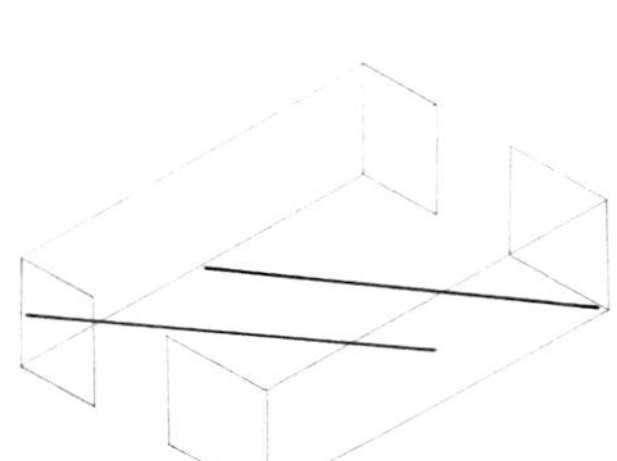

1980.118.1-2

1980.115.1-2

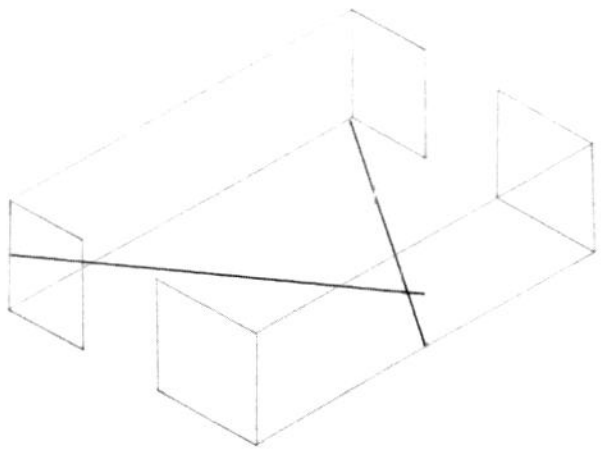

1980.119.1-2

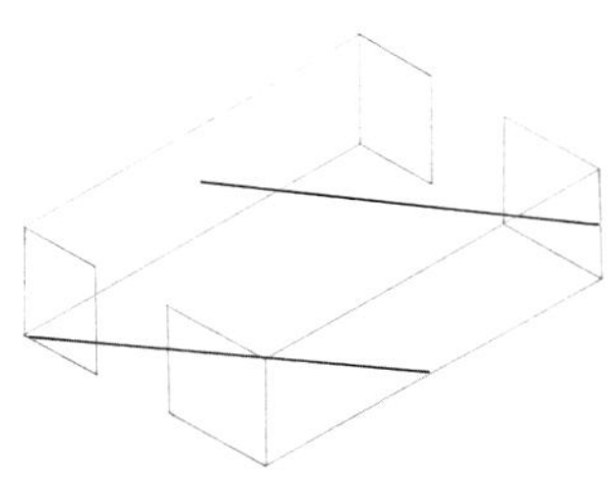

1980.116.1-2

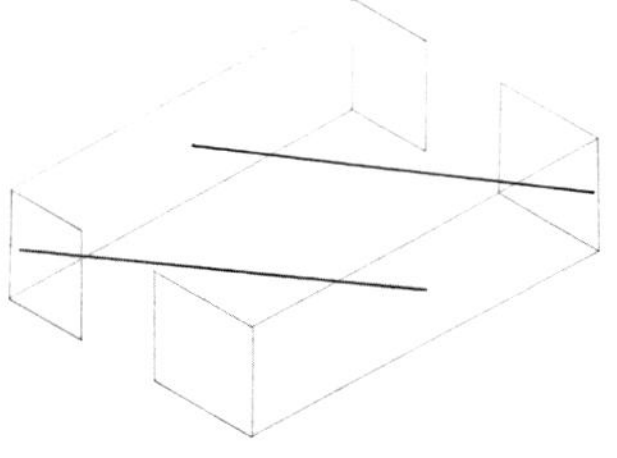

1980.120.1-2

Sixteen Two-part Pieces (Closed Series), 1974
Acrylic yarn (black)

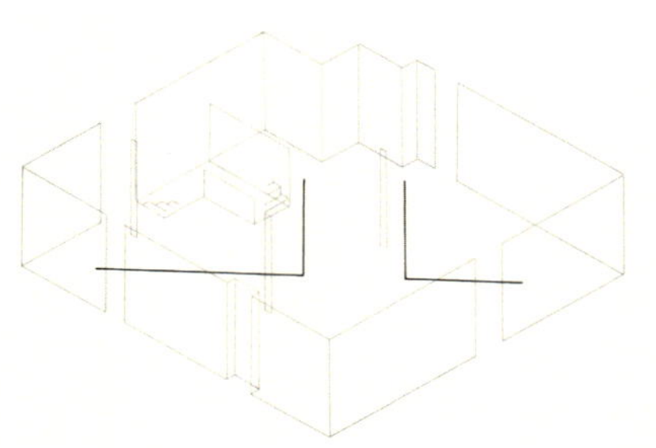

Untitled (from Ten Vertical Constructions), 1977–79
Acrylic yarn (black)
1980.273.1-2

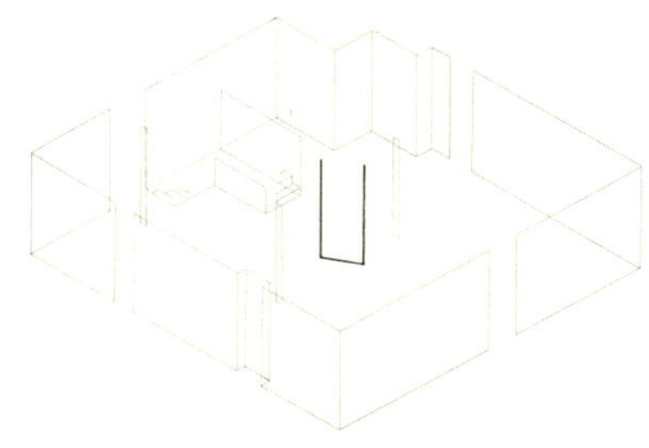

Untitled (from Ten Vertical Constructions), 1977–79
Acrylic yarn (black)
1980.542

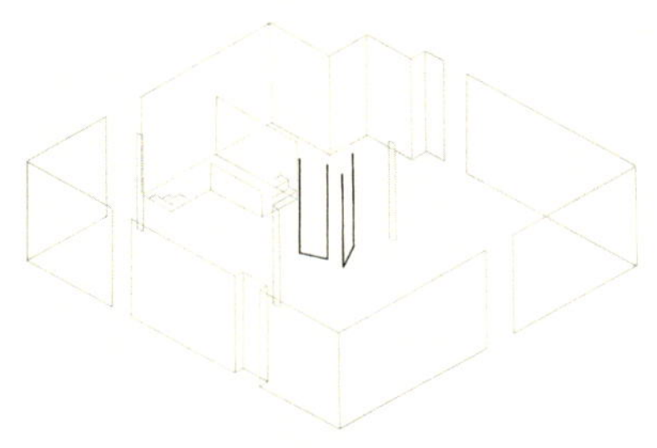

Untitled (Two-part Vertical Construction, from Ten Vertical Constructions), 1977–79
Acrylic yarn (black)
1980.540

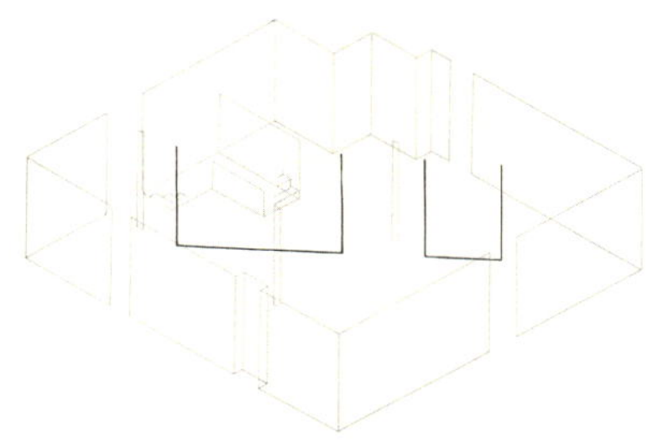

Untitled (from Ten Vertical Constructions), 1977–79
Acrylic yarn (black)
1980.543.1-2

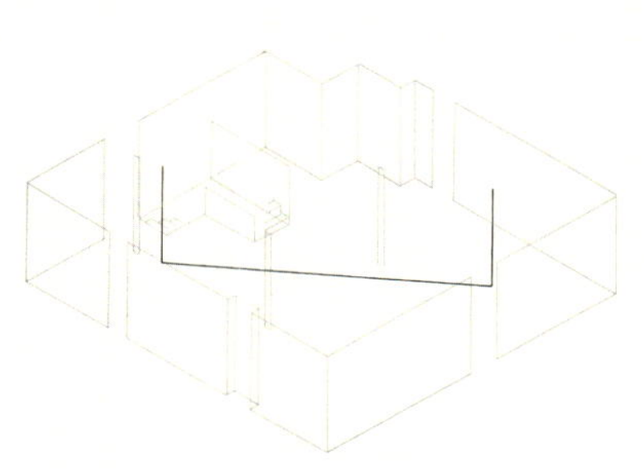

Untitled (from Ten Vertical Constructions), 1977–79
Acrylic yarn (black)
1980.541

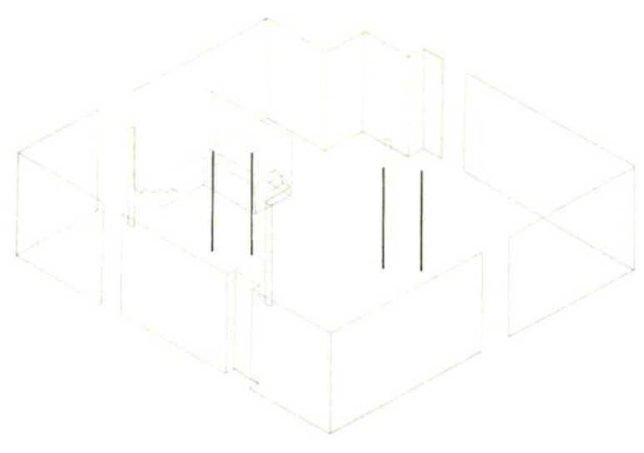

Untitled (from Ten Vertical Constructions), 1977–79
Acrylic yarn (black)
1980.544.1-4

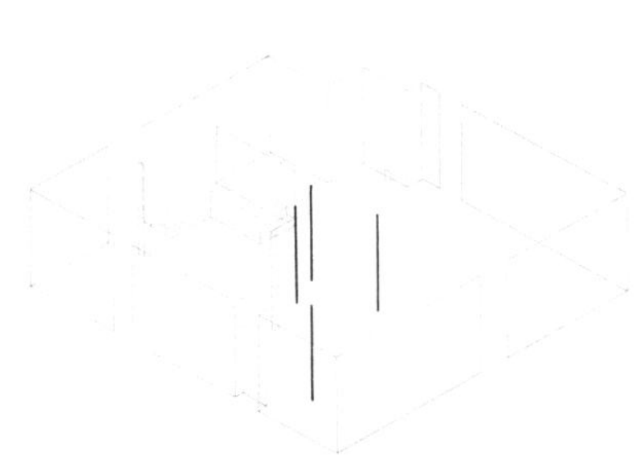

Untitled (from Ten Vertical Constructions), 1977–79
Acrylic yarn (black)
1980.545.1-4

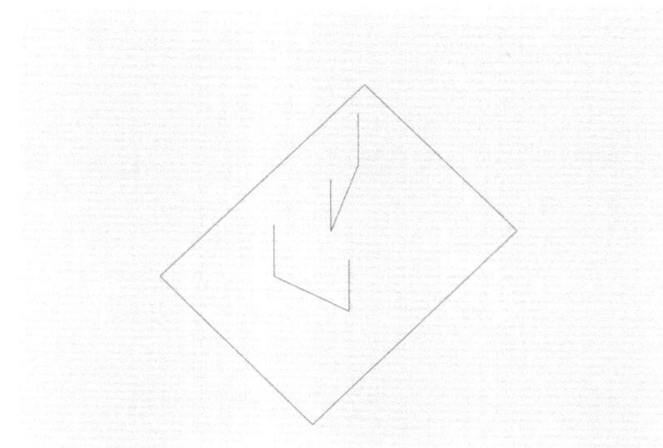

Untitled (from Ten Vertical Constructions), 1977–79
Acrylic yarn (rust red)
2014.003.1-2

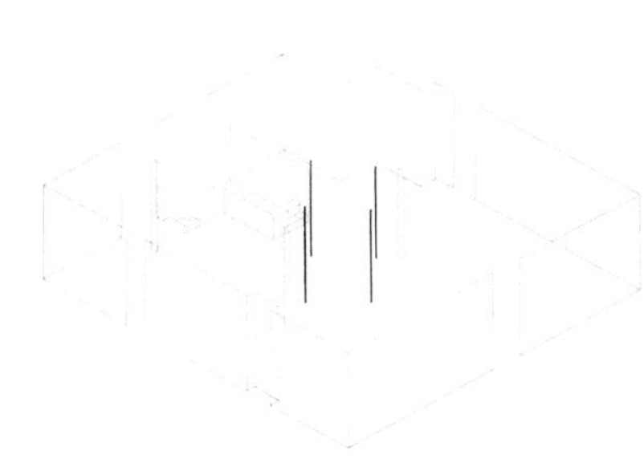

Untitled (from Ten Vertical Constructions), 1977–79
Acrylic yarn (black)
1980.546.1-4

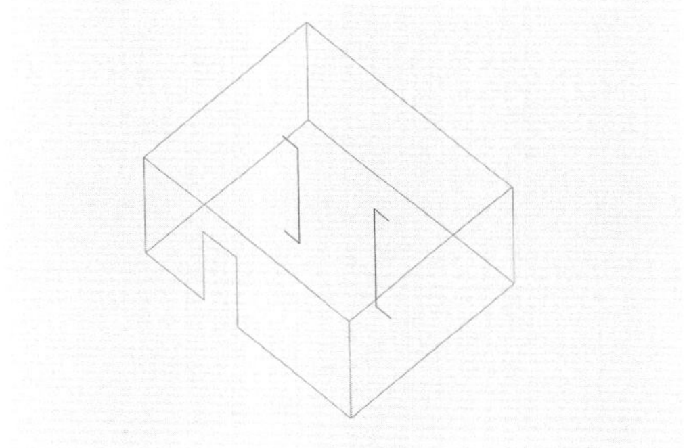

Untitled (Two-part Vertical Construction), 1978
Acrylic yarn (ultramarine blue)
1980.566

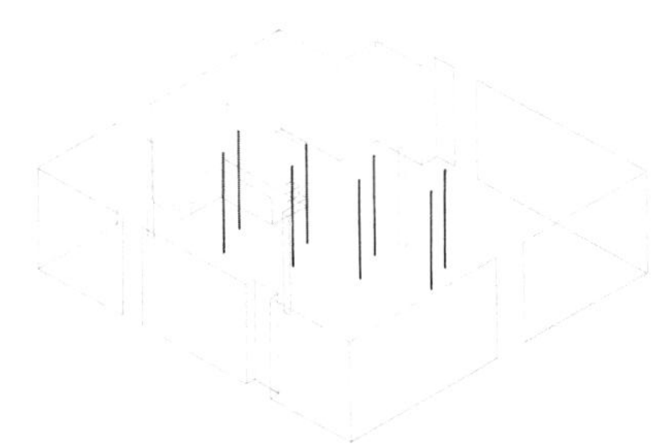

Untitled (from Ten Vertical Constructions), 1977–79
Acrylic yarn (black)
1980.547.1-10

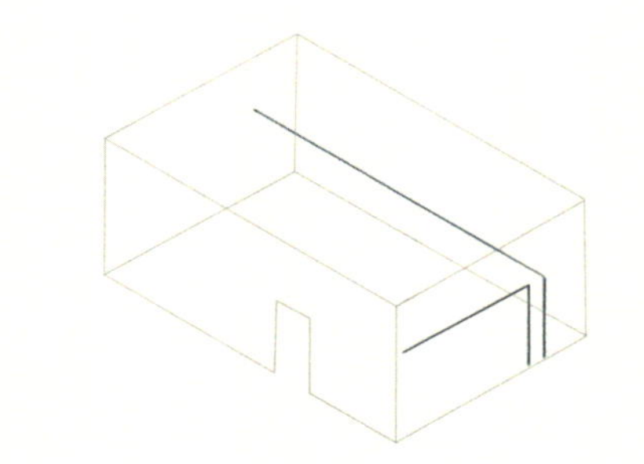

First Construction for the Rindge Studio, 1979
Acrylic yarn (blue)
1981.035.1-2

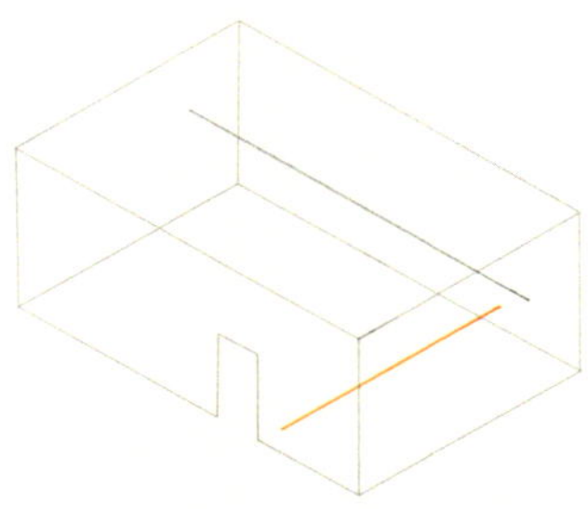

Fourth Construction for the Rindge Studio, 1979
Acrylic yarn (gray and yellow)
1981.038.1-2

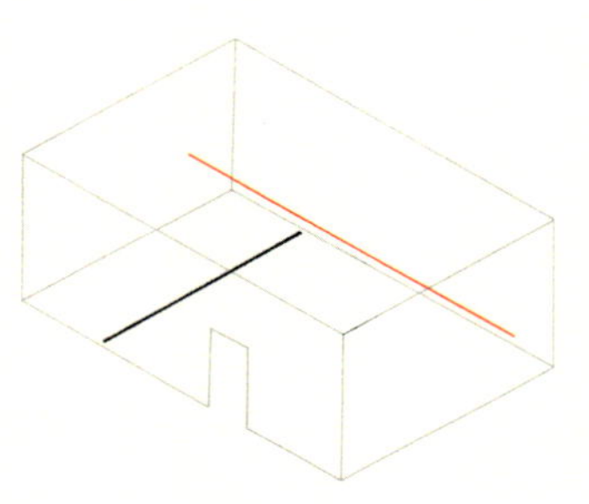

Second Construction for the Rindge Studio, 1979
Acrylic yarn (umber and sienna)
1981.036.1-2

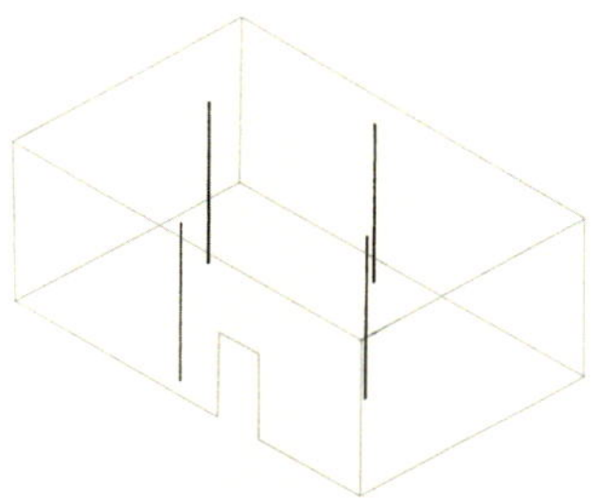

Sixth Construction for the Rindge Studio, 1979
Acrylic yarn (black)
1980.040

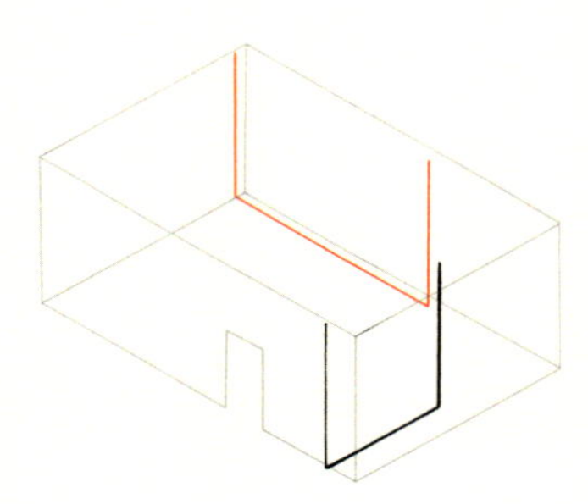

Third Construction for the Rindge Studio, 1979
Acrylic yarn (sienna and umber)
1981.037.1-2

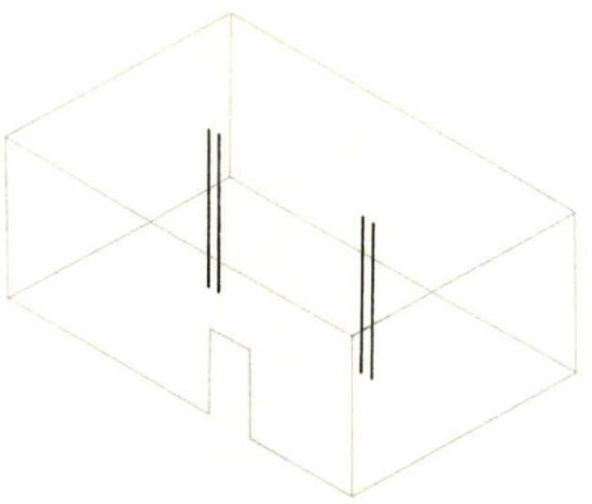

Seventh Construction for the Rindge Studio, 1979
Acrylic yarn (black)
1981.041.1-2

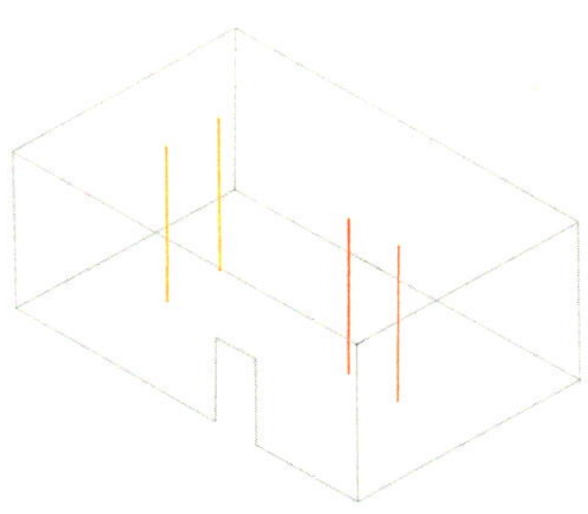

Eighth Construction for the Rindge Studio, 1979
Acrylic yarn (yellow and pink)
1980.042.1-4

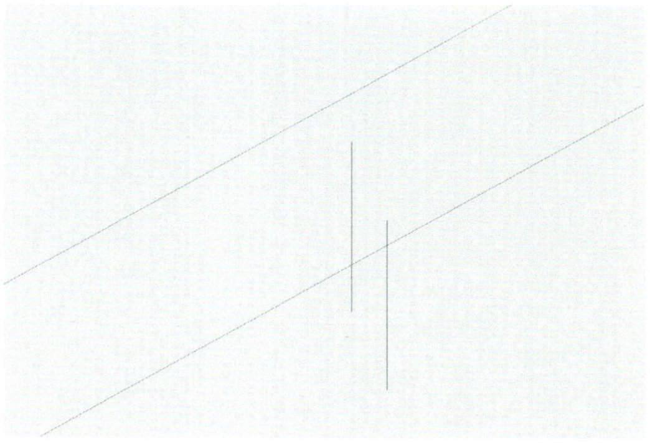

Untitled (Two-part Vertical Construction), 1979
Acrylic yarn (black)
2014.004.1-2

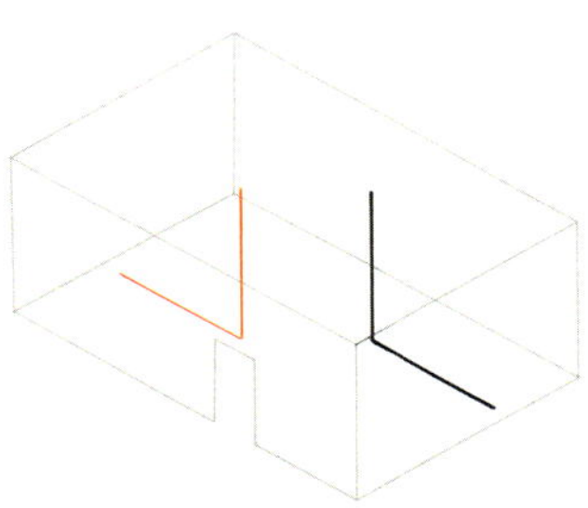

Ninth Construction for the Rindge Studio, 1979
Acrylic yarn (orange and black)
1981.043

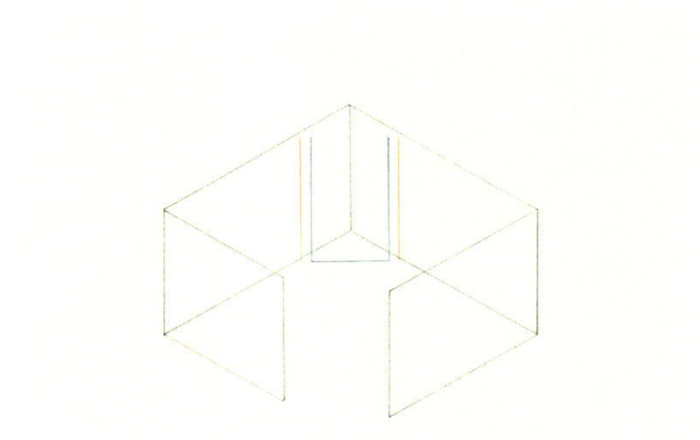

Untitled (First of Ten Cornered Constructions), 1981
Acrylic yarn (gray and pink)
Ceiling height × 64½ × 64½ inches (163.8 × 163.8 cm)
1981.010.1-3

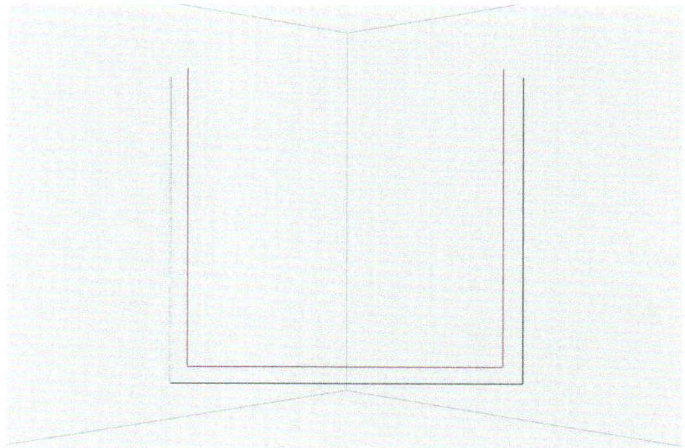

Untitled (Fourth of Ten Corner Constructions), 1983
Acrylic yarn (maroon and black)
99½ × 70 × 70 inches (252.7 × 177.8 × 177.8 cm)
1983.040.1-2

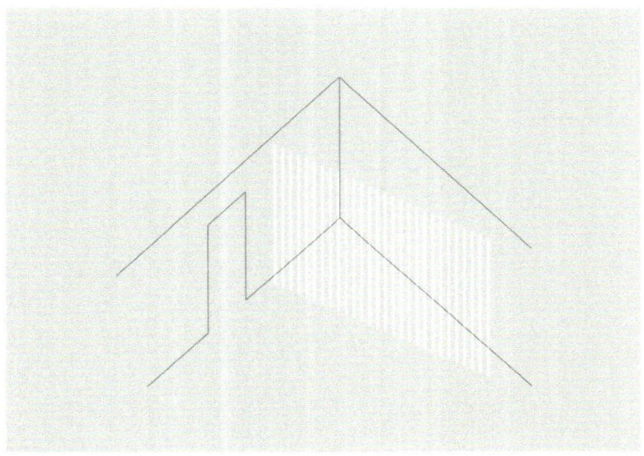

Untitled, 1983
Acrylic yarn (off-white)
1983.042.1-28

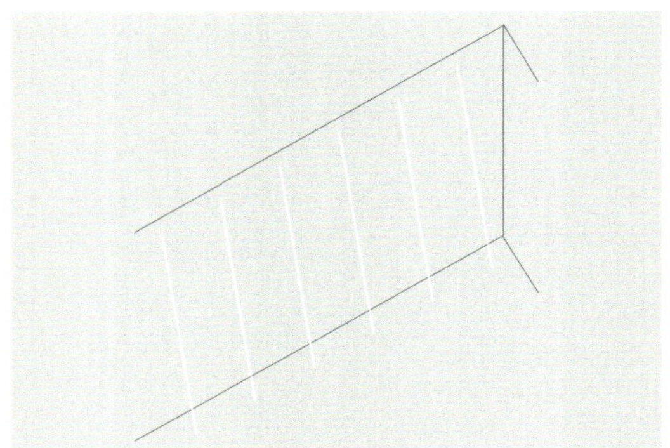

Untitled (Six-part Vertical Construction), 1996
Acrylic yarn (white)
2003.040.1-6

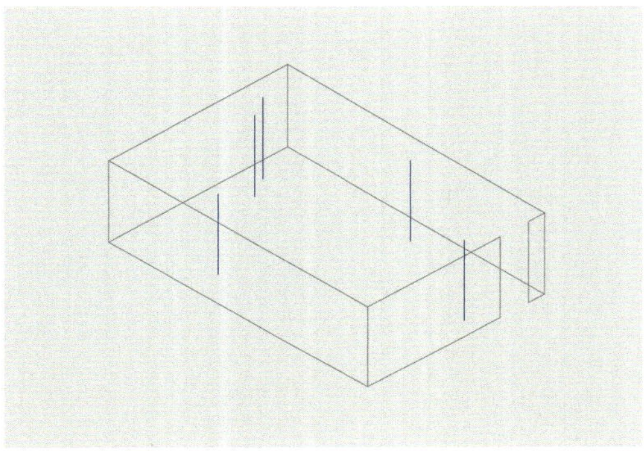

Untitled, 1983
Acrylic yarn (ultramarine)
1983.043.1-5

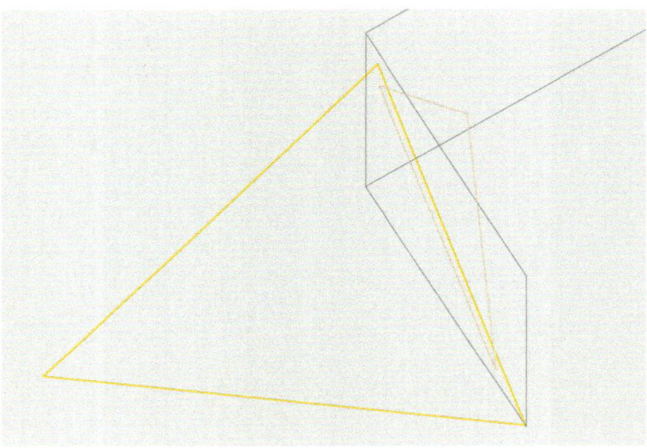

Untitled (Two-part Construction), 1996
Acrylic yarn (ocher and beige)
2014.005.1-2

Untitled (Four-part Relief Construction), 1983
Acrylic yarn (gray, chrome yellow, and green)
2015.002.1-4

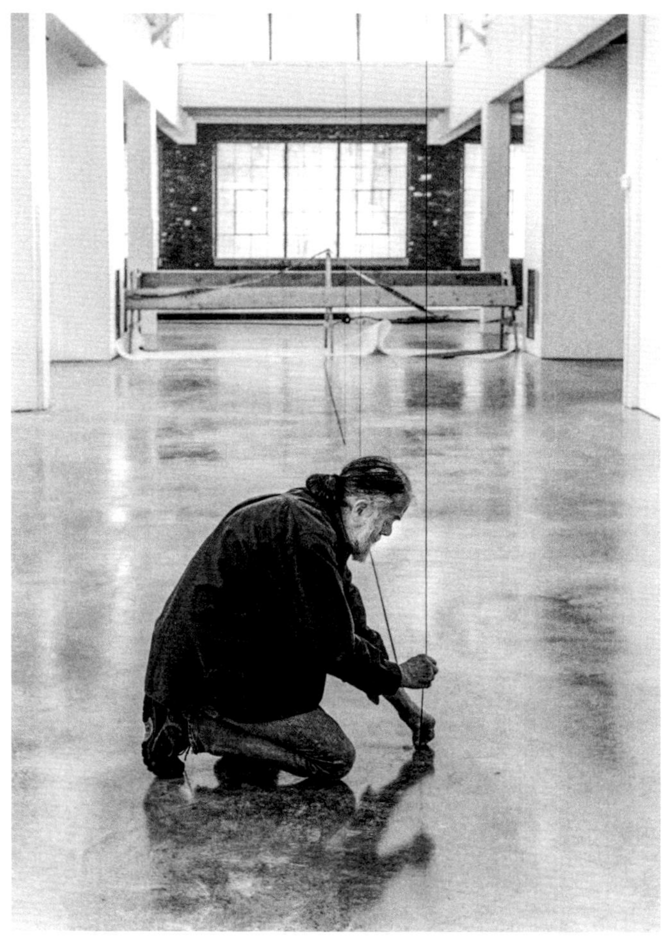

Fred Sandback installing his work at Dia Beacon, 2003

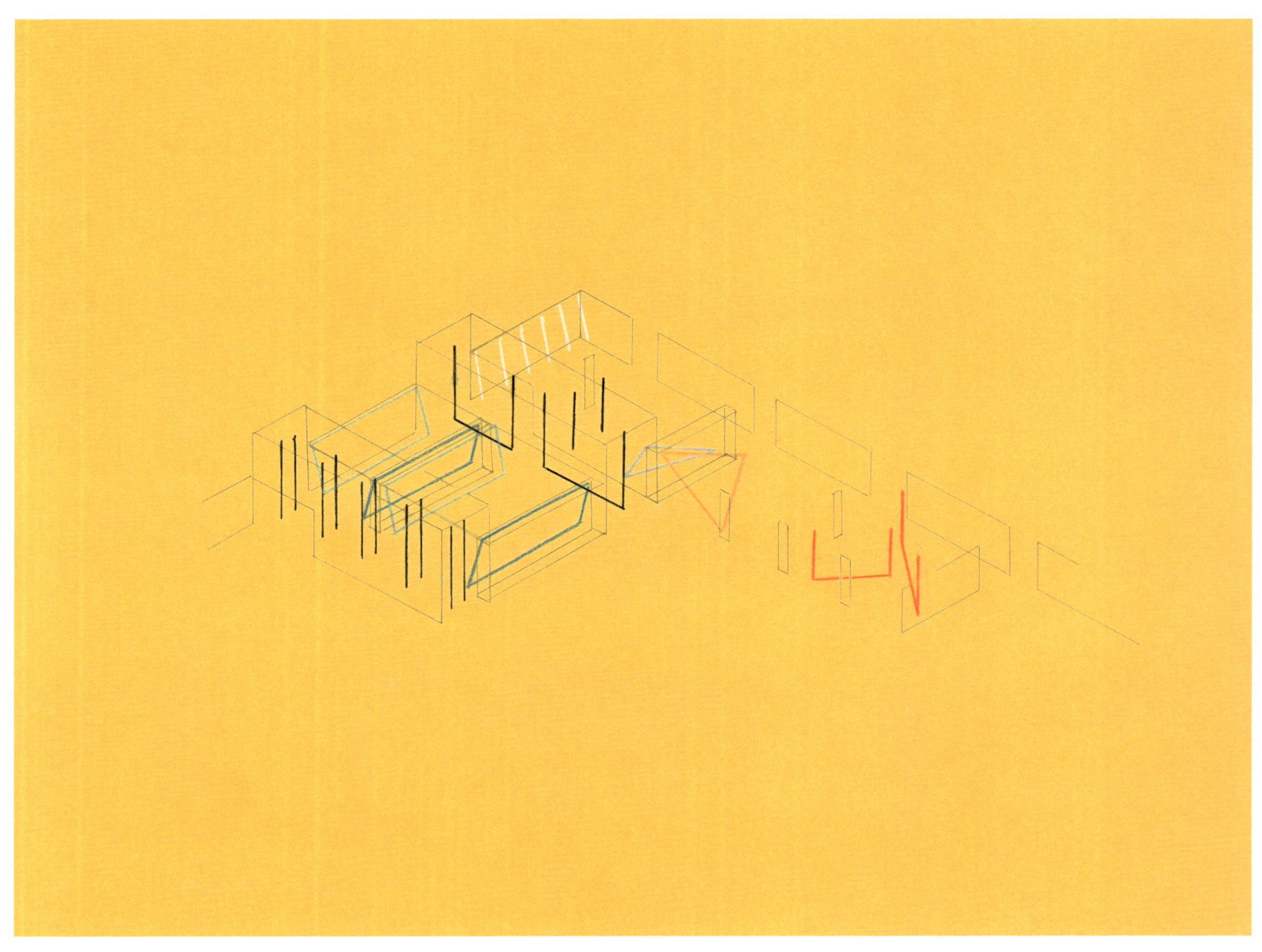

Untitled (Study for Dia:Beacon), c. 2003.
Pastel and pencil on paper, 8½ × 11 inches
(21.6 × 27.9 cm)

Fred Sandback at Dia Beacon

Lynne Cooke

"The first sculpture I made with a piece of string and a little wire was the outline of a rectangular solid . . . lying on the floor. It was a casual act, but it seemed to open up a lot of possibilities for me," Fred Sandback wrote in 1986, looking back on almost twenty years of activity to a seminal sculpture he had executed in 1967.[1] The key implications of that determining impulse remained at the heart of his practice until his death in 2003. In wanting to create sculpture that did not have an inside, he found through this seemingly "casual act" the means to "assert a certain place or volume in its full materiality without occupying and obscuring it."[2]

For more than three decades, Sandback pursued these governing insights with remarkable consistency and inventiveness, creating a body of work that is informed by a signature style and yet, as a result of the close interdependence of each work with the architectural site in which it is realized, ever different in its manifestations. Arguably still the best commentator on his own work, he elucidated his abiding wish "to be in some sort of constituting material relationship with my environment" in limpid forthright terms. "My feeling persists," he avowed in that same article from 1986, "that all of my sculpture is part of a continuing attitude and relationship to things. . . . The sculptures address themselves to the particular space and time that they're in, but it may be that the more complete situation that I'm after is only constructed in time slowly, with the individual sculptures as its constituent parts."[3]

For his presentation at Dia Beacon, Sandback seamlessly integrated older pieces with newer ones to orient and ground the viewer in a particular place, a specific situation. Part of a stringent selection from his deliberately circumscribed lexicon, each sculpture was newly parsed for the site. "I don't feel that once a piece is made, then it's done with," he explained. "I continue to work with older schemata and formats, and often begin to get what I want out of them only after many reworkings. Though the same substructure may be used many times, it appears each time in a new light. It is the measure of the relative success of a piece, not necessarily that a new structure emerges, but that a familiar one attains, in its present manifestation, a particular vibrancy or actuality."[4]

1. Fred Sandback, "Remarks on My Sculpture 1966–86," *Fred Sandback Sculpture 1966–1986* (Mannheim, Germany: Kunsthalle Mannheim, 1986), 12. This text and all other published writings by Fred Sandback are online at https://www.fredsandbackarchive.org/publications.

2. Ibid.

3. Ibid., 12–13.

4. Ibid., 13.

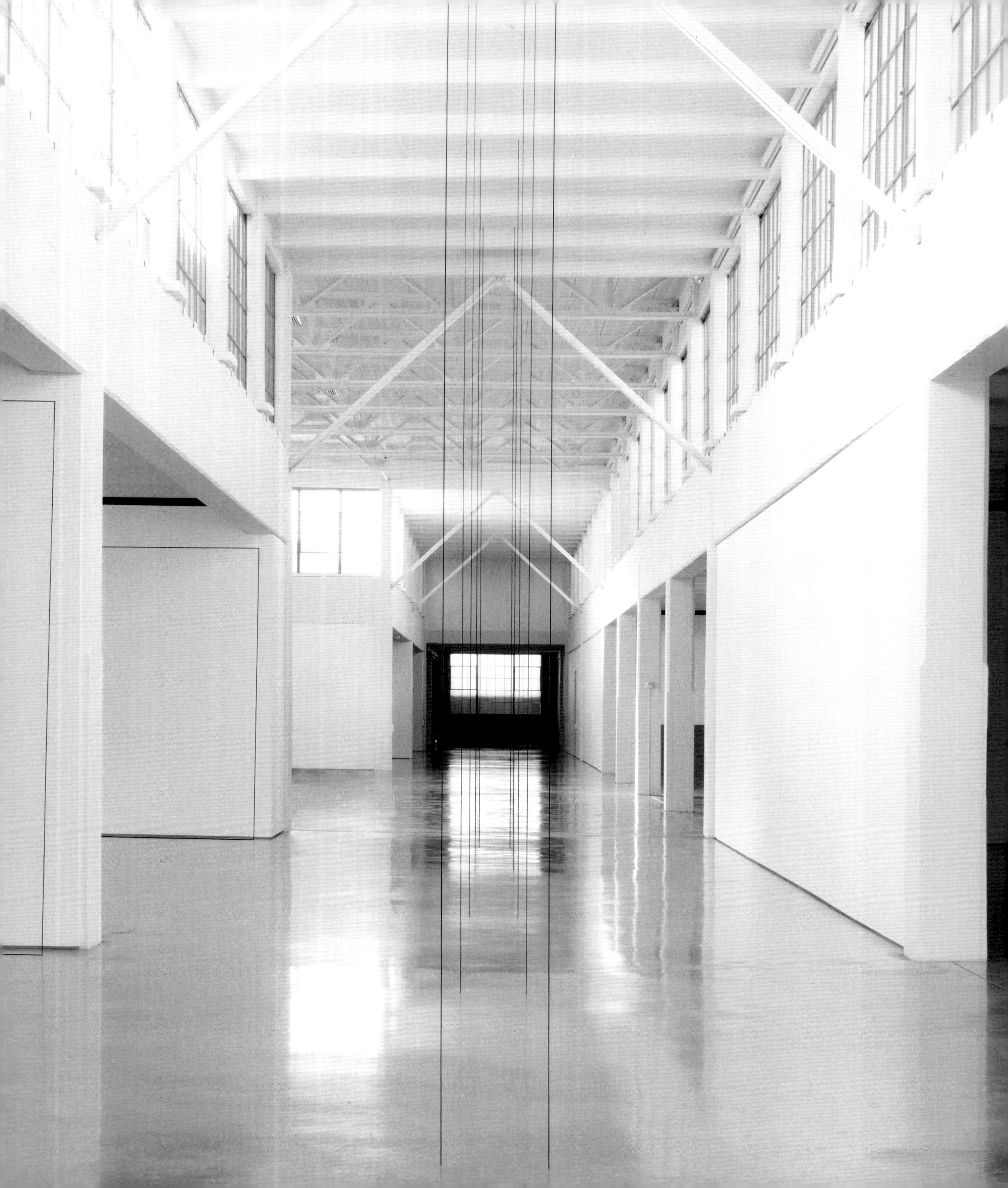

5. Sandback and a friend coined the
term to define space that was "literal,
flat-footed, and everyday. The idea was
to have the work right there along with
everything else in the world, not up on a
spatial pedestal. The term also involved
the idea of utility—that a sculpture was
there to be engaged actively, and it had
utopian glimmerings of art and life hap-
pily cohabitating." Ibid.

6. Fred Sandback, "Notes," in *74 Front
Street: The Fred Sandback Museum*.
Installation view, Dia Beacon, Beacon,
New York (New York: Dia Art Foundation,
1982), 4.

The character of any particular work is relative to its site, its proportions
and form subtly calibrated in response to the architectonics of the area it inhabits.
Thus not only the specific measurements and proportions but the tone or hue of the
yarn may be adapted or intuitively adjusted in relation to both its neighbors and to its
new location. In these sculptures, space is both defined and imbued with an incorporeal palpability, so that often the spectator concentrates less on the edges, on the
yarn demarcating the forms, than on the planar or volumetric components within.
Whether transparent geometries, as in *Untitled (Two-part Vertical Construction, from
Ten Vertical Constructions)* (1977–79) and *Untitled* (1996)—two triangles—or simple
linear trajectories, as in *Untitled* (1996)—a six-part vertical construction—Sandback's
sculptures unequivocally occupy the same physical site as the viewer. Inhabiting what
the artist dubbed "pedestrian space"—the ordinary matter-of-fact space coextensive
with that of the spectator and the site—they reveal themselves over time, from different vantages, and according to different perspectives.[5] While any apprehension of his
works involves a process of kinesthetic viewing, a phenomenological experience of
each piece in situ, Sandback was careful to distinguish his sculpture from so-called
installation art, from the creation of a holistic place set apart, in and of itself, sui
generis. His work is never "environmental," if that implies transforming the context.
On the contrary, as he stated, "it incorporates specific parts of the environment, but it's
always coexistent with that environment, as opposed to overwhelming or destroying
that environment in favor of a different one."[6]

In a low gallery at Dia Beacon, the brightly colored vectors of two works,
initially glimpsed from afar, skim through the air. When confronted directly, they
radically reorient the spectator's relation to the dominant axial configuration of the
architecture, dramatically skewing one's circuit away from the strongly accented horizontal and vertical sight lines that elsewhere prevail. The vivid terra-cotta contours of
the two-part vertical construction limn two planes positioned almost at right angles
to each other, creating dynamic diagonal vectors on the west side of the gallery. To
the east, a vibrant ocher triangle tilting out from the wall ventures beyond its half of
the space to invade the transitional passage opening into the adjacent gallery. As the
viewer passes into that room, a second triangle, angled almost parallel to the back-
side of the dividing wall, is revealed. Canted only slightly off the vertical and more
subdued in hue, it deftly counters and stabilizes the bold thrust of its more monumen-
tal partner. Sandback actively incorporated the wall as a pivot rather than treating it
simply and conventionally as a passive element whose function is to separate the two

Untitled (Six-part Vertical Construction),
**1996. Acrylic yarn (white), situational
dimensions, overall dimensions vary with
each installation using spatial relationships
established by the artist. Installation view,
Dia Beacon, Beacon, New York**

spaces. The delicate equilibrium established between the works activates the viewer's sense of engagement in the immediate context, the world at hand.

Like the others on view here, these two sculptures are made from acrylic yarn, a material that carried no significant connotations for Sandback. He preferred it over other materials because its slightly soft, fuzzy contours conjure a less crisp, less rigid line than that produced by metal and because its matte surface absorbs rather than reflects light. Taken together, these qualities permit the works made from yarn to coexist more subtly with their ambience than did their predecessors made from wire or metal rods.

Emerging during the heyday of Minimalism, Sandback's art has distinguished and differentiated itself from that of his immediate forbears by its eschewal of the reductively literal and of the material as its primary mode of being.[7] In his exploration of physical relationships via the incorporeal rather than through concrete matter—via the interplay of vacancy and volume—he recognized that the illusory and the factual are inextricably intertwined. "Fact and illusion are equivalents," he asserted: "Trying to weed one out in favor of the other is dealing with an incomplete situation."[8] Nevertheless, he stressed, "in no way is my work illusionistic. Illusionistic art refers you away from its factual existence towards something else. My work is full of illusions, but they don't refer to anything."[9]

7. While a student at Yale School of Art and Architecture in 1967, Sandback took courses from both Robert Morris and Donald Judd.

8. Sandback, "Notes," 4.

9. Ibid.

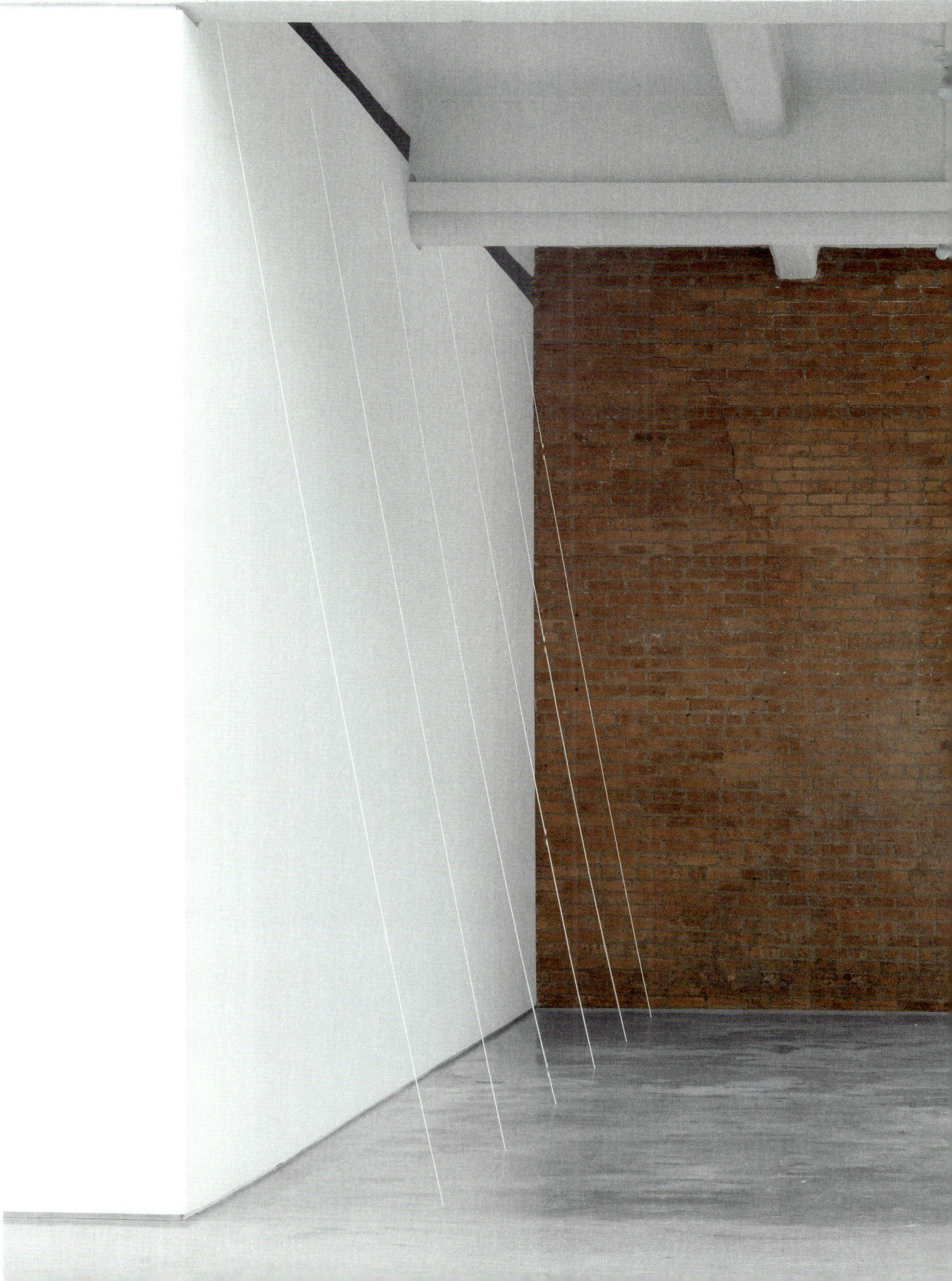

Construction of Four Parallel Leaning Planes (from 133 Proposals for the Heiner Friedrich Gallery), 1969. Acrylic yarn (blue and green), situational dimensions, overall dimensions vary with each installation using spatial relationships established by the artist. Installation views, Dia Beacon, Beacon, New York

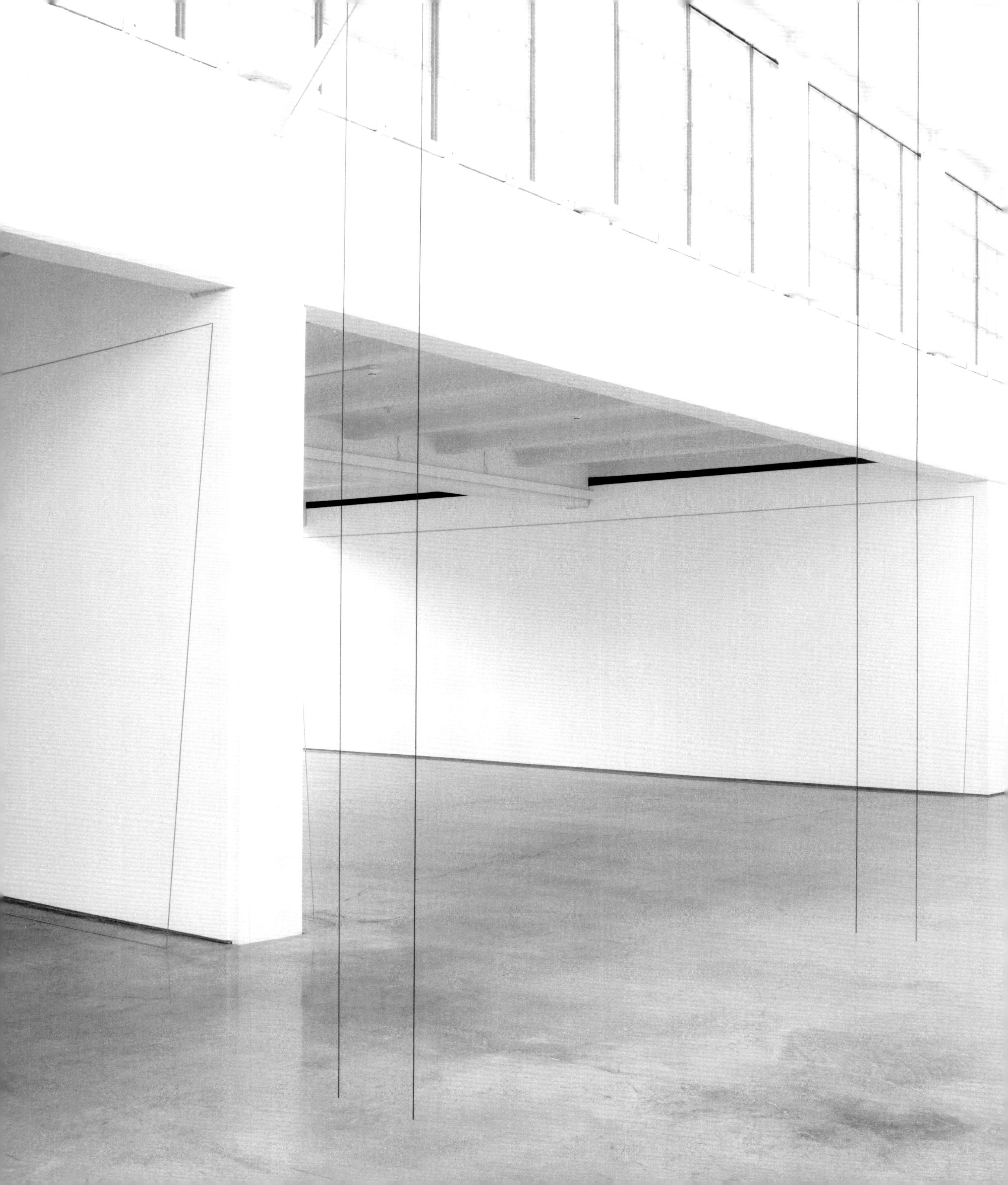

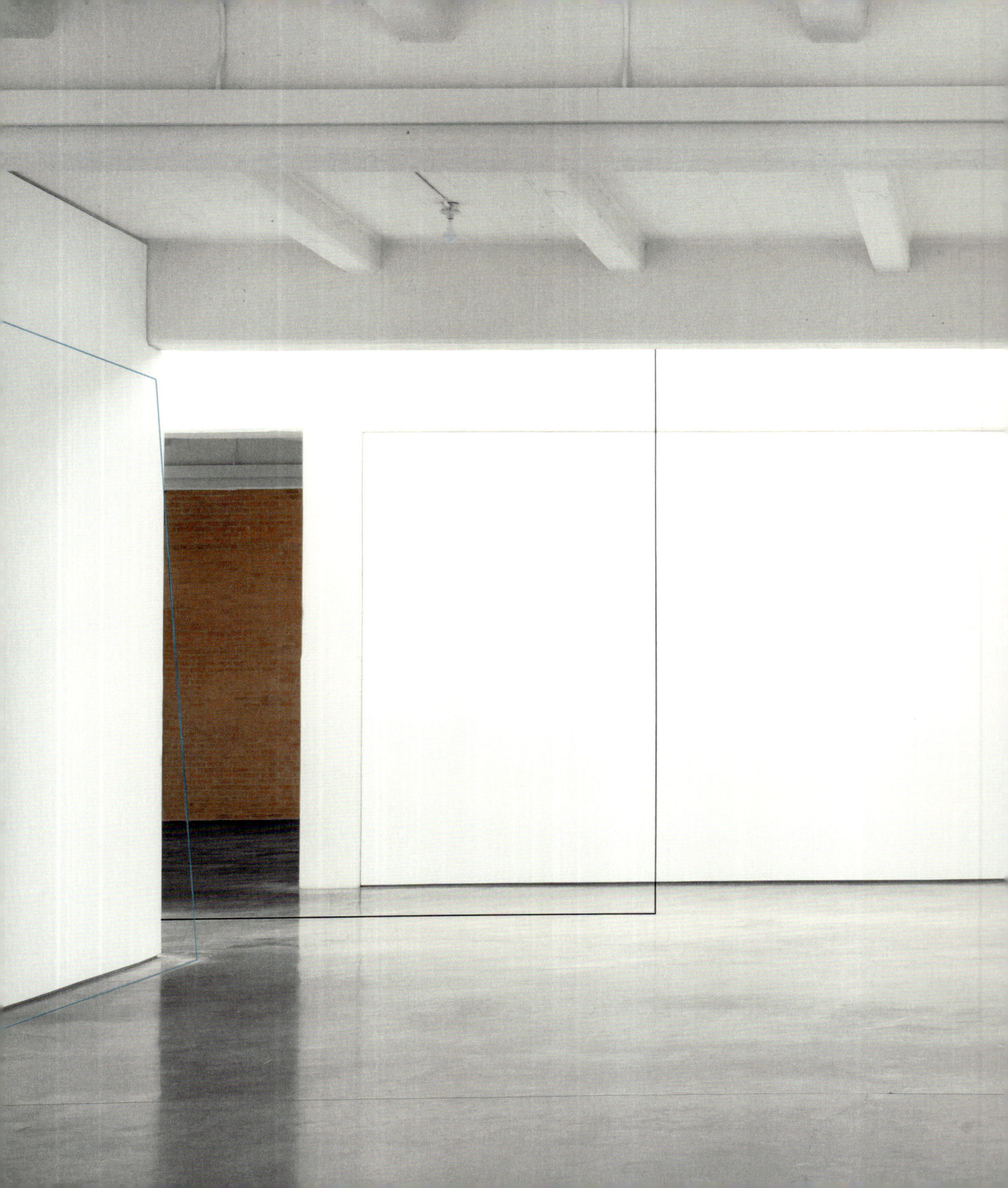

*Untitled (Two-part Vertical Construction, from
Ten Vertical Constructions)*, 1977–79. Acrylic yarn
(rust red), situational dimensions, overall dimensions vary with each installation using spatial
relationships established by the artist. Installation
view, Dia Beacon, Beacon, New York

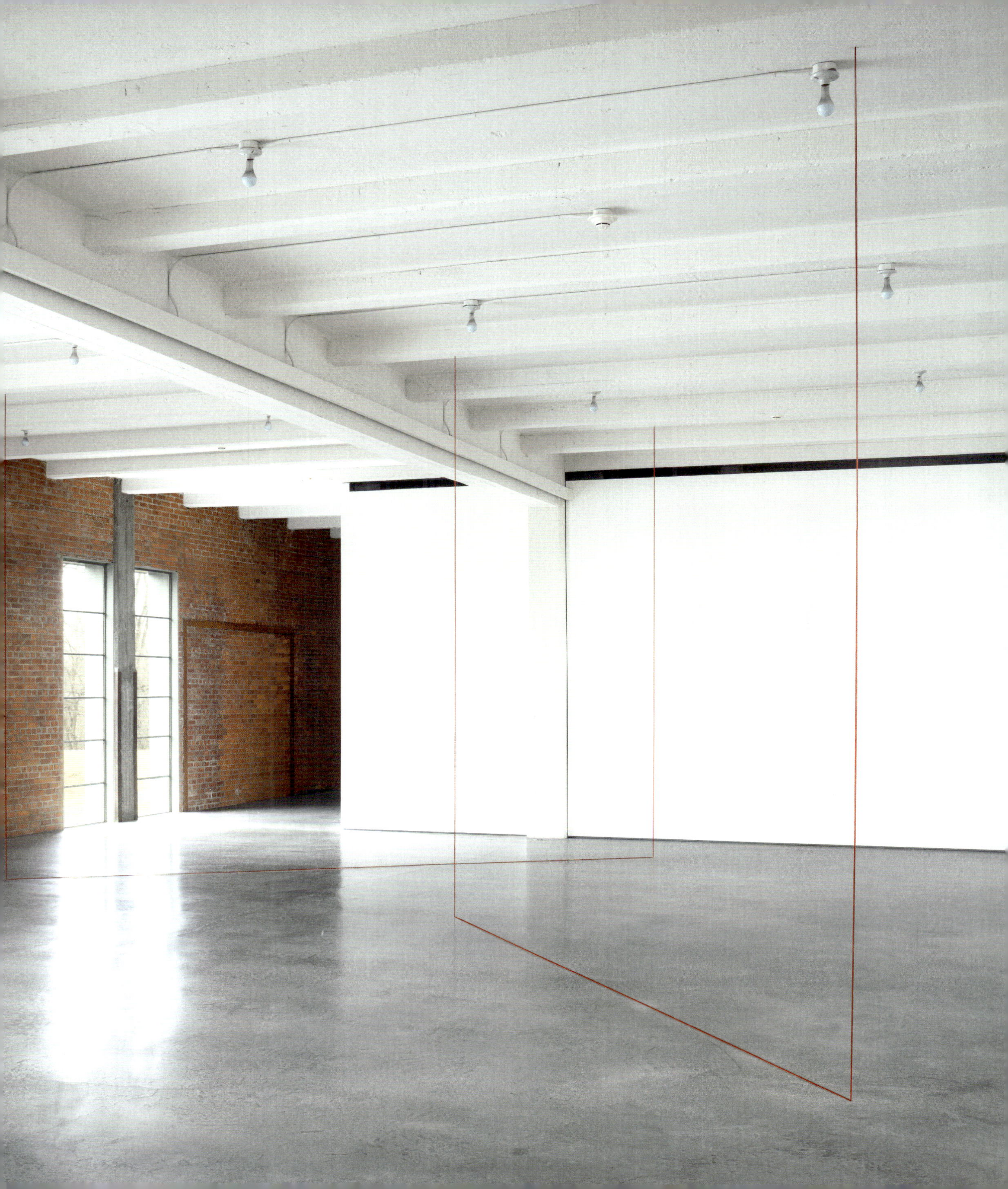

*Untitled (Two-part Vertical Construction, from
Ten Vertical Constructions)*, 1977–79. Acrylic yarn
(rust red), situational dimensions, overall dimensions vary with each installation using spatial
relationships established by the artist. Installation
view, Dia Beacon, Beacon, New York

Following pages:

Untitled (Two-part Construction), 1996. Acrylic
yarn (ocher and beige), situational dimensions,
overall dimensions vary with each installation.
Installation views, Dia Beacon, Beacon, New York
using spatial relationships established by the artist

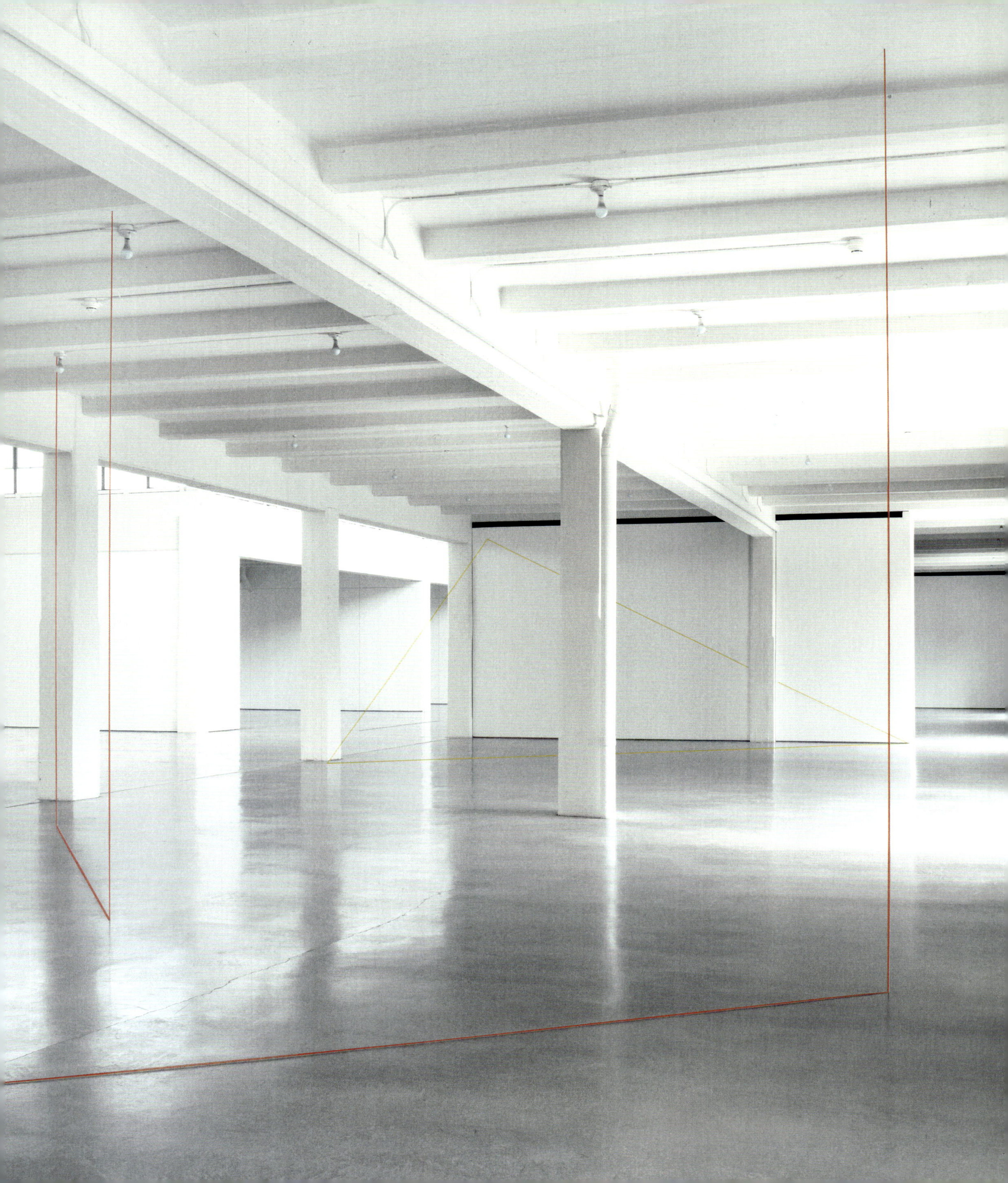

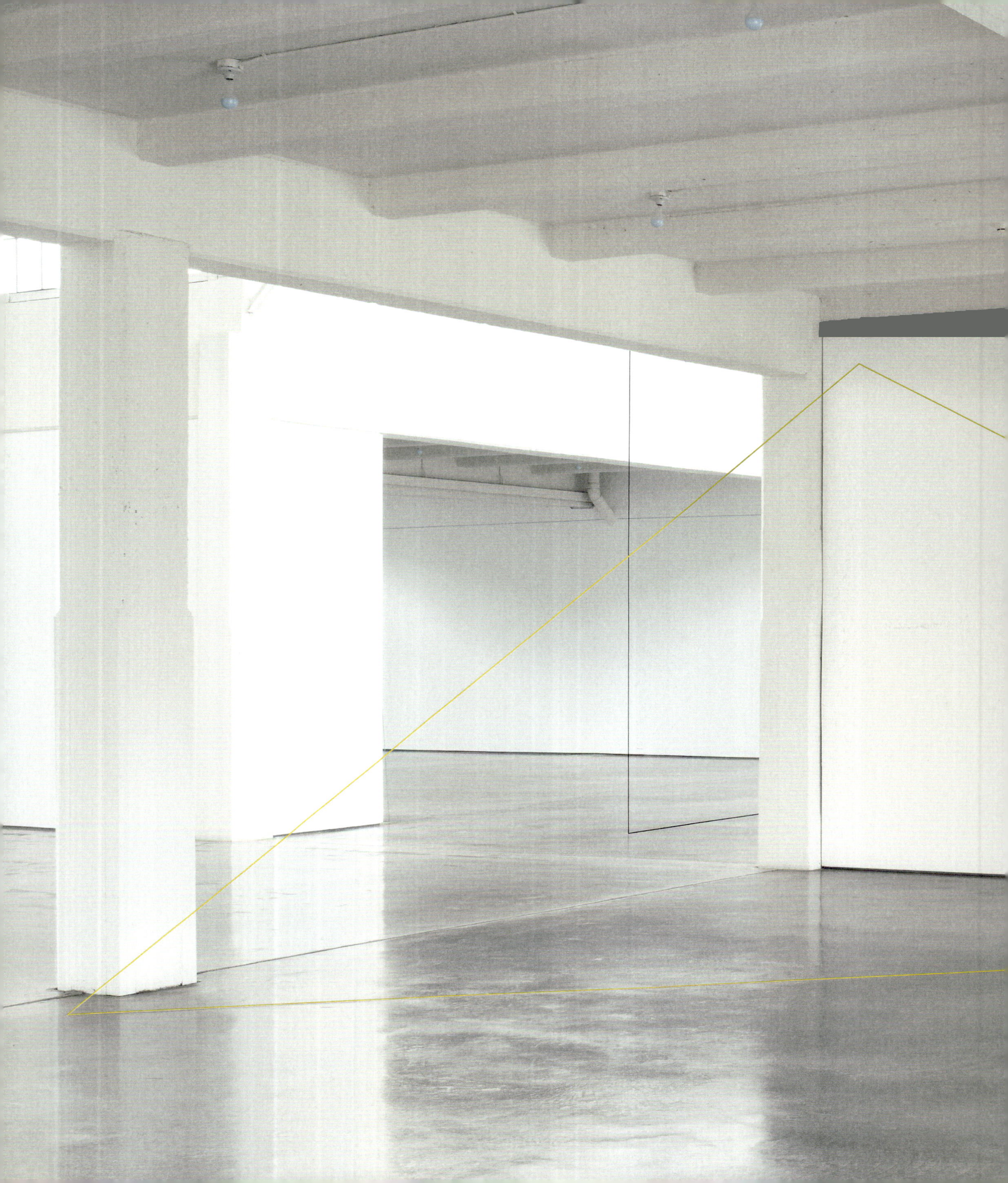

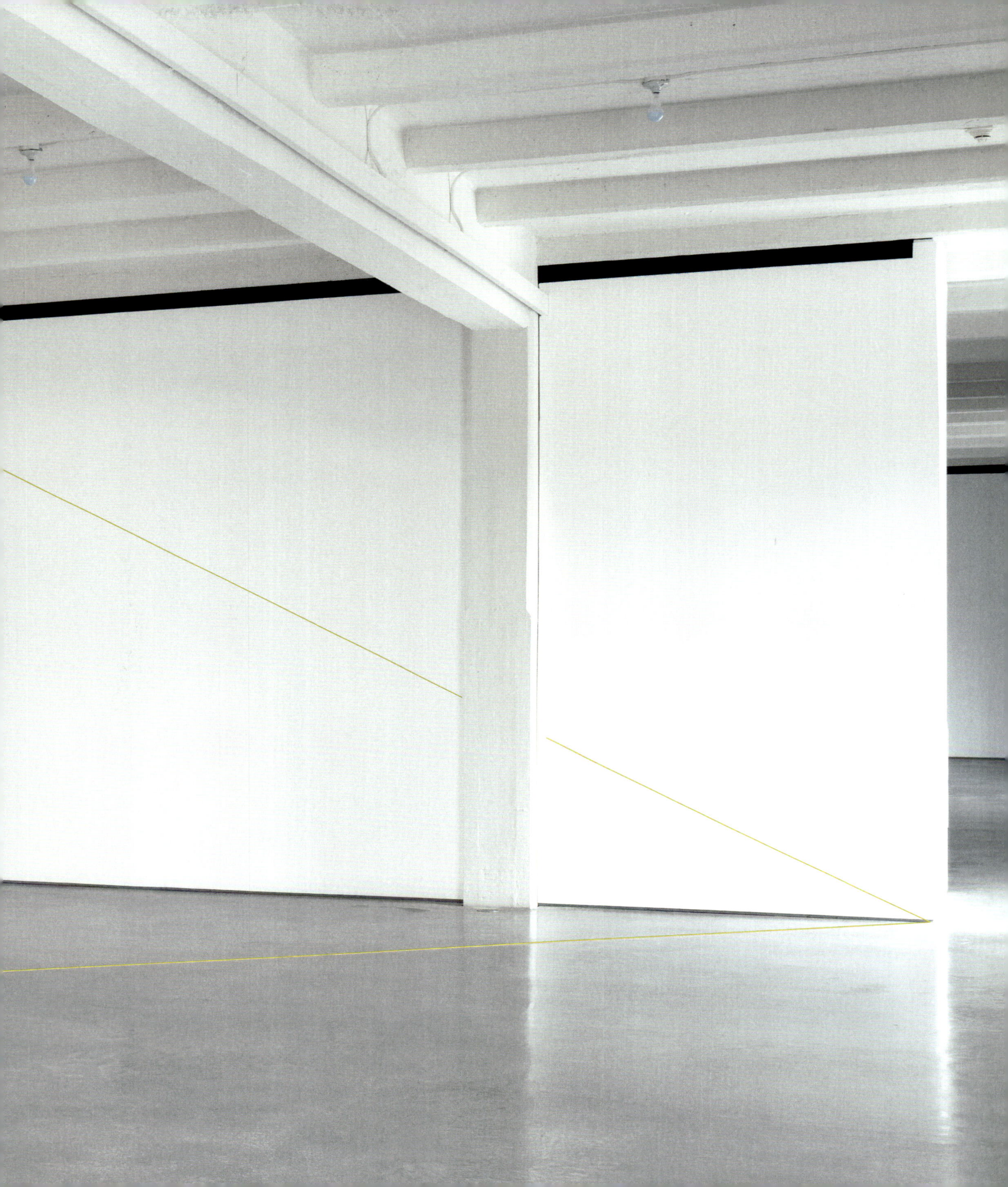

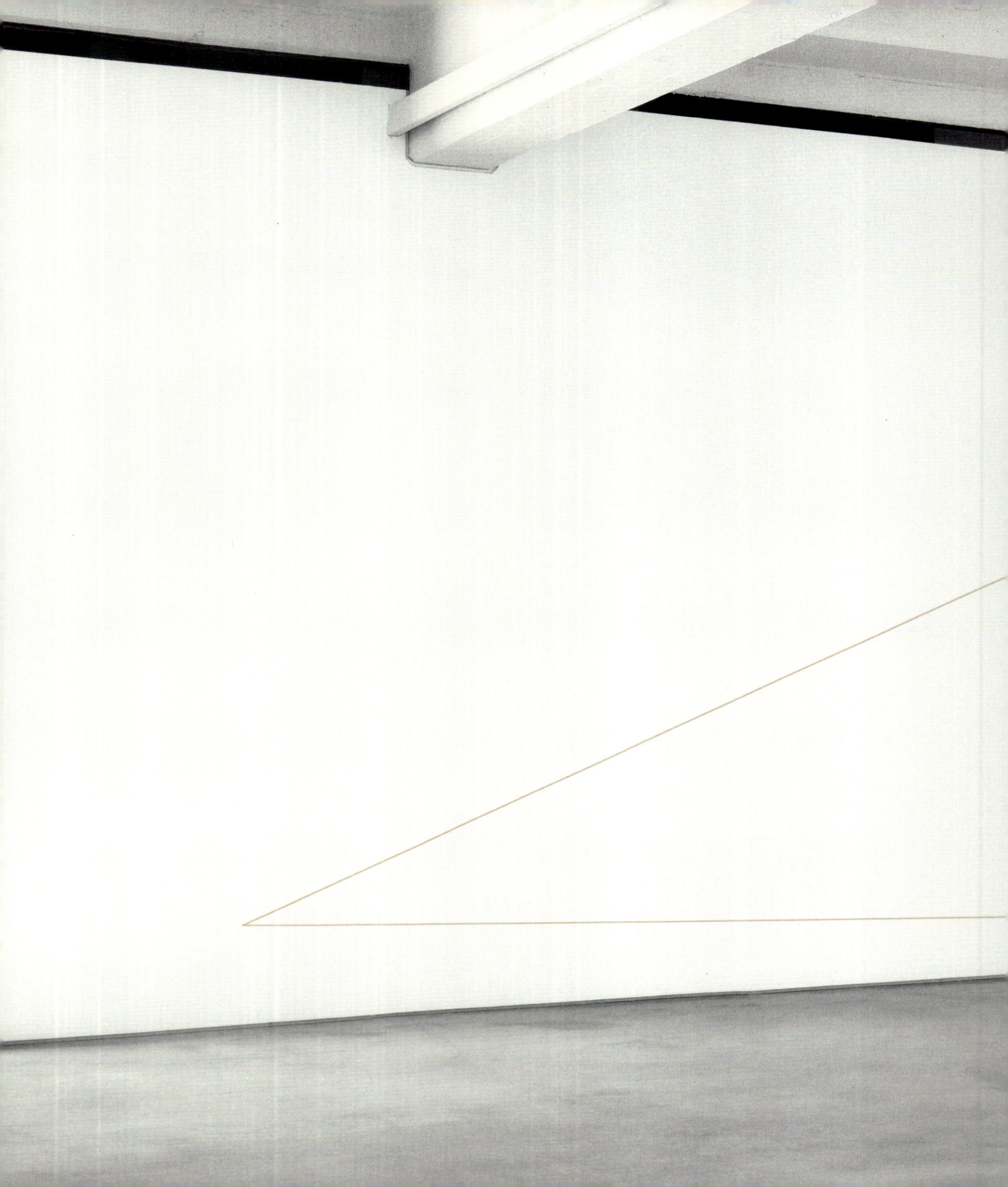

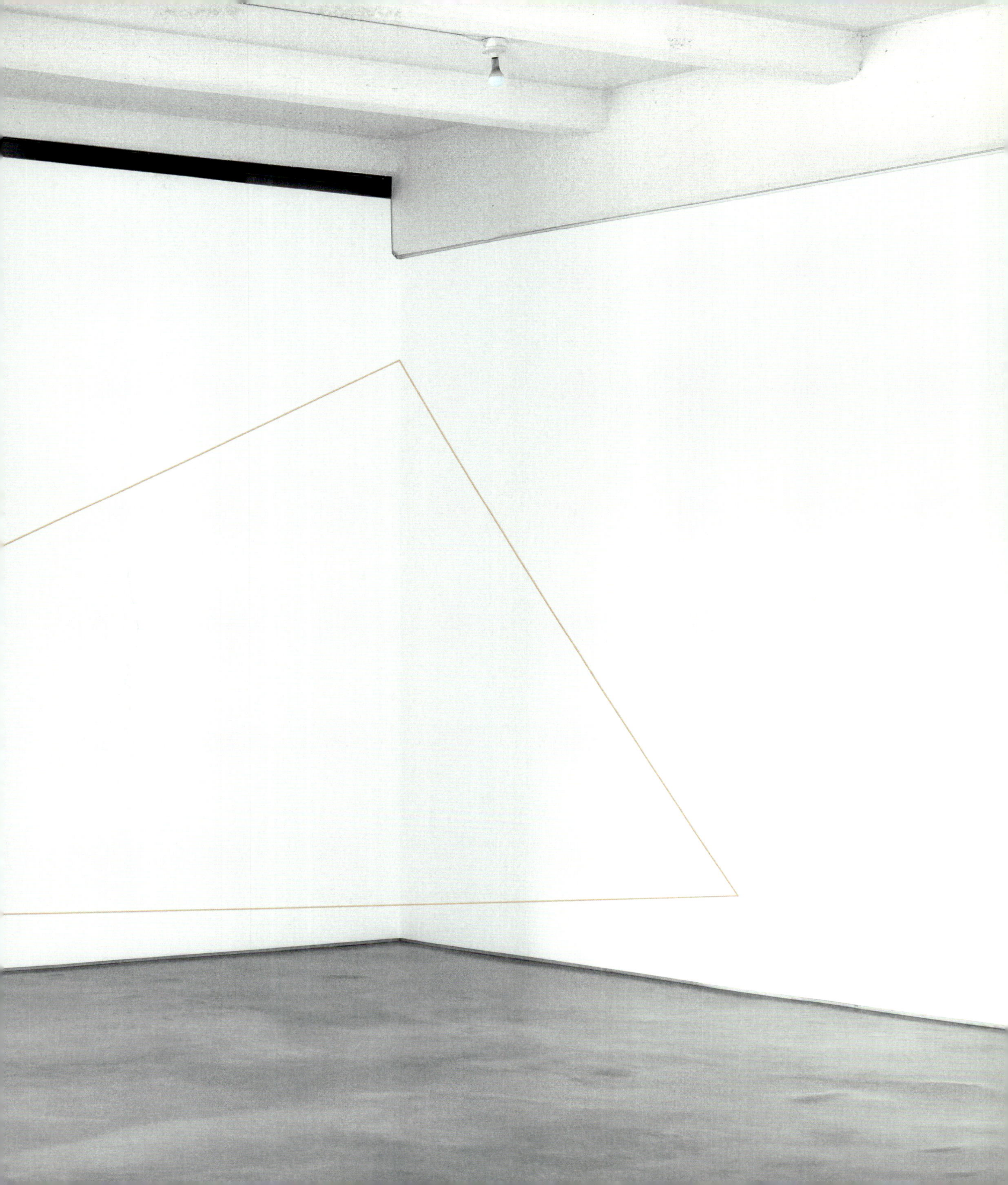

Untitled (Two-part Vertical Construction), 1979.
Acrylic yarn (black), situational dimensions, overall dimensions vary with each installation using
spatial relationships established by the artist.
Installation view, Dia Beacon, Beacon, New York

Untitled (from Ten Vertical Constructions),
1977–79. Acrylic yarn (black), situational dimensions, overall dimensions vary with each installation
using spatial relationships established by the artist.
Installation view, Dia Beacon, Beacon, New York

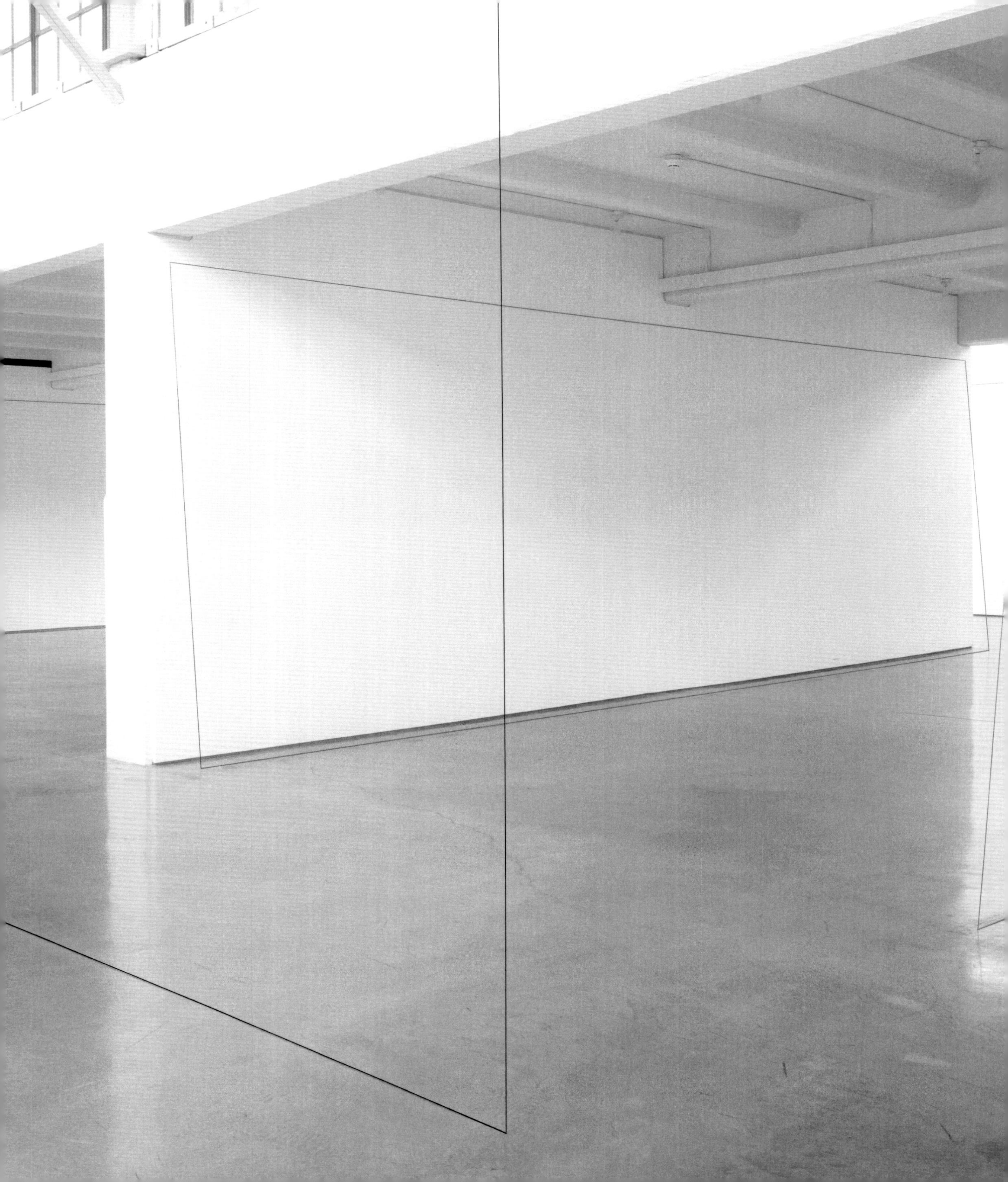

Contributors

Lynne Cooke is a senior curator in the Department of Modern and Contemporary Art at the National Gallery of Art, Washington, DC, where she organized the exhibitions *Woven Histories: Textiles and Modern Abstraction* and *Outliers and American Vanguard Art*. Previously, Cooke was deputy director and chief curator at the Museo Nacional Centro de Arte Reina Sofía in Madrid (2008–2012); curator at Dia Art Foundation, New York (1991–2008); artistic director at the Tenth Biennale of Sydney (1994–1996); cocurator of 1991 Carnegie International at the Carnegie Museum of Art in Pittsburgh; and lecturer in history of art at University College, London University. She has curated exhibitions on the work of Francis Alÿs, Cristina Iglesias, Zoe Leonard, Blinky Palermo, Richard Serra, and Rosemarie Trockel, among many others. Cooke has written for magazines and journals, including *Artforum* and *The Burlington Magazine*.

Matilde Guidelli-Guidi is the curator and cohead of the curatorial department at Dia Art Foundation, where she has organized exhibitions of work by Leslie Hewitt, Jill Magid, Mario Merz, Senga Nengudi, Cameron Rowland, Fred Sandback, Jack Whitten, and Meg Webster, among others. As the curator of Dia's Artists on Artists Lecture Series, she has commissioned work by a growing number of artists including Charles Atlas, Olga Balema, Aria Dean, Duane Linklater, Naeem Mohaiemen, Precious Okoyomon, Marina Rosenfeld, Tiffany Sia, and Cheney Thompson. Guidelli-Guidi has edited books including *Dia: An Introduction to Dia's Locations and Sites* (Dia Art Foundation, 2021), a translation of Carla Lonzi's *Self-Portrait* (Divided Publishing, 2021), and *Jack Whitten: The Greek Alphabet Paintings* (Dia Art Foundation, 2023). Liaising with Dia's archivist, she contributed to studies of Dia's institutional history and shepherded several acquisitions, most notably the extended loan agreement that stipulates the terms of stewardship of Cameron Rowland's *Depreciation* (2018) as a new Dia site, in collaboration with Jordan Carter. Prior to joining Dia, she worked at institutions including the International Center of Photography, New York; Paula Cooper Gallery, New York; and the Whitney Museum of American Art, New York.

Curtis Harvey is director of exhibitions at Dia Art Foundation, where he has worked with artists including Robert Irwin, Joan Jonas, Fred Sandback, Meg Webster, Robert Whitman, and most recently Steve McQueen to install their works at Dia Beacon. Harvey has been collaborating, fabricating, and installing art since 1984. He is also an artist and musician, who plays in such bands as Rex and Pullman, a folk-rock band whose lineup also includes Chris Brokaw, Doug McCombs, and Bundy K. Brown. He has two solo records; his most recent, *The Wheel*, was released in 2014.

Julian Rose is a historian and critic of art and architecture. From 2012 to 2018, he was a senior editor at *Artforum*, and he regularly contributes to a wide range of publications, including *Aperture*, *Architectural Review*, *Artforum*, *Bookforum*, *Log*, *Perspecta*, and *October*. His work as a cofounder of the award-winning design studio Formlessfinder has been exhibited internationally at venues including the Chicago Architecture Biennial; the Museum of Modern Art, New York; and the Venice Biennale of Architecture. Rose received a BA in the history of art and architecture from Harvard University and an MA in architecture from Princeton University and has taught architectural design and history at Columbia University and Princeton

University. His latest book, *Building Culture: Sixteen Architects on How Museums Are Shaping the Future of Art, Architecture, and Public Space* (Princeton Architectural Press, 2024), focuses on the architecture of contemporary art museums.

Fred Sandback was born in Bronxville, New York, in 1943. After receiving a BA in philosophy at Yale University, New Haven, Connecticut, he studied sculpture at Yale's School of Art and Architecture. His first solo exhibitions took place at Galerie Konrad Fischer, Düsseldorf, and Galerie Heiner Friedrich, Munich, both in 1968. His work has been presented in numerous solo museum exhibitions, including at Pinakothek der Moderne, Munich (2003); Whitechapel Gallery, London (2011); and Glenstone, Potomac, Maryland (2015). Dia initiated and maintained the Fred Sandback Museum in Winchendon, Massachusetts, between 1981 and 1996. For the opening of Dia Beacon in 2003, a selection of Sandback's sculptures from the collection were placed on long-term view. Sandback died in 2003 in New York. The Fred Sandback Archive was established in 2007 to create and maintain an archival resource on his art.

Corinna Thierolf is an art historian and founding curator of the Pinakothek der Moderne in Munich, where she served as chief curator for over twenty-five years. At the Pinakothek, she significantly expanded the museum's collection of postwar art, curated numerous exhibitions and published books and essays on Georg Baselitz, Joseph Beuys, John Cage, Walter De Maria, Dan Flavin, Anselm Kiefer, Donald Judd, Arnulf Rainer, and Andy Warhol, among others. Her exhibition series *Königsklasse* (2013 to 2020) set contemporary works from the museum's collection in the historic Herrenchiemsee Palace. Since 2020, she has been a freelance curator, writer, and consultant for two museums opening in the Netherlands and Slovenia in 2025. Her most recent publications are dedicated to the work of Wolfgang Laib and Fabienne Verdier and the art program for the 1972 Olympic Games in Munich.

Edward A. Vazquez is an associate professor in the Department of the History of Art and Architecture at Middlebury College in Vermont, where he has taught since 2009. He is the author of *Aspects: Fred Sandback's Sculpture* (University of Chicago Press, 2017) and *Alfredo Jaar: Studies on Happiness* (Afterall Books, 2023), and his essays have appeared in *Art Journal* and *Res*, among other publications. His research and writing have been supported by the American Council of Learned Societies; the Graham Foundation for Advanced Studies in the Fine Arts; and the Center for Advanced Study in the Visual Arts at the National Gallery of Art, Washington, DC.

I have relied on a subjective construction method based on the specifics of a given moment. These specifics include a chosen form, or structure, which is usually quite straightforward, e.g., "the sculpture." The records are the specifics of the *location*—light, time of year, color, structure, duration, etc. Because my use of this set of specifics is casual, playful, and not codifiable as a constant, the curator will have to rely on her influences for the nuance of iterations gone by, interpreted. This should not be cause for alarm. To expect permanence from the ephemeral is a recipe for disaster.

The . . . set of specifics evolve to free [the] subjectivity of the curator/constructor, which is always larger than the run of historical precedent. It is my wish that the moment should be one of play and pleasure.

—Fred Sandback, from "Curators' Preparation and Conservation Guide to Maintenance, Repair, and Installation of Fred Sandback Sculpture," 2003